IN NATURE'S REALM

Early Naturalists Explore Vancouver Island

MICHAEL LAYLAND

TOUCHWOOD

Editing by Jean Layland
Design by Colin Parks
Cover image: *An Island in Bird's Eye Cove*, by E. J. Hughes, used with the kind permission of the artist's executors.

LIBRARY AND ARCHIVES CANADA CATALOGUING IN PUBLICATION
Title: In nature's realm : early naturalists explore Vancouver Island / Michael Layland.
Names: Layland, Michael, 1938- author.
Description: Includes bibliographical references and index.
Identifiers: Canadiana 20190121793 | ISBN 9781771513067 (hardcover)
Subjects: LCSH: Natural history—British Columbia—Vancouver Island. | LCSH: Naturalists—British Columbia—Vancouver Island—History. | LCSH: Vancouver Island (B.C.)—Description and travel. | LCSH: Vancouver Island (B.C.)—Discovery and exploration. | LCSH: Vancouver Island (B.C.)—History. Classification: LCC QH106.2.B7 L39 2019 | DDC 578.09711/2—DC23

We acknowledge the financial support of the Government of Canada through the Canada Book Fund and the Canada Council for the Arts, and of the Province of British Columbia through the British Columbia Arts Council and the Book Publishing Tax Credit.

PRINTED IN CHINA

23 22 21 20 19   1 2 3 4 5

To Terry and Tiny, who sparked and nurtured
my fascination with the natural world

❋ ❋ ❋

"I may say that . . . there is no better field in Canada than [Vancouver] island for collecting interesting things."

PROFESSOR JOHN MACOUN'S LETTER TO DR. C.F. NEWCOMBE, MARCH 18, 1890

CONTENTS

FOREWORD

ON READING THE PROOFS OF Michael Layland's *In Nature's Realm: Early Naturalists Explore Vancouver Island*, my first thought was, "Why hasn't this book been available for 50 years?" Scholars of early British Columbia tend to be compartmentalized into some aspect of archaeology, anthropology, ethnobotany, or into the specific histories of the maritime fur trade, the land-based fur trade, the colonial era, or the early provincial era. For 18th- and 19th-century studies alone, scholars are further pigeonholed into specialists in the Spanish, British, or American expeditions, or in the main land-based fur-trading companies—the North West, Pacific Fur, and Hudson's Bay companies. Such scholars tend to be familiar only with the naturalists who intersect with their particular era or interest.

What Layland has done here is consider the botanists of Vancouver Island, starting with Indigenous people, "the island's first true naturalists," and continue through the voyages and trading expeditions of the first century of contact, to end in the 1880s with the formation of the Natural History Society of British Columbia and the British Columbia Provincial Museum. He examines the broad continuum of naturalists and natural history regardless of the national, regional, or temporal specialties that scholars traditionally work within. He collects and unites many individual strands to tell a larger overarching story of naming and species reconnaissance. In the process, he provides an overdue public service to anyone interested in the natural history, history, and achievements of the early settler culture of Vancouver Island.

But the audience for *In Nature's Realm* will extend far beyond Vancouver Island. The island was, after all, the linchpin and physical centre of the entire ethnographic "Northwest Coast" and the historic "North West Coast." Therefore the book will be of particular interest to all coastal British Columbians and to our neighbours in Washington, Oregon, and Alaska.

Indeed, I can think of no more accessible introduction to the early history of coastal British Columbia than *In Nature's Realm*. The many colour illustrations—painstakingly gathered from dozens of archives, museums, and galleries—of botanists, Indigenous hosts and traders, ships, birds, mammals, plants, and sea life make for a work of great range, breadth, and synthesis. But *In Nature's Realm* is more than this. Layland has resurrected the careers and contributions of the scientific intelligentsia that helped define and name the natural variety that, as newcomers, they encountered in this ancient landscape.

For example, Layland features two eminent naturalists whose names are commemorated in the trees that are most representative of the Coastal Douglas-fir ecosystem or bio-geoclimatic zone, which stretches in a narrow low-elevation coastal strip from Victoria to Bowser and includes the many Gulf Islands south of Cortes Island as well as a narrow band along the Sunshine Coast near Halfmoon Bay. The smallest major ecosystem in British Columbia, the Coastal Douglas-fir zone occupies only 0.25 to 0.3 per cent of the province.

To the west, the Vancouver Island range and the Olympic Mountains in Washington State create a rainshadow that protects the Coastal Douglas-fir region from incoming precipitation and the raw and exposed power and fury of the open Pacific. This major outer mountain barrier creates a large, sheltered, and temperate refuge characterized by warm and relatively dry summers and long, mild, and wet winters. The result, on the leeward side of the mountains and the southeast coast of Vancouver Island, is a Mediterranean-type climate.

The characteristic trees of the Coastal Douglas-fir ecoregion are the coastal variety of Douglas-fir (*Pseudotsuga menziesii* var. *menziesii*), the Garry oak (*Quercus garryana*), and the arbutus (*Arbutus menziesii*). Douglas-fir—which is hyphenated because it is a member of the pine family and not a true fir—is the dominant tree of this ecosystem; Garry oak and arbutus, which are found nowhere else in Canada, tend to grow in well-drained, sunny, dry, and rocky sites within this ecoregion.

The common English and Latin names are, of course, absent in the Indigenous languages of the region. For example, in SENĆOŦEN, the Saanich language, Douglas-fir is JSₓ,IŁ, Garry oak is ĆEN,IŁ, and arbutus is ḰEḰEYIŁĆ.

The English and scientific names reflect the visits and connections of the working naturalists. The Latin names of arbutus and Douglas-fir honour Archibald Menzies (1754–1842), the Scottish botanist and surgeon who accompanied both James Colnett's fur-trading expedition to the North West Coast between 1786 and 1789 and Captain Vancouver's expedition of 1791–1795. Douglas-fir was named for the botanist David Douglas (1799–1834), who, like Menzies, came from Perthshire. Garry oak was named by David Douglas after his patron Nicholas Garry (circa 1782–1856), the deputy governor of the Hudson's Bay Company, for helping him arrange his travels to the North West Coast.

Thus the three iconic trees of the Coastal Douglas-fir ecoregion owe their names to two botanists who visited the North West Coast with the maritime and land-based fur trades between the 1780s and the 1830s. In this way their names have entered and persisted in the everyday lexicon of millions of people on Canada's west coast.

But this is just a teaser. This beautiful book, *In Nature's Realm*, provides the full stories of Menzies, Douglas, and Garry—and many more naturalists and their important work of reconnaissance, collecting, and naming.

RICHARD SOMERSET MACKIE
EDITOR, *The Ormsby Review*
JUNE 2019

PREFACE

THIS WORK COMPLEMENTS MY BOOKS *The Land of Heart's Delight* and *A Perfect Eden*. It covers many of the same episodes of European exploration and early colonial settlement of Vancouver Island as the earlier volumes. In those, however, emphasis on the stories of the explorers and mapmakers diverted attention from the revelation of fauna, flora, and ecosystems they found, some of them previously unknown to European science.

Learning about these aspects of a new world was an important factor driving the exploration. The resources were potentially valuable, and gaining the knowledge was a strategic advantage in an age of scientific competition. The botanists, surgeons, and scientists shared the same perils and hardships of voyages to far-flung lands as did the ships' complements, but their achievements have been less celebrated. This is unjustified, since their findings constituted important advances in knowledge about this scientifically significant region. As crucial components of the encounter, these findings warrant proper recognition and acknowledgement.

In Nature's Realm is about Vancouver Island's natural environment as it was experienced by early European explorers and settlers, naturalists of many stripes. My research is based on the written record, and therefore reflects the biases of the original writers and their times. Fortunately times have changed, if too little and too slowly. I could not have written this book without paying tribute to the island's first true naturalists, its Indigenous Peoples, whose Traditional Knowledge is now informing efforts toward sustainability. In recent years, Indigenous and non-Indigenous experts have worked with surviving Traditional Knowledge Keepers to document information about ethnobotany and ethnoecology.[1] They have raised awareness about the deep and complex relationship between the First Peoples of this coast and the fauna and flora of their environment.

Modern society needs to combat the depredations of the industrial era and current ecological imbalances. I am hopeful that such cooperative wisdom will offer a way forward.

For the title, I was inspired by a piece of music. In 1891, just before his visit to the New World, the Bohemian composer Antonin Dvořák composed his Opus 91, *In Nature's Realm*, an orchestral overture "closely resembling a landscape painting evoking his home in the forest of Vysoká."[2]

FIG. INT-0 Old-growth forest on Edinburgh Mountain, near Port Renfrew.
Photo © courtesy of TJ Watt.

INTRODUCTION

*I*n *Nature's Realm* FALLS INTO four phases. The first phase concerns the Indigenous Peoples of the island, who became highly skilled, technically sophisticated hunter-gatherers, fishers, and cultivators. The first people to arrive were probably early voyagers, coasting down the kelp highway from Beringia; others came, conveyed by ocean currents, out of eastern Asia and probably Polynesia, but they left little tangible record of their landings, what they encountered, or how they lived.

Over the last few thousand years further waves of people followed, and many chose to settle here as the conditions improved. Their success, indeed their survival, depended on developing an intimate knowledge of the island's flora and fauna, their interdependencies, and how to sustain them. Such knowledge, built on and refined over millennia, continues to evolve. This book gives just a very few examples from the written record showing interesting practices of some Indigenous Peoples on Vancouver Island. There are, of course, many others that could have been equally highlighted. To omit Indigenous science and technology from the overall discussion would have been unpardonable.

Some suggestions for readers to further investigate certain aspects appear as endnotes to the text.

Starting in the 18th century, explorers and settlers from Europe profited from Indigenous wisdom and know-how in their exploration endeavours, but to their detriment they undervalued them because they underestimated Indigenous people and their ways. Their highly detailed, complex scientific knowledge was mostly ignored. Much Indigenous Knowledge was nearly lost or was driven underground in the process of European colonization, which threatened the collective memory by disrupting and dislocating the Indigenous Peoples' way of life.

Indigenous Knowledge is at last becoming recognized by the non-Indigenous population for its immense value, particularly now, with the growing awareness that survival of the human race on the planet depends on sustainable practices. In the Indigenous Knowledge that is being shared, we have a magnificent example of how sustainability may be achieved.

The second phase of *In Nature's Realm* deals with the first written records. They were left by the European explorers of the

FIG. INT-1 Indigenous Peoples used the natural world around them to provide their food, housing, clothing, transportation, tools, and weapons, while respecting and protecting its bounty. This 1902 photo by H. Muskett shows a Kaigani Haida woman weaving baskets from split cedar roots. Note the fish nets behind and the woven rush matting beneath her. *Image G-04232, courtesy of the Royal BC Museum and Archives.*

late 18th century: Spanish, English, French, and American. Some of these were exploring to increase knowledge of "unknown" lands, adding to the body of knowledge about these newly encountered lands and the inhabitants; others were intent on commercial ventures, or imperial expansion and rivalry. Some included trained scientists; others, amateurs noting curiosities in their journals. This reflected the flowering of science in the Age of Enlightenment.

The third phase covers the era of settlement by Europeans. They brought a wide variety of objectives, knowledge, and interests, and they added in different ways to the body of knowledge of the geography, fauna, and flora of their new abode. It was socially acceptable for a respectable, educated gentleman to devote his attention to acquiring a collection of butterflies, birds' eggs, or seashells. These amateur collector-naturalists formed clubs and published papers to share their findings with fellow enthusiasts and the public locally, and to contribute to the global body of knowledge. They created museums as focal points for such interests.

The last phase deals with structured expeditions sent forth by learned institutions or clubs with special interests, in search of specific knowledge or to collect specimens on behalf of the sponsoring bodies. Included in this phase were scientific missions sent by government departments to investigate natural resources of economic significance.

As with *The Land of Heart's Delight*, I have chosen to conclude the main narrative at the start of the First World War. I have, however, succumbed to the temptation to include a few elements and stories that fall outside this time frame but contribute to the overall theme. Similarly, I have not limited the account strictly to the geographical bounds of Vancouver Island, as many of the discoveries that apply to the island were made in its immediate vicinity, for instance, Menzies's first sighting of the arbutus on the southern shore of the Strait of Juan de Fuca. I see them as essential elements of the story.

In this book, I have considered as naturalists those people who took an interest in, and reported on—by oral tradition, the written word, or in graphic illustration—the natural world they encountered, in all its complexity. Over the course of this process of discovery, and particularly in the later colonial and early provincial periods, a major shift occurred in the approach to natural sciences. Prior to that shift, studying natural history was usually just a sideline to the main occupation of the observer—an intellectual pastime.

Later, a more scientific and increasingly specialized focus took precedence. The hobbyists continued collecting and reporting their findings to their peers, but more serious work, usually of greater economic significance, was carried out by academically trained biologists. This shift was especially evident in entomology, the study of insects, with its obvious connection to food production.

A word about nomenclature: Since the theme of this book is the stories of the naturalists, I have opted, for readability, to generally omit scientific/Latin names from the text. I have, however, attempted to provide, where necessary, the names in English according to current usage. This process is, of course, made more difficult by the variety of vernacular names, changing through time, and the evolving structures of scientific taxonomy.

Similarly, names of Indigenous Peoples, places, organizations, and institutions changed over time. I have attempted to use the name current at the time under discussion.

FIG. 1-0 These small islands and adjacent shores near Quadra Island are sites of extensive mariculture activity by Indigenous Peoples. The constructions multiplied harvests of clams and other seafood, major elements of their diet. *Drone photo courtesy of Keith Holmes, Hakai Institute.*

CHAPTER ONE

THE FIRST NATURALISTS
ON VANCOUVER ISLAND

IN THE NORTHEASTERN REACHES OF the Pacific Ocean stretches a large island blessed with an exceptional abundance of life in all its forms. It was formed over geological epochs by the successive arrival of the crusts of various tectonic plates to create a series called "accreted terranes," and was modified by flows of ice and weathering. The island's substance is rich and variegated; its shores are bathed in a constant flow of cold, nutrient-rich water from the North Pacific Gyre, which also brings ample rainfall.

Today known as Vancouver Island, it has been settled by people from all parts of the globe. But for millennia before the first Europeans arrived, it was home to flourishing, complex cultures, whose peoples lived in close relationship with the environment. They thrived on the bounty of its ocean, shores, and forests, developing sophisticated methods of hunting, fishing, foraging, and cultivation, of food preservation and storage. They used its resources for housing, clothing, transportation, tools, and weapons, while respecting and protecting the sources of its bounty. The peoples developed myriad social and governance structures, traditions, arts, and spiritual beliefs reflecting their strong ties to the natural world.

Generation over generation, they acquired a profound understanding of and insight into the ecosystem. They knew the island's fauna, flora, lakes and rivers, minerals, climate, weather, tides and oceanic currents, and their interconnections. The whole existence of these First Peoples was intimately tied to the natural world. They were the first true naturalists in this extraordinary place.

The island's rich flora and fauna also interested many of the area's earliest explorers and settlers, who left written narratives of what they found, adding to the growing body of scientific knowledge. Particularly during the earliest phases of these investigations, the newcomers relied on the knowledge and assistance of the local people. Had they but known it, the newcomers could have learned so much more. In recent years, realization has grown about the need for living sustainably on and with the land. This process has led to ever-increasing awareness of and respect for Indigenous Knowledge and tradition.[1]

Archaeologists have long known that during the most recent glaciation, areas habitable by humans remained available along the northwest coast of North America, including on Vancouver Island. As the glaciers receded, these refugia increased in both number and extent, while the resulting meltwater altered sea levels. These changes, together with the elastic rebounding of the land freed from the weight of ice, resulted in significant fluctuations in the position of shorelines.

Between the time of the receding ice cap and about 9,000 years BP (before the present), the sea level was much lower than it is today, revealing large stretches of the continental shelf and a quite different shoreline. The earliest migrants travelling along the coast would have passed over these previous shores, some staying to settle. Traces of their passing are few in the archaeological record. Most sites are now many metres underwater, difficult to find and study.

In the sea level's next fluctuation, it overshot today's level before receding, with the result that coastal sites were then located on what is now higher ground, often deep within the forest.

Recent evidence confirms humans were present in some of those areas for at least the past 14,000 years. They appear to have arrived from Beringia, the land bridge that once connected Asia with North America, and probably travelled down the coastline in watercraft, along what has been called the "kelp highway." Relying mainly on marine and coastal resources, the people lived close to shorelines that were, in places, up to 300 feet (91 metres) below today's sea level. A few ancient occupation sites, however, have been discovered above sea level, and archaeologists are seeking others on dry land and underwater.

Scientists from BC's Hakai Institute have found and investigated human campsites on islands just north of Vancouver Island. The first, on Calvert Island, across Queen Charlotte Sound from Vancouver Island's northern tip, contained a firepit with footprints of two adults and a child. Carbon dated at 13,200 years BP, these footprints are among the oldest found in North America.[2] This finding appears to prove that the first arrivals to this part of the world came along the Pacific coast, rather than from east of the Rockies through a corridor between retreating ice sheets, as was long believed.

In a second campsite discovery, beneath layers of sediment and peat on nearby Triquet Island, scientists found fire-lighting tools, charcoal, an anvil stone with toolmaking debris, fish hooks, wooden spears, and the remains of sea mammals, dating as early as 14,000 years BP. Up next for investigation is a nearby shell midden, 16 feet (5 metres) deep. This site, in an area where the shoreline remained unchanged, corroborates Heiltsuk First Nation's oral tradition that a strip of land in that location remained ice-free and provided emergency village sites for their people since ancient times.[3]

Across the Strait of Juan de Fuca from Victoria, near Sequim on the Olympic Peninsula in the traditional territory of the Jamestown S'Klallam People, archaeologists found another important clue to these early arrivals. In 1977, farmer Emanuel Manis was digging a pond with his backhoe when he uncovered the tusks of a mastodon. Recognizing the potential importance of his find, he called in experts from Washington State University to investigate. They revealed the butchered remains of the animal, including a rib bone in which a spear point made from the bone of a different mastodon was embedded.

DNA testing and CT scans confirmed that humans had shaped the spear point, and that the date of the site was 13,800 years BP.[4] This finding helped refute the long-held and fiercely defended "Clovis First" theory of North American human population.[5]

These early peoples were active during the Younger Dryas, the last part of the geological epoch of the Pleistocene, which

FIG. 1-1   A mastodon rib bone with an embedded spear point made from a different mastodon, dating to 13,800 years BP. Found in 1977 at the Manis farm near Sequim, Washington. *Photo courtesy of Grant Keddie.*

corresponded with archaeology's Neolithic period. There followed the Holocene epoch. During this time, as Earth's climate warmed, the landscape and ecosystems of the northern Pacific coast of North America changed from a subarctic tundra—comprising a few small and stunted trees amid muskeg swamps—to the lush, temperate rainforest that still survives in areas spared from industrial logging.

What remained constant was the littoral—the waters above the continental shelf—the ecosystem of the kelp forest, home to a wealth of fishes, sea mammals, seabirds, crustaceans, and algae. The prevailing current of the North Pacific Gyre, flowing toward and along the coast year-round, kept these waters rich in minerals and plankton. At the mouths of rivers created by ample rainfall and seasonal snowmelt, herbaceous vegetation of great

FIG. 1-2 The kelp forest, an environment rich in food resources, provided a continuous coastal "highway" for early navigator-settlers from Asia along the Pacific coast of North America as far south as California. *Photo © courtesy of Gabriel Lu, Ocean Safari Outdoors Inc., San Gabriel, California.*

variety and nutritional value developed and flourished. This habitat supported healthy populations of land-based species.

The rivers also formed a channel for vast stocks of salmon to migrate between the open ocean and their freshwater spawning grounds. As the fish died, they provided the primary source of essential nitrogen for the forest giants, which sheltered other components of this complex and vigorous web of life.

It is little wonder that successive waves of people—adept at boat building and seamanship, and accustomed to thriving on the bounty of the sea and shore—would retrace the steps of their pioneering ancestors. They followed the kelp highway south, to settle and prosper on these lush shores. They sought shelter from the furies of the winter storms within the intricacies of the rocky archipelagos and inlets that complicate the shoreline from Alaska to Cape Flattery. From an assortment of trees and plants, they found sustainable supplies for spiritual, cultural, and artistic expression, and for constructing dwellings, canoes, clothing, utensils, and weapons for hunting and defence.

For food, the people fished, hunted sea and land mammals, trapped waterfowl and other birds, and harvested shellfish, crustaceans, roots, tubers, leafy plants, fruits, fungi, and algae. Most of these resources were plentiful but seasonal, so people developed methods of preserving and storing the harvests, animal and vegetable, for the winter months. In addition, they ensured the success of future harvests by tending and propagating the plants, and by weeding and controlled burning.[6] They also learned how to access and process the wealth of the forest for their tools and many manufactures.[7]

Groups preserved surpluses from locally abundant harvests and managed them through extensive and efficient regional trading networks, through which they could acquire resources not available in their own territories. These networks were reinforced through intergroup arranged marriages and the system of distribution of wealth through Potlatches, although relationships were complicated by traditional rivalries and feuding.

These early peoples studied and learned every aspect of the natural world around them to support and reinforce their enduring coexistence within the ecosystem. Their well-being, indeed their survival, depended on it.

THE LINGUISTIC PERSPECTIVE

A key to tracing the arrival and dispersal of the waves of migrations is the study of linguistics. Prior to 1790—and the disruptive impacts of European culture, metal artifacts, diseases, and languages—the population of this coast was highly disparate linguistically. Between the Alaskan Panhandle and Cape Alava, south of Flattery, "at least 45 distinct languages" were spoken, from five distinct language families.[8] The exceptional complexity of the region's ethnography makes it difficult to differentiate between groups. These language families provide the most effective way of doing so.

On Vancouver Island, most Indigenous Peoples identify as belonging to three language groups: the Nuu-chah-nulth; the Kwak'wala-speaking Kwakwaka'wakw; and the Coast Salish Peoples, who speak a number of variations within the Salishan language family. Many alternative names and spellings have been used when referring to nations and communities, as well as languages within these groupings.[9]

The three groups had many techniques in common for acquiring sustenance from their natural world—the sea, shoreline, lakes and rivers, and forests. There are, however, some that seem to have been the exclusive practice of a particular group. Considered in combination, they emphasize the spectrum of ingenuity the Indigenous Peoples brought to bear on feeding themselves and their associated communities through times of plenty and of scarcity.

HUNTERS OF THE WHALE

Along the west coast of Vancouver Island lie the territories of people who actively hunted migrating whales. They, the Nuu-chah-nulth, lived in coastal communities between Cape Cook and the northern shore of the Strait of Juan de Fuca, as far as today's Port San Juan, on the southwest coast of the island, and on the northwestern tip of the Olympic Peninsula. They hunted in open dugout canoes, powered solely by paddlers wielding hand-launched harpoons, spears, and knives.

In common with other coastal groups, they also hunted smaller marine mammals such as sea lions, fur and hair seals, porpoises, and sea otters, and took advantage of "drift whales"—floating dead, stranded, or beached animals—whenever an opportunity arose. As revealed by archaeologists, the sophistication of these hunters' tools—fashioned from different woods, stone, bone, and antler—developed over time. Improved tools permitted successful hunting of larger mammals. Better hooks caught more and larger fish. Advancing thread and rope construction led to better nets and fishing and harpoon lines.

During the last millennium before the arrival of Europeans, enhanced technologies enabled the effective pursuit of the enormous, healthy cetaceans that passed along their coast. Hunters used their new tools in combination with exceptional courage, seamanship, technique, coordination, and a close understanding of the behaviour patterns and anatomy of their prey.

They primarily hunted the California grey whale but also the northern right and humpback whales. The greys, migrating north between April and June and often accompanied by calves, came closer to shore, but the right whales swam more slowly and were therefore easier to approach. They also provided tastier meat. Some humpbacks remained in local waters year-round. While successful hunts were not frequent, the vast amount of protein and storable fat from a single animal brought to a village beach could mean survival for a community through a poor fishing season followed by a prolonged winter.

Archaeologist John Dewhirst, who has studied Yuquot intensively, feels that whaling held more significance for a chief's prestige than as a source of basic subsistence.[10]

In 1951 anthropologist Charles Borden published a paper linking the "Nootkan" whale hunting with that of the Eskimo (Inuit) of the Bering Strait and Siberia.[11] He identified 19 traits—characteristics of the equipment, methods, protocols, and rituals—which they had in common. These, he deduced, indicated that

> the contact may be assumed to have extended over considerable time to allow for the complete adoption of such highly specialized activity as Eskimo whaling along with the associated whale cult. Nootka contact with Eskimo may even antedate the advent of whale hunting.[12]

This theory attracted some debate, but more recently, the Siberian connection is being revisited.[13]

THE BIRD NETTERS

Within the traditional territory of the Central Coast Salish Peoples, many estuaries and wetlands teem with migratory and wintering wildfowl, providing enormous opportunities for skilful hunters. One of their techniques was to deploy huge nets, suspended between tall poles, across the path of flocks of geese and ducks in flight.[14]

The nets had to withstand the impact of a flock of heavy, strong-flying geese at speed, and hold them until the net could be lowered and the hunters could dispatch the captives.

Moreover, the nets needed to be fine enough to be invisible to the birds, sufficiently flexible and light to be rolled up for con-

The first European to observe bird-net poles was Gonzalo López de Haro, pilot of Manuel Quimper's expedition of 1790, whose report noted this:

> The [sand bank] ended at the entrance to the port where [I] found in various places on the beach many high poles which look like flagpoles, with some props at the bottom to prevent the wind from breaking them. . . . They were placed at the very edge of the sand bank.[15]

Two years later, George Vancouver and Archibald Menzies wondered at arrays of poles at Dungeness and 17 of them near Port Townsend, and were similarly mystified at their purpose. The artist Paul Kane saw them at Port Angeles. Estimates of the height of the poles varied from 30 to 100 feet (9–30 metres).

In 1825 botanist John Scouler also saw the Dungeness poles, and his local guides were able to explain how they were used to trap waterfowl.[16] Apparently, they were deployed at dawn and dusk during the migration seasons. The nets would be dropped immediately after a flock of geese struck, to avoid damage to the nets. Hunters would hide below the nets, or in canoes if they were deployed over water, to quickly dispatch the birds.[17] Second flocks would often follow the first down to the ground and were also captured and killed.

In 1868 an American mountaineer, Edmund Coleman,[18] set out by canoe from Victoria, with a party of climbers, intent on making the first ascent of Mount Baker. As they passed between San Juan and Orcas Islands they saw a single pole and were told by their Lekwungen[19] guides what it had been used for. In 1908 G.D. Sprot[20] saw similar poles at the mouth of the Chemainus River. He learned from local settlers that they were no longer in use but had been there for at least 70, perhaps 100 years.

veying to the site, hauled up into position, tightened, and then stored until the next use. Individually, none of these problems would have been simple to solve. Achieving all these parameters, using only materials available locally, demanded both intimate knowledge of the characteristics of plant fibres, and generations of experimentation and development.

Effective location of the arrays also required detailed awareness of the flight patterns and behaviour of the target species. Hunters deployed the arrays at spits and sandbanks, or across streams, passes, and estuaries—places where they knew migrating or wintering birds, mainly geese and widgeons, regularly flew. The hunters would often light smudge fires upwind to further hide the nets in smoke.

Another form of net was used to catch ducks on the surface at night. Two hunters in a canoe, with a fire in a pot or sand-filled box on a platform at the stern, would paddle stealthily toward a flock of roosting waterfowl. The hunter in the bow would grip, horizontally with his teeth, a stick from which a mat of woven bulrushes was draped, leaving his hands free to wield a wide net on a pole. The mat would cast a shadow on the water ahead of the canoe. As the canoe approached the flock, the birds, wary of the fire, would seek the shelter of the shadow of the mat, bringing them within range of the hunter's net.

W. Alexander del: from a Sketch taken on the Spot by J. Sykes.

J. Heath Sculp.

FOUR remarkable, supported POLES, in PORT TOWNSHEND, GULPH of GEORGIA.

London Published May 1st 1798, by R. Edwards New Bond Street J. Edwards Pall Mall & G. Robinson Paternoster Row

FIG. 1-3 The first depiction in European literature of the mysterious poles seen by the Vancouver expedition in 1792. The visitors were unaware that the poles were there to support huge, suspended nets to catch waterfowl in flight. *Drawing by J. Sykes from Vancouver's Voyage.*

Wildfowl not susceptible to these nets, such as diving ducks or higher-flying swans, were hunted by other methods. For the former, a large, flat net was suspended underwater between floats and anchor weights, above a patch of eelgrass or seaweed known to attract spawning herring. The edge nearer the shore was lower than the outer one. Herring eggs deposited on the beds of grass would attract diving ducks, such as mergansers, harlequins, scoters, and grebes, which would swim under the net to graze and become trapped when they surfaced for air. Hunters would be waiting for them there.

Swans and cranes were stalked and shot with bows and arrows from behind cover, or from canoes camouflaged with leafy branches. Few other Vancouver Island people used the nets slung from tall poles, but many used the other forms of netting. All such techniques called for an intimate awareness of avian behaviour achievable only through generations of observation and cultural transmission.

CULTIVATORS OF THE SEA GARDENS

"When the tide goes out, the table is set" is a popular adage among people of the west coast of North America, referring to the rich harvests of intertidal seafood available to them.

It was only in the last few years of the 20th century that the scientific community took notice of some strange structures in and around the Broughton and Discovery archipelagos. They were underwater ridges of boulders apparently created by human effort. The local peoples, the Kwakwa̲ka̲'wakw and Northern Coast Salish, whose forebears had built those structures, knew of them and their purpose, but that knowledge had remained unappreciated by the newcomers. The ridges are curving berms about 3 feet (1 metre) high, made of piled-up rocks. They created landward-side terraces that are underwater except at low tide. At that point, the berms close off bays and inlets, except for a gap at one end.[21] On the nearby beach, there is often a deep shell midden, and traces of ancient habitation. A recent archaeological study has shown that on northern Quadra Island, clam gardens have been in use for 3,500 years.[22]

Mention of such berms and terraces farther to the south first appeared in 1934, but it seems to have been ignored:

> At a place called Klelung, or Orcas Island, there is a clam bed cultivated by its owners. They took the largest rocks that were in the clam bed and moved them out to the extreme low water marks, setting them in rows like a fence along the edge of the water. This made clam digging very easy compared to what it had been previously been because there are only small pebbles and sand to dig in. It is exceptional to cultivate clam beds in this manner and while other clam beds are used by everyone in the tribe, here only the owners who cultivated the bed gathered.[23]

From recent research, it is now understood that construction of the *loxiwey* walls creates a second ecosystem conducive to harvesting food from the sea. The seaward side of the wall becomes, in effect, an artificial reef. It provides good anchorage for kelp, wrack and other algae, whelks, red turban shells, and chitons. The nooks and crannies formed between the boulders make excellent hiding places for octopuses, crabs, sea cucumbers, sea urchins, and juvenile fish. At high tide, larger fish patrol the reef in search of prey, in turn becoming accessible to hunters standing on the wall with spears or dip nets. This realization is causing some researchers to reconsider the name "clam gardens" for the more general "sea gardens."

Kwaxistalla (Clan Chief Adam Dick)[24] remembered the words of a traditional song from Gilford Island, in the Broughtons, which included a verse about children helping their mother build a clam garden. He also recalled going to one beach where a *Bukwis* (Sasquatch) stole four bags of clams from them. Families had passed down these clam gardens and managed them for untold generations. The Kwak'wala name for them was *loxiwey*, meaning "rolled rocks forming a wall." These were rock-walled, terrace-like constructions across the mouth of a small bay, which provide an ideal habitat for butter clams and other edible shellfish.[25]

A published summary of Kwaxistalla's first-hand account of the traditions associated with *loxiwey* walls provides a crucial contribution to the current scientific study of Indigenous mariculture in the region.[26] The chief describes the four species of clams cultivated (horse, butter, littleneck, and cockle); harvesting, cooking, and preserving them; the construction and maintenance of the *loxiwey* walls and clam beds; and the role played by clams in Kwakwaka'wakw cosmology. They were not only a regular and emergency source of food, but also valuable in trade.

HOW *LOXIWEY* WORK

For clams to thrive on a beach, it is critical that the depths of water at high and low tides suit them. On an unmodified beach, constructing a *loxiwey* wall creates the ideal strip of sandy environment, within the intertidal zone, where those levels meet the animal's needs. Throughout many generations, diggers would learn the location of such zones. When establishing a clam garden, the builders chose the position and best height for the wall so as to increase both the width of the ideal zone and the volume of sand within that zone. The wall

FIG. 1-4 A Quadra Island clam garden at low tide with researchers from the Hakai Institute at work. Note how all boulders have been cleared from the beach to construct the wall. *Photo by author.*

FIG. 1-5 Part of the same *loxiwey* wall seen from the water. Note the grass-covered midden, 10 metres deep, behind the beach. *Photo by author.*

should be located along the line of the bottom of the ideal zone, and its height should be level with the zone's upper limit and below the high tide. In this way, oxygenated, nutrient-rich water regularly flows over the terrace. The wall also prevents the outflowing tide from carrying all the sediment with it.

In many cases, communities constructed the rock walls gradually, during the times of harvest. They removed any rocks and medium-sized boulders and added them to the wall or to the sides. In other cases, to start a new clam bed, they carried out the initial engineering as a project, later adding rocks cleared during the harvests. In either case, the walls and terraces need regular attention to repair damage from waves during storms.

Once the wall is in place, each incoming tide brings additional sand to deposit onto the beach, making the gradient flatter until the bed, a mixture of sand and finely ground old clamshells, reaches the top of the wall. This new, engineered habitat has advantages for both the clams and the diggers: behind the wall, the modified beach is more extensive, providing room for more clams within the zone of optimum water depth, and clamming is easier without the rocks.

Removing boulders and selectively digging and harvesting mature clams has the beneficial effect of "tilling" the garden to aerate it. The clams move around more easily and develop in the loose, rock-free medium, leading to their faster reproduction and growth. They are healthy and, as their reputed disposition claims, "happy."

Researchers have found many previous sites of clam gardens now neglected and fallen into poor productivity. In some of those places, where the water is not polluted, there are now initiatives to restore those walls and gardens, to regain an important source of food, and to train a new generation of gardeners.[27]

FIG. 1-6 A small family group waits while their harvest of butter clams, covered in mats, bakes over heated rocks in this 1902 photo by H. Muskett. The line of collected boulders at the water's edge is probably a *loxiwey*. *Image G-04230 courtesy of the Royal BC Museum and Archives.*

Nancy Turner's career has been devoted to bridging the chasm between two mountains of cognition: that of scientific, Linnaean botany, and the wealth of Indigenous wisdom concerning the vegetable kingdom of this region. As an ethnoecologist, and following the path of Erna Gunther, she has spoken with Elders, mostly women, from many different language groups. She learned how they understand, name, and make use of local plants for food and medicine, and in many other ways. She has recorded traditional harvesting, food preparation, preservation, and storage techniques, the making of textiles and cordage, and other non-food uses of trees, shrubs, herbs, ferns, fungi, marine algae, and lichens. She has transferred this lore into scientific and popular books, articles, and talks.

Nancy Turner has done so in the nick of time: one or two decades later, this chasm would not have been bridgeable. In these matters, the didactic chain through the generations was about to be broken. Apart from the now-recognized operational savagery of the residential school system, it was deliberate policy to sever the transmission of Traditional Knowledge and practices from Elders to children. This gap is starting to be filled by Nancy Turner, working in collaboration with Indigenous specialists, and Indigenous writers like Mary Siisip Geniusz and Robin Wall Kimmerer.

Two examples will serve to show how Turner bridges the chasm. They are from the authoritative but very accessible guidebook *Plants of Coastal British Columbia*.[28] Her contribution to the book was to add an ethnobotanical note to most of the entries. The examples are from part entries for two familiar plants, both of great significance to the Indigenous Peoples of this area.

DEVIL'S CLUB

This spiny shrub, related to ginseng, is still highly important as a medicine and protective agent to aboriginal peoples throughout its range. At least on the B.C. coast it is one of the most important of medicinal plants. . . . Numerous ailments including arthritis, ulcers, and digestive tract ailments and diabetes, were treated with Devil's club. . . . The Washington Klallam and Vancouver Island Nuu-chah-nulth made fish lures by peeling devil's club sticks and cutting them into small pieces. The Manhousat Nootka carved small fish out of devil's club sticks which would be tied near fishhooks and reeled in to snag the fish. . . . Cowlitz [People] dried the bark and pulverized it for perfume and baby talc, and made an infusion drink for colds and applied topically for rheumatism and stomach trouble. . . . Tea made from the inner bark is taken by many people today for diabetes.

WESTERN REDCEDAR

Redcedar has been called "the cornerstone of northwest coast Indian culture" and large-scale use of its wood and bark delineates the cultural boundary of the northwest coast peoples within its range. The easily split, rot resistant wood was used to make important cultural items such as dugout canoes, house planks and posts, totem and mortuary poles, bentwood boxes, baskets, clothing and hats, and a variety of tools and implements such as dishes, arrow shafts, harpoon shafts, spear poles, barbecue sticks, fish spreaders and hangers, dip-net hooks, fish clubs, masks, rattles, benches, cradles, coffins, herring rakes, canoe bailers, ceremonial drum logs, combs, fishing floats, berry-drying racks, fish weirs, spirit whistles, and paddles. . . . The power of the redcedar was said to be so strong that a person could receive strength by standing with his or her back to the tree. . . . Western redcedar is B.C.'s provincial tree.

APPRECIATION OF TRADITIONAL KNOWLEDGE

The First Peoples of the island relied on the knowledge of the natural world passed down the generations by traditional learning: stories, songs, art, and dance, as well as involving children in traditional activities to enable their learning-by-doing. Communicating the extent and detail of that knowledge to the newcomers did not happen easily or quickly. There were, of course, significant language barriers. These were exacerbated by reluctance on the part of non-Indigenous society to study the local languages in sufficient depth to understand Traditional Knowledge. Moreover, some technologies were considered the property of particular clans. As a result, the incomers tended to underrate or even disparage such knowledge. All this was overlaid with a Eurocentric world view of cultural and racial superiority, disdain, and exploitation.

Only relatively recently has the scientific establishment appreciated the depth and complexity of the understanding that Indigenous Peoples enjoyed about their ecosystem. This change has come about through the work of anthropologists, linguists, ethnoecologists, and archaeologists, working in close consultation with keepers of Traditional Knowledge. Even so, that process was often distorted or limited through intrinsic bias. Usually, the investigators were men, asking questions of men. This ignored the vast body of knowledge held by women. More recently, this bias has been identified and begun to be corrected. Notwithstanding such omissions, it has become clear to scientists raised within the European system of "enlightenment" that Traditional Knowledge can support, stimulate, confirm or question, and add to the reasoning and conclusions of the scientific method.

Modern non-Indigenous people are at last coming to realize, respect, and value the contribution that such learning could have made to living more sustainably on this precious land. Bitter examples abound of the errors that have been made: industrial clear-cutting; overfishing; river and seashore engineering; pollution of the atmosphere, rivers, and oceans; devastating forest fires due to having prevented natural, annual, low-intensity fires; government bounties for eliminating natural predators; and blanket application of pesticides and herbicides. Had we but understood or even cared!

FIG. 2-0 *Short-tailed albatross.* Archaeology has revealed that these, now rare, oceanic birds provided an important food source for the ancestors of the Mowachaht people of Yuquot. *Hand-coloured lithographic plate from John Cassin's* Illustrations of the Birds of California, Texas, Oregon, British and Russian America, *1856.*

CHAPTER TWO

COUNTING WILDLIFE AT NOOTKA

NOOTKA SOUND WAS THE FIRST location on Vancouver Island to be studied by Europeans, and subsequently was the centre of much activity by fur traders, Spanish scientists, and colonizers. Consequently, it has the earliest and longest series of visitors' descriptions of its natural history. From these, it is possible to deduce the earliest stages of Europe's growing knowledge of the island.

Several factors restricted wildlife sightings by the early Spanish expeditions and those of Cook and Vancouver/Menzies. First, counting types of birds and other wildlife was just a peripheral reason for their being there. Since they visited only during the summer months, they missed bird migration passages and winter-resident birds. They lacked the benefits of binoculars for distance viewing and shotguns for collecting. Also, because most of their observations were made on or close to shore, their ability to study land mammals was restricted and confined to daylight hours, or to examining skins brought to them by the local people.

What bird species and population sizes the explorers might have encountered is a matter of speculation. There will have been changes in avian populations between the early 1790s and modern times, but a useful starting point for comparison is the BC Provincial Museum's 1978 publication of *Birds of Pacific Rim National Park*, a study by three ornithologists. It lists sightings along 75 miles (120 kilometres) of coastline near, and similar to, the Nootka area.[1] The ornithologists examined 16,000 records—historic and more recent sightings, specimens collected, and other reports—to produce statistics on species seen during the year, including a breakdown by month.

The study notes 247 species "known or strongly suspected to be there," 90 of them seen 50 or more times, indicating they should reasonably have been present. Of those, 27 species were sighted more than 200 times, which means they were there to be seen by anyone looking for them.

In the summer of 1910, professional zoologist-collector Harry Swarth, with guide-trapper Ned Despard, spent just under three weeks at Yuquot and Tahsis, seeking birds and mammals for the research collections of Berkeley University.[2] The men collected specimens of 45 bird species, and "besides these, numbers

FIG. 2-1 (LEFT) Archaeologists investigating the midden at Yuquot in 1966. The distinct boundary between the historic (upper, whitish) layers and the prehistoric (lower, darker) is attributed to the abundance of clams following the extirpation of sea otters. *Photo courtesy of John Dewhirst.*

FIG. 2-2 (BELOW) Deeper into the Yuquot midden, the team uncovered the scapula of a whale. *Photo courtesy of John Dewhirst.*

of gulls, scoters, and phalaropes were seen, but under circumstances not permitting of absolute specific identification."[3]

ARCHAEOLOGICAL STUDIES

In 1980, the National Historic Parks and Sites branch of Parks Canada published the results of a 1966–79 archaeological investigation of the midden at Yuquot, the Mowachaht summer village site in Nootka Sound. The midden showed that the site was occupied continuously from about 4,300 years BP (before the present).[4] Biologist Nancy McAllister of the University of Ottawa analyzed the 6,000 bird bones excavated from the midden.[5]

McAllister identified 67 species, of which she deduced 23 were significant sources of food. These were mainly large- or medium-sized seabirds such as glaucous-winged gulls, murres, three species of cormorant, mostly Brandt's (a winter species), Canada geese, diving ducks, and, to her astonishment, a large number of short-tailed albatrosses, now almost extinct worldwide. She calculated that the midden contained at least 80 individuals and even suggested that "it could be referred to as an albatross midden." These birds were most prolific during the millennium prior to the Europeans' arrival. They were available during the summer, when ducks and geese were not. When boiled, the albatross provided a lot of fat, an important dietary supplement. McAllister calculated that, based on the contents of this midden, more than 30 per cent of the bird meat consumed by the Mowachaht may have come from albatross.[6] Their extirpation does not seem related to hunting by west coast Indigenous Peoples, but from depredation by plumage traders in the 19th and early 20th centuries at the birds' nesting grounds on islands near Japan.

McAllister considered that the most probable method for hunting albatrosses and similar sea-surface scavengers was by baited lines with gorges.[7] Hunters used this from canoes, even though these birds are now found only far beyond the continental shelf.[8] Some of the accounts by early European arrivals mentioned "Quebrantahuessos gulls." Theed Pearse[9] suspected that these were short-tailed albatrosses, since the brownish immature birds appear similar to the giant petrel of Patagonia, which mariners knew by that name.

The inhabitants of Yuquot do not seem to have consumed forest birds, since few such bones emerged from the midden. The team found bones of crows and ravens, but those species were considered taboo as food,[10] so they might have been tamed or died there while scavenging. Also, the children probably practised their hunting skills on small birds, which could account for the presence of some of the bones in the midden. Youngsters also trapped hummingbirds by smearing slug slime on twigs, keeping the tiny birds as pets or for trade with the newcomers.

A series of archaeological digs at a Huu-ay-aht village on a small island at the mouth of Barkley Sound between 2005 and 2008[11] revealed the inhabitants' patterns of harvesting fauna. The site seems to have been occupied, not always continuously, for about 5,000 years. The inhabitants' diet changed somewhat over time, but since the villagers lived close to the open Pacific, their protein derived principally from marine and coastal animals. Gay Frederick analyzed the bones found during the digs.[12] Her species lists indicated that the local people knew and exploited a great variety of fauna including the following.

- Fishes: 42 kinds, varying in size from sand lance to halibut and bluefin tuna, but mainly hake, salmon, rockfish, and dogfish. In the earliest period of the record, herring comprised the predominant species harvested, later replaced by hake. There is some suspicion that the count of herring was skewed because the sifting mesh was too coarse.

- Marine mammals: 14 kinds, including dolphins, seals, sea lions, whales, and sea otters.
- Land mammals: 12 kinds, including mule deer, elk, river otters, and a surprising number of mink, the latter presumably taken for their pelts. The bones of the deer and elk were mainly those of limbs, indicating that they had been hunted and butchered in the inland forests. Bones were also found of small dogs, adults and many pups, suggesting that they were domesticated and not hunted.
- Birds: 68 different species, ranging in size from sparrow to albatross. The greatest numbers of specimens found were ducks and geese, pelagic birds (petrels, shearwaters, albatrosses), alcids (auks such as murres and puffins), loons, gulls, cormorants, bald eagles, and northwestern crows. Many of the land birds, such as eagles, owls, thrushes, and towhees, were probably sought for their decorative feathers or ceremonial purposes, rather than for food.

The studies also investigated evidence for consumption of invertebrates, finding that 13 shellfish species were harvested, by far the most frequent being California mussel. While butter and littleneck clams were harvested in the earlier phases of the site's occupation, they were significantly absent from later layers. The report suggested this could have been the result of cultural restrictions such as local harvesting rights owned by other groups, or seasonal factors, for example, winter village use only.[13]

Harvesting of some other marine invertebrates, like sea cucumbers and shrimp, would have provided additional protein without appearing in the archaeological evidence. Octopuses and sea urchins would leave some traces in the midden, such as beaks and spines, but were not always included in archaeological studies.

The combination of archaeological investigations and recent studies of faunal occurrence provides a reasonable basis for appreciation of the reported findings by the early-arriving European naturalists.

FIG. 2-3   Male rufous hummingbird, noted by both Spanish and British explorers at Friendly Cove. *William Ellis, Natural History Museum plate #32, © Trustees of the Natural History Museum, London.*

FIG. 3-0   William Ellis's *Alca cirrhata* (tufted puffin) in breeding plumage.
Natural History Museum, plate #37, © *Trustees of the Natural History Museum, London.*

CHAPTER THREE

COOK'S NATURALISTS

"You are to carefully observe . . . the animals and fowls . . ."

I N 1776, UNDER A COVER story that he was to repatriate a native Tahitian, Captain James Cook set sail on his third great voyage of oceanic exploration. He carried, however, secret instructions to investigate the existence of a long-suspected northwest passage. Such a route, if it existed, would be of enormous strategic importance to a trading nation such as Britain. It would not only provide British merchants with a closer connection to the wealth of China, but also have other potential advantages. It would bypass both the Arab control of the western end of the Silk Road and the "Spanish Lake," as Britain's archrivals considered the southern Pacific Ocean. If the passage were there, the British needed to be the first to find and control it.

Cook's covert instructions also included the scope of his scientific mandate:

> You are also carefully to observe the nature of the Soil & the produce thereof; the Animals & Fowls that inhabit or frequent it; the Fishes that are to be found in the Rivers or upon the Coast, and in what plenty; and in case there are any, peculiar to such places, to describe them as minutely, and to make accurate drawings of them, you can; And, if you find any Metals, Minerals, or valuable Stones, or any extraneous Fossils, you are to bring home Specimens of each, as also of the Seeds of such Trees, Shrubs, Plants, Fruits and Grains, peculiar to those Places, as you may be able to collect, and to transmit them to our Secretary, that proper examination and experiments may be made of them,—You are likewise to observe the Genius, Temper, Disposition, and Number of the Natives and Inhabitants, where you find any; and to endeavour, by all proper means to cultivate a friendship with them.[1]

For this ill-fated voyage, Cook would take two ships: his own HMS *Resolution* with the supporting HMS *Discovery*, Captain Charles Clerke, RN, as master. James King, *Resolution*'s second lieutenant, was aware of the biological and ethnographic work that had been major elements of Cook's first two voyages of discovery.[2]

King respectfully enquired why Cook would not be taking professional naturalists with him on this, his third great voyage. Cook responded, with deep-seated passion, "Curse all scientists and all science into the bargain!"[3] King would later write the official record of the third voyage, after Cook's death in Hawaii.

Cook's experience with scientific supernumeraries on his previous expeditions had been far from positive. On the first, he had been obliged to welcome aboard—and cede his own cabin to—the strong-willed young dilettante Joseph Banks, who had brought a retinue of eight servants and two greyhounds.

The wealthy and well-connected Banks, a scientist of repute in his own right, was particularly interested in botanical discovery. He had provided the Royal Society with ample funds to cover the expenses of the scientific team that would join the voyage. Two other botanists had accompanied Banks, contributing valuable additional skills to the mission. One was Daniel Solander, an eminent Swedish scientist, who had studied the naming and classification of species under the renowned Linnaeus. The other was a Finn, Herman Spöring, who was both surgeon and watchmaker. Despite the contributions of the scientific team, Cook resented the publicity surrounding Banks and his work on natural history. This had upstaged the geographical discoveries, the original purpose and achievements of the voyage.

For the second of the expeditions—by then, to Cook's displeasure, known generally as "Mr. Banks's voyages"—the scientific entourage was to number 17, including two horn players and Solander. A young Scottish surgeon and astronomer, James Lind, would replace Spöring. However, after a dispute with the Royal Society over command of the voyage, the Admiralty withdrew permission for Banks and companions to participate.

They were replaced by a father-and-son team of German naturalists, the Forsters: Johann Reinhold and Georg. The former, a dour, irritable, Calvinist pastor, had up to then made a precarious living as a teacher, translator, and writer. His son Georg had, from boyhood, accompanied him on scientific expeditions, learning how to collect, identify, preserve, and describe animals and plant specimens. In so doing, Georg had honed innate talents for drawing and writing. During the voyage, the father managed to infuriate Cook and all levels of his shipmates, but the somewhat more personable son fared better.

At the end of the voyage, and six weeks before Cook's official report appeared, Georg published an unauthorized account, well received by the scientific community and by the general public. Once more, Cook was upstaged.

Cook's jaundiced view of scientists had derived from direct, bitter experience of the snobbish Banks, the insufferable elder Forster, and his son's pre-emptive publication. With much relief, Cook learned that scientific supernumeraries would not be on his third voyage. Instead, suitable members of the crew would take on the mission's natural history and ethnographic research.

Cook's instructions were to make landfall on the Pacific coast about 45° north and then head northward as far as "65° or farther, if you are not obstructed by Lands or Ice; taking care not to lose any time in exploring Rivers or Inlets," but he was permitted to stop to collect wood, water, or "Refreshments."

SCIENTIFIC STUDIES AT NOOTKA

Under the Refreshment provision, Cook anchored on March 30, 1778, in King George's Sound, the place that would become known as Nootka. He needed to replenish his freshwater supplies. More significantly, he wanted to replace some rotted masts and spars before facing the rigours of the Arctic. For this, he could take advantage of the splendid stands of timber he had seen there. That process took until April 26, providing a window of almost four weeks for Cook and the astronomers to measure their longitude accurately. Others used the time to investigate local natural history and ethnology. These were the first such studies by any European on the Pacific northwest coast.

FIG. 3-1 Cook's men meeting Mowachaht people below their village of Yuquot. *Webber's plate in Cook's published journal. From author's collection.*

An earlier voyage by the Spanish frigate *Santiago*, under the command of Juan Pérez, had preceded Cook's arrival at Nootka by four years. At an anchorage they called San Lorenzo, Pérez and his crew had traded with the locals but had not landed. Pérez recorded nothing of the natural history of the coast he had seen and was criticized for the lack of specific detail in his report.

CHARLES CLERKE

A major contributor to Cook's natural history reports was Captain Charles Clerke. He had sailed with Cook on both earlier expeditions, during which he had spoken with Banks, Solander, and the Forsters about their work and findings. Clerke's personal journal included notes on the birds, animals, and plants they found.

Clerke had served in the Royal Navy from the age of 13. While still a midshipman, he had seen active service in the Seven Years War. He had been aboard John Byron's HMS *Dolphin* during a 22-month circumnavigation to explore the Pacific. This included, he reported, encountering the notorious giants of Patagonia.[4] Between Cook's second and third voyages, he voluntarily served time in London's notorious Fleet prison for a debt incurred by his brother. During his incarceration, he contracted the tuberculosis that would later prove fatal. Clerke's strong sense of duty to his leader kept him at his post, further weakening his condition, as the expedition entered the Arctic Circle on two occasions.

Clerke kept a personal journal during the third voyage, but it was discovered only after the official version, James King's edition of Cook's narrative, had been published. Clerke's very significant contribution was included in an important new edition in 1968 under the supervision of John Beaglehole. This will be discussed later in the chapter.

WILLIAM ANDERSON

Another contributor to the reports was the Scottish surgeon William Anderson. He, too, had served aboard *Resolution* on Cook's second voyage, assembling a large collection of botanical specimens for Banks and impressing Cook. His health failing, Anderson broke off his journal in early September 1777, while they were still in Tahiti. Nevertheless, it seems he was still able to study the natural history and local language of King George's (Nootka) Sound. His 275-entry Nootkan word list given in the official account included several related to the natural world: 15 plants, 14 animals, 7 birds, and 6 fishes. Curiously absent were the words for sea otter, gull, salal, salmon, or halibut, all of which must have been very present at Yuquot village on Nootka Sound.

Tragically, Anderson, like Clerke, had contracted tuberculosis before the third voyage sailed, and during its course, their conditions deteriorated. Anderson succumbed while in the Bering Sea, not long after visiting Nootka, and Clerke a year later at Kamchatka. These two deaths, coupled with Cook's own demise at the hands of Hawaiians in February 1779, complicated preparing the official account of the voyage.

The task of compiling the section covering the Nootka interlude fell to James King, by then promoted to the rank of captain. He did not clarify the original sources for the lists of species he reported, nor is it certain exactly where the species were observed or collected. King, too, died of tuberculosis in 1784, barely a year after he had completed his work on the voyage's official account.

JOHN WEBBER AND WILLIAM ELLIS

Two artists were part of the expedition's complement and illustrated elements of natural history they saw: John Webber and William Ellis. Webber studied at Cambridge and then trained

FIG. 3-2 John Webber's drawing in Cook's published journal of a sea otter. He probably drew it from a skin, without having seen one on land. *From author's collection.*

as a painter of landscapes and portraits in London and Paris. After exhibiting at the Royal Academy, he was noticed by the Admiralty, which appointed him official artist for the voyage, and he sailed aboard *Resolution*. He mainly produced views, ships, interiors of houses, and portraits of people, but he also made sketches of some local cultural objects, birds, and animals, including a well-known one of a sea otter.

William Ellis, through Banks's patronage, sailed as assistant surgeon's mate aboard Clerke's *Discovery*. A gifted and prolific artist, he drew coastal views and scenes of local village life, and he compiled a portfolio of 150 pencil and watercolour natural history drawings, including 90 of birds. In contravention of Admiralty orders, he delivered the portfolio to Banks at the end of the voyage. He also published, without permission, his journal of the voyage,[5] mentioning briefly some of the birds, animals, and plants he had seen. The book proved so popular that it ran to three editions.

SUBSEQUENT IDENTIFICATION ATTEMPTS

Later, attempts were made to identify the species noted in the various accounts of the voyage. A major work of this kind was by Theed Pearse, who was born and well educated in Bedford, England, and qualified to practise law. Coming to British Columbia in 1909, he worked in Vancouver until 1916, then moved to Courtenay, where he continued until he retired in 1941. Thereafter he devoted his attention to his lifelong hobby, the study of birds. In 1968 he published *Birds of the Early Explorers in the Northern Pacific.*[6] In it, he identified the birds mentioned in the various accounts from the exploration expeditions. His research included the official account, James King's, of Cook's third voyage, not just from the time he was at Nootka, but also from the voyage's continuation to Alaska and Kamchatka. Pearse covered the birds of not only the Cook voyage, but other British and several Spanish, Russian, French, and American expeditions as well.

Pearse included a list—made in 1949 by Erwin Stresemann, an ornithologist at the Berlin Museum—of the birds collected on the Cook voyages into the north Pacific.[7]

About the time Pearse's book was ready for publication, another major work appeared about Cook's third voyage, this one by New Zealander John Beaglehole. It was a scholarly, annotated edition of Cook's third voyage, in the series published by the Hakluyt Society of London.[8] The editor consulted eminent specialists in London to identify the species mentioned in the text.

Beaglehole's edition contained a long extract from Clerke's journal,[9] including 10 pages on the Nootka Sound anchorage. In the section on birds, Clerke had written:

> We arriv'd at this place in so early a part of the Year [April] that very few Birds had begun to make their appearance; as the more common in all Country's are generally those that are seen we may reasonably suppose the following may be placed in that Class.[10]

Beaglehole had consulted specialists at the University of British Columbia and the Natural History Museum in London to help identify the species of birds mentioned in the journal, including a few not recorded in King's account.

BIRDS MENTIONED IN JAMES KING'S ACCOUNT

King's official account included a record of the wildlife at Nootka in greater detail. It began with a lengthy description of the sea otter, and then continued:

> Birds are not only rare as to the different species but very scarce as to numbers, and these are so shy that in all probability they are continually harassed by the natives, perhaps to eat them as

FIG. 3-4 *Trumpeter swans migrating south*, a 1945 painting by Frank Beebe, long-serving illustrator for the Royal BC Museum's series of handbooks. *From a postcard in author's collection.*

FIG. 3-3 (FACING PAGE) The "large crested American kingfisher" noted in Cook's journal is now known as the belted kingfisher, still common throughout Vancouver Island. *From Audubon's* Birds of America *[image edited].*

food; certainly to get possession of their feathers, which they use as ornaments. Those which frequent the woods are crows and ravens, not at all different from our English ones; a bluish jay or magpie; common wrens, which are the only singing bird that we heard; the Canadian or migrating thrush, and a considerable number of brown eagles with white heads and tails; which, though they seem principally to frequent the coast, come into the Sound in bad weather and perch in the trees. Amongst some other birds, of which the natives either brought fragments or dried skins, we could distinguish a small species of hawk, a heron, and the alcyon, or large crested American kingfisher.[11]

Of the birds appearing in the preceding excerpt, Pearse recognized northwestern crow, Steller's jay, winter wren, American robin (noting that Ellis painted this bird and a varied thrush on the same plate), and bald eagle. Pearse leaves the raven, small hawk, heron, and kingfisher without comment as, presumably, obvious or unidentifiable from the description.

King's account went on to describe water birds:

The birds which frequent the waters and shores are not more numerous than the others. The Quebrantahuessos gulls and shags were seen off the coast; and the two last frequent the Sound. They are of the common sorts; the shag being our cormorant or water crow. We saw two sorts of wild-ducks; one black with a white head, which were in considerable flocks; the other, white with a red bill, but of a larger size; and the great lumme, or diver, found in our northern countries. There were also seen, once or twice, some swans flying across the Sound to the northward; but we knew nothing of their haunts. On the shore, besides the sandpiper described above, we found another, about the size of a lark, which bears a great affinity to the burre; and a plover differing very little from our common sea-lark.

Pearse speculated that "Quebrantahuessos" was most likely the short-tailed albatross.[12] He is more confident in identifying the pelagic cormorant, surf scoter, common merganser, and common loon. He did not identify the swans—they were probably migrating trumpeters—or either of the sandpipers, but he considered the "burre" to be a dunlin, noting that Ellis had also depicted that species. King's account continued:

> There are also some, which I believe are not mentioned, or at least vary, very considerably from the accounts given of them by any writers who have treated professionally on this part of natural history. The first two of these are species of woodpeckers. One less than a thrush, of a black colour above, with white spots on the wings, a crimson head, neck and breast, and a yellowish olive-coloured belly; from which last circumstances it might be called the yellow-bellied woodpecker. The other is a larger, and much more elegant bird, of a dusky colour on the upper part, richly waved with black, except about the head, the belly of a reddish cast, with round black spots; a black spot on the breast; and the underside of the wings and tail of a plain scarlet colour, though blackish above, with a crimson streak running from the angle of the mouth, a little down the neck on each side. The third and fourth, are a small bird of the finch kind, about the size of a linnet, of a dark dusky colour, whitish below, with a black head and neck and white bill, and a sandpiper of the size of a small pigeon, of a dusky brown colour and white below, except the throat and breast with a broad band across the wings. There are also humming birds; which yet seem to differ from the numerous sorts of this delicate animal already known, unless they be a mere variety of the Trochilus colubris of Linneus [sic]. These perhaps, inhabit to the Southward and spread to the northward as a season advances; because we saw none at first, though, near the time of our departure the natives brought them to the ships in great numbers.

In this passage, Pearse recognized what have later been listed as the red-breasted sapsucker and the northern flicker, birds both also drawn by Ellis, and the Oregon form of the dark-eyed junco. The third sandpiper of the account could have been, he thought, either a black turnstone or a surfbird. Again, Ellis drew this ambiguous bird. He also mislabelled his drawing of the rufous hummingbird, for which Pearse corrected the identification.

The last part of King's account dealing with the Nootka sightings reads:

> The gulls were of the common sort and those which fly in flocks. The shags were large and black, with a white spot behind the wings as they flew. But probably on the large water cormorant. Also a single bird flying about, to appearances of the gull kind of a snowy white colour with black along part of the upper side of the wings.

Pearse had difficulty identifying the lone white gull. He wondered if it might have been a herring gull, a Thayer's gull in faded plumage, a Sabine's gull, or possibly a mew gull. The white patch confirmed his earlier identification of the pelagic cormorant. Later in his coverage of the Cook voyage, Pearse notes that "there is no doubt that some of the birds described as crows were Ravens which would be quite common but not listed anywhere."

He tried to trace where the collection of specimens ended up but describes the history as "unfortunate." At the time of his writing, he noted "few are left; one in Vienna is the type specimen of the Marbled Murrelet [probably taken at Kayak Island in Alaska]. There are still others in the Berlin Museum."

For the Nootka Sound episode, Stresemann listed 16 species. In addition to those identified by Pearse were golden-crowned

FIG. 3-5 *Picus auratus* (northern flicker), drawn by William Ellis and described in detail in Cook's journal. *Natural History Museum, plate #19* © *Trustees of the Natural History Museum, London.*

sparrow, varied thrush, snow goose, wandering tattler, least sandpiper, red knot, and green sandpiper.

Pearse provided a biography of Ellis, who, he felt, had received inadequate recognition by Cook or King, particularly after having taken over the role of naturalist following Anderson's death. He quoted the following from Ellis's account of the voyage referring to Nootka:

> These people [Mowachaht] are very ingenious in making calls to imitate the notes of different birds and animals; by which means they take great numbers; they likewise make use of whalebone springs, like those used with us to catch snipes. Among other articles of trade, they frequently brought birds of several kinds for sale, particularly a beautiful species of humming bird and a bird of the snipe kind, it is not improbable that some of these are caught in this manner.[13]

In other quotes from Ellis, Pearse recorded that Nootka "afforded excellent shelter for all kinds of waterfowl but they are shy to a degree. . . . Principal land birds we saw were eagle, thrushes, growse [*sic*], owls, snipes and several smaller kinds." And shortly after leaving Nootka, they saw "a large flock of geese," which Pearse suspected to be Brant.

The portfolio of Ellis's paintings, delivered to Banks at the end of the voyage, now forms part of the collections held at the Natural History Museum. Pearse noted that the paintings had received acclaim by art experts. He quoted Elsa Allen—"External parts, such as bills, feet and eyes, which today are not always accurately executed, are drawn with great care"—and Averil Lysaght, who considered them to be "of considerable charm and delicacy." Pearse concluded: "Having had the pleasure of examining the paintings, I thoroughly concur." Even so, he later recorded that Webber also painted many of the same birds as

FIG. 3-6 William Ellis's paintings of the varied thrush (upper) and American robin (lower), both very familiar to Vancouver Islanders today. *Natural History Museum plate #74,* © *Trustees of the Natural History Museum, London.*

Ellis, adding, "I am of the opinion that Webber's are distinctly the better; he introduces some background and his plumages show more detail."[14]

Pearse devoted a page to Captain Charles Clerke, mentioning that his log contains a few brief entries of bird sightings, but that he "does not appear to have kept a diary[15] or record other than his logbook, though evidently, he contributed to Captain King's narrative."

The following compares Clerke's identifications with those of Beaglehole's specialists.

BIRDS NOTED IN CLERKE'S JOURNAL	SPECIALISTS' IDENTIFICATION [WITH AUTHOR NOTES]
"small kind of eagle"	"probably a Buteo Hawk" [most likely a red-tailed hawk]
"blue titmouse"	"probably the Red-breasted Nuthatch"
"the small brown Godwit, and the spotted Godwit"	"likely that these . . . were the same species, the Pacific Godwit" [or bar-tailed godwit]
"Gulls of 2 kinds viz: the common brown & white, and the ash colour'd"	"Perhaps the immature Western Gull, and probably the Glaucous-winged Gull"
"2 or 3 species of Ducks, among which was the Mallard; the red-breasted Goosander and a small species of Geese, of a dark, dirty brown colour"	"Red-breasted Merganser" "The Black Brant"

In his "Vegetable Productions" section, Clerke listed 26 species of trees, including the strawberry tree (arbutus), but also raspberry, bramble, and whortleberry. He also provided a list of 26 flowering plants, adding, "Besides the plants above mention'd, there were great numbers just making their appearance; likewise, 4 or 5 kinds of Shrubs which were not known." These unknown shrubs would certainly have included salal, abundant in the area; a curious omission is what would become known as the Nootka rose.

Clerke concluded, "These People seldom leave the waterside, but live a great deal in their Canoes and supply themselves with the principal part of their Provender from the Water." He listed some fishes that seemed most abundant:

FISHES NOTED IN CLERKE'S JOURNAL	SPECIALISTS' IDENTIFICATION
"Species of Roach or Dace"	"types of Sea Perch, one the Striped, the other unidentifiable"
"a smaller one resembling a Sprat"	"California Anchovy"
"Rock Cod"	"Pacific Cod"
"Elephant Fish—the ugliest and most uncouth form'd Fish I ever saw"	"Ratfish"
"a small fish of the Perch kind . . . the colour a fine Red"	"Perhaps the Redtail Sea Perch"

Clerke noted, "I have reason to believe that the abundance which reign'd during our visit by no means continues throughout the Year." He was correct in that the runs of fish are seasonal, and for that same reason, he will have been unaware of the equally abundant runs of different species of salmon and of halibut, and so made no mention of these. He described the sailors' attempts to catch fish:

> We tried with Hooks and Lines but had no Success, however here is an inexhaustible abundance of large and excellent Muscles [California mussels], which are with the utmost ease and convenience procured at low Water.

In discussing fish, Clerke included whales and described the local peoples' abilities and techniques for hunting these creatures:

> I believe they must be very clever at this kind of business, as they certainly destroy a number of these Fish: they sometimes had Porpusses & once a Sea Beaver [sea otter], all procured by means of this Instrument [harpoon].

Clerke's other note of the local mammals is in a passage concerning the clothing used by the Mowachaht Peoples.

> [It] consists of Garments made of Skins, of which they have several kinds; those of the black Bear, Wolf, Wild Cat, Martin, Sea Beaver, Seal, and a very large, thick Skin, which I think most probably is it of the Elk. . . . They sometimes work with a fine, long fur, which they get from some animal or other, that we at present know nothing of ["Mountain Goat" according to Beaglehole].

James King's own journal recorded:

> We saw but few Animals, & these only the Raccoon, Polecat, & Squirrel; but in the natives possession were the Skins of Black Bears, Wolves, foxes, wildcats, Raccoons, Polecats, Deer, Martins, Ermines, & Squirrels.[16]

JOHN LEDYARD

Another member of James Cook's crew was the corporal of the marine detachment, John Ledyard. He also published his journal before the official account appeared. In it, he too described the vegetation at Nootka:

> It is intirely [sic] covered with woods such as maple, ash, birch, oak, hemlock, but mostly with tall, well grown pine. We also found currant bushes, wild raspberry and juniper bushes, and little crabbed apple-trees, but could not learn whether they bore any fruit, neither is it probable that they do.

Ledyard was an American, and so would have been more familiar with New World species than were the English officers. He continued:

The light in which this county will appear most to advantage respects the variety of its animals, and the richness of their furr [*sic*]. They have foxes, sables, hares, marmosets, ermines, weazles, bears, wolves, deer, moose, dogs, otters, beavers, and a species of weazle called the glutton; the skin of this animal was sold at Kamchatka . . . for sixty rubles, which is near 12 guineas, and had it been sold in China it would have been worth 30 guineas.[17]

Beaglehole also consulted botanist Helen Gilkey, who was not able to shed much light on the tree species noted by Ledyard. The zoologist Robert Storm attempted to identify some of the animals. Storm pointed out that the members of the expedition had no time for hunting or seeking wildlife, so the only indications of the local mammal population were the pelts worn, or offered in trade, by the Mowachaht. Such pelts were often damaged or lacking in heads or extremities, adding to the difficulty of identification. Also, the Mowachaht could have obtained those pelts from elsewhere, in trade.

Storm thought the "foxes" were the red fox, native to the island, and similarly, the "sables" the marten. The "hares" were possibly the snowshoe hare, traded from the interior or northern communities. He thought Ledyard's "marmoset" could well have been a Vancouver Island marmot—if so, this would have been the first record of this subspecies. The "glutton" might have been a mink, marten, or wolverine, all present on the island. The "wolves" were probably the endemic subspecies of grey wolf.[18] Storm understood correctly that the "moose" did not occur on the island and thought that the large hides might have been those of elk, as did Cook.

Beavers were found in the Nootka region in that era, and the Mowachaht chief Maquinna even presented Cook with his personal status cape made from what Cook thought were beaver pelts. More likely, they were of prime, male sea otters. Clerke's references to sea beaver probably also referred to sea otter.

Pelts of the latter became an important item of trade with Cook's officers and men, ideal for the warm clothing and bunk covers that they would shortly need farther north. Sea otters have the highest hair density of any animal, compensating for their lack of blubber. In all, the two ships' companies acquired 1,500 prime sea otter pelts by the time they left Nootka. They subsequently discovered that such pelts were worth a fortune in China. When the news got out, it triggered a rush of trading vessels arriving to exploit the opportunity.

FIG. 3-7 *Tais de Nutka*. N. Moncayo's portrait of a Mowachaht chieftain in his status cloak of prime sea otter pelts and wearing the hat of a distinguished whaler. *Archivo General del Ministerio de Asuntos Exteriores y de Cooperación, Madrid, ms. 146, lám. 30.*

FIG. 4-0 The black-banded rockfish is one of 68 species of "rock cod" found off the coasts of Vancouver Island. *Plate 6 from* Fishes of the Pacific Coast of Canada, *Fisheries Research Board of Canada, 1961.*

CHAPTER FOUR

IN THE AFTERMATH OF COOK

URING THE LAST DECADE OF the 18th century, several expeditions retraced Cook's visit to Nootka and the surrounding coastline. Bearing flags from several nations, the missions sailed with varying motives. Early among those voyagers were traders seeking to exploit the opportunity offered by acquiring sea otter pelts to sell to the Chinese market. All these traders came and went without the knowledge of the Spanish authorities in Mexico who considered the whole coast to be under their jurisdiction

Seeking new sources of pelts, the traders explored the coastline. In 1787 one of them, Charles Barkley, discovered an entrance that he realized corresponded with one reportedly discovered in 1592 by Juan de Fuca. He so named it but did not enter what appeared to be a strait.

Few such trading missions wasted time recording "irrelevant" observations on local birdlife or vegetation; however, two did. One of those was a member of a group of American traders, known generally as "Bostonmen."

BOSTONMEN HASWELL AND HOSKIN

Three ships, *Columbia Rediviva*, *Lady Washington*, and the locally assembled *Adventure*, spent several months in the area during winter of 1788. The following season, using Nootka as their base, the Bostonmen traded for sea otters along the coast between the Juan de Fuca entrance and Alaska. One of the officers, Robert Haswell, kept a journal, later published,[1] in which he summarized the aspects of natural history he had seen in the area.

In a long, curiously spelled, and barely punctuated entry dated March 16, 1789, Haswell wrote "a short account of Nootka Sound and its enverence [environs]," which included:

> In the woods we find Fir spruce of several sorts white pine Red and white Cedar white Cypruss Ash Alder Burch Hemlock popple maple Crab tree Wilde cherry and a small tree that resembles a Hemlock the wood is close graned and resembling mahogany but heavyer. And the natives tell me there is oak at Matchlat [Muchalaht]. A village far up the Sound we frequently meet with gooseberrys raspberrys in the spring there is plenty of small wild

onions [probably camas bulbs] but late in the season they are not so well flavoured. the rivers produce water creeses and the marshes Samphire. Their is pulin wild celery hogweed sorrel wild peas and mullin.

Turning to mammals and birdlife, he continued:

> Here are Bears Wolves Moose fallow and rain deer Foxes raccoons squrrels Land and sea otters Dogs Beavers Martins wild Cats and Mice.
>
> In the woods we find several sorts of woodpickers, Robbins the Vergina red bird, snow birds, yellow birds, long tailed thrush ground birds, tomtits, s[p]arrows wrens, parterages, Quales, hawks owls, Eagles of several sorts Ravens, Crow, swallous Doves and pidgeons.
>
> Of water fowl are Geese, Duck, Brants two sorts of shags several sorts of Shrill drake, two sorts of teel, large Loons several sorts of divers and Gulls, Murs, Marsh larks, kingfishers, and swans.[2]
>
> Fish their air plenty of whales, but fue spermasity [sperm whales] maney right Whales and an abunants of humpbacks, Porpoises Salmon of various species Breem flounders Cod and halibut Sculpins Frost fish There are fish resembling the West india Red and white snapers black fish Dog fish Herrins Serdenas and Seals The shell fish are Oisters Scollops Clams Limpts coules mussels pearl sea egs [urchins] and starfish.[3]

That group of Bostonmen made a second trading voyage to the area in 1891. Haswell was again aboard, along with a new man, John Hoskins, a supercargo sent by the owners to watch out for their interest. Better educated than Haswell, Hoskins wrote a journal that is easier to read. He too noted wildlife he observed; his lists replicate many of Haswell's entries, adding a few more.[4]

A FRENCHMAN EN PASSANT

In August 1786 a two-ship scientific expedition, intended as France's response to Cook's voyages, sailed southward along the Pacific coast of North America. In command was a distinguished naval officer, prominent figure of the Enlightenment, and admirer of Cook, Jean-François de Galaup, comte de la Pérouse. The overt purpose for being in the region was to investigate the trade in sea otter pelts. The more confidential objective was to find the Northwest Passage; in this, the expedition was unsuccessful. The complement included several naturalists, with this instruction:

> To investigate the natural history resources. The Naturalists to make observations peculiar to their studies and act according to instructions from the French Academy.... [The commander] will ensure that natural, terrestrial and marine curiosities are collected from each of the three kingdoms;[5] he will get them classified according to category, and will have drawn up, for each species, a descriptive catalogue indicating where they have been found, and the use to which the local natives put them; and if they are plants, the virtues they attribute to them.[6]

Behind schedule and making a hurried departure following a serious misadventure at Lituya Bay in Alaska, the ships headed for Monterey in California. Passing Breaker Point at the south side of the entrance to Nootka Sound in fog, they noted, "We were surrounded by small land birds resting in our rigging; we caught several that are so common in Europe they do not warrant a description."[7]

Fifteen months later, both ships of the Pérouse expedition were lost with all hands, presumably in a typhoon, off the northern coast of Australia.

FIG. 4-1 *Pileated woodpecker*, one of the most dramatic birds of the forests around Nootka seen by early European visitors. *From* Audubon's Birds of America.

James Colnett was a British exception to the rule that, amid the keen competition for pelts, fur traders found little time to observe natural history. As a midshipman, he had sailed with Cook on the first two voyages, had seen eminent naturalists at work, and had gained some knowledge of, and interest in, the topic. During his first visit to Nootka in 1787, Colnett made lists of the vegetation and wildlife found there. His ship's surgeon, a Scottish botanist named Archibald Menzies, probably helped him create the lists. (If Menzies kept his own journal of the 1787 voyage, it has not survived.) In his journal, Colnett recorded:

> Vegetable productions are numerous.... Strawberries, raspberries, currants, gooseberries, alder, partridge berries [possibly kinnikinnick], & Apples about the size of a small Cherry [crabapple] there are several other kinds of berries the best of them are Red & purple ones growing on Bushes a little larger than currant.... Many plants that were found promiscuously on the shore were eaten of and agreed with us. The most common ones us'd were leeks [nodding onion], and a green call'd Lamb's Quarters [goosefoot or wild spinach] this last we were fondest of & most easily procured.
>
> The Quadrupeds must be numerous from the different Skins the natives wear, the only ones I saw were dogs, a small land Otter, & Deer.
>
> The Sea Animals were Seal, Whales, porpoises, & sea Otters, of the latter great numbers were seen in different parts of the Sound.
>
> Birds are not numerous & very Shy, Crows, Ravens, White headed Eagles, Fishing Hawks [osprey], Herons, King Fisher, wood peckers, a bird like the English Hedge Sparrow, Swallows, a small bird of a dirty green colour, sand Piper, Humming birds and Pigeons [band-tailed].

FIG. 4-2 (COUNTER-CLOCKWISE FROM TOP LEFT) Birds seen and sketched in James Colnett's journals: tufted puffin, pigeon guillemot, bufflehead, harlequin, and Steller's jay. *Images from James Colnett's journals, ms. 1519, courtesy of the Royal BC Museum and Archives [image edited].*

Sea & water Birds are found in no great plenty & are the Quebrantehuesses [short-tailed albatrosses; see Pearse, pp. 156–57] Gulls, Shags, Divers and wild Ducks.

Fish are in great plenty the Principal sorts are the small sardine, a silver fish like a Bream, also a Gold colour'd one with Blue Longitudinal stripes . . . Salmon, Salmon trout, Flounders, Skate Eels [Pacific lamprey], Sculpins, Cod . . . Starfish sea Eggs [urchins] & Crabs haul'd on shore at times.

Great quantities of Cockles & Clams are found by digging in the sand at low water, & on the Rocks are abundance of large muscles & a few welks & snails & caught in the seine a very small scallop. Of the Reptile kind were snakes Brown lizards, Centipedes, Caterpillars, & earth worms. Insect tribe common Butterfly, Bumble Bee, small Bee, Wasps, Moths two or three kinds of flies, a few Beetles. Musquitoes & Spiders.

Besides the Rocks that constitute the Mountains and the Shores there, a Black one like the Oil Stone of Carpenters & one of a dirty pea Green colour both of which they polish for working tools and war weapons, a piece of Rock Crystal was purchas'd. I believe it to be scarce as it was the only piece seen.[8]

Menzies did some botanical collecting in the area, accompanied by Maquinna's sister-in-law and another young woman.

These guides knew their local food and medicinal plants well, and seemed to him to be intrigued by his interest. He later realized that they had also been provided for his protection. Lone strangers had often been attacked, even killed; the women's high status probably deterred such threats to him. Within a few years, Menzies returned and continued the work he had started, making a substantial contribution to the scientific record of the region.

FIG. 4-3 *Mujer de Nuca.* José Cardero's portrait of a young Mowachaht woman dressed in cedar-fibre clothing. Two of them accompanied Menzies as he searched for plants around Yuquot. *Museo de América, Madrid.*

The Age of Enlightenment was an intellectual movement in which empirical evidence, rational discussion, and the scientific method gained favour over obedience to faith-based dogma, mysticism, or superstition. The trend came slowly to Spain, resisted by conservative forces, particularly the clergy. It did, however, benefit from the 1759 accession of a new Bourbon monarch, Carlos III. An enlightened despot, the new king wanted to know more about the resources of the Indies, to make better use of them. He sent out botanical expeditions to Chile, Peru, and New Granada (Colombia / Venezuela).

In 1768 Spain established a naval shipbuilding base at San Blas in New Spain (Mexico), near the important centre of Guadalajara and only a few days' sailing from Acapulco. Six years later, a group of junior officers and technicians trained in navigation and chart making, called pilots, arrived there and began a series of exploratory voyages northward. One early sortie was that of Juan Pérez in 1774.

In 1785 in Seville, Carlos III established the Archives of the Indies, to bring together all documents related to the Spanish Empire. That same year, he ordered the construction of a magnificent neoclassical edifice in the centre of Madrid to house the imperial natural history collection. That building is now the renowned art museum El Prado, "the meadow." Carlos also authorized a voyage of scientific research into the Pacific in 1789, led by Alejandro Malaspina.

MARTÍN DE SESSÉ'S GRAND BOTANICAL PROJECT

In New Spain, military physician Dr. Martín de Sessé y Lacasta proposed a multi-purpose botanical initiative. In addition to mounting collecting expeditions, the project would establish a botanical garden, a chair in botany at the university, and an academy of pharmacy and medicine. The viceroy and the new

king both endorsed the concept, which would "examine, draw and describe methodically the natural products of the most fertile dominions of New Spain . . . to banish the doubts and uncertainties then existing in medicine, dyeing and other useful arts."[9]

Appointed director with a six-year commission, Sessé was to have a staff of qualified scientists. He also needed technical illustrators for work on the natural history descriptions and sought recommendations from the director of the Royal Art Academy. The best of these, 18-year-old Atanasio Echeverría, proved his worth in the field and the laboratory. An eminent botanist in Madrid described one of Echeverría's drawings of a butterfly as "so completely charming that it appeared to want to escape from the paper." This talent made Echeverría an invaluable member of the expedition.

Among the students enrolling in the first course in botany offered by Sessé's new organization, two stood out as exceptional: José María Maldonado and José Mariano Moziño. Both, together with the artist Echeverría, would make enormous contributions to the natural history knowledge of the Viceroyalty of New Spain. This included at the time Mexico, Alta California, and the area around San Lorenzo de Nuca, known to the British as Nootka.

Moziño, born a pure-blood Spaniard in a small town in Mexico, excelled in all sciences leading to a medical degree. Instead of taking up that career, he continued his studies in botany and pharmacy. Moziño's aptitude soon attracted the attention of Sessé, who arranged for him to be part of the botanical field team. His classmate Maldonado also joined the expedition.

In December 1788 Sessé's royal sponsor died, with the crown passing to his second son. The new king, Carlos IV, did not share his father's enthusiasms for scientific progress nor for the affairs of the Indies. The situation in France concerned him more, where, a few months later, revolutionaries would storm the Bastille.

FIG. 4-4 Atanasio Echeverría painted butterflies "so completely charming that [they] appeared to want to escape from the paper." *Biological Illustrations #6331.1269, Torner Collection of Sessé and Mociño, Hunt Institute for Biological Documentation, Pittsburgh, PA.*

Esteban Martínez, who had been second-in-command to Juan Pérez on the 1774 voyage,[10] realized that the place they had called San Lorenzo was the same as King George's Sound, or Nootka, in the published accounts of Cook's voyage. He suggested to the viceroy that, to counter rumoured intentions of the Russians, the place should be identified as part of Alta California and therefore under Spanish dominion. The viceroy gave him command of two ships and orders to establish a fort at the entrance to the harbour.

When Martínez arrived at Nootka in 1789, he discovered to his astonishment that foreign ships were already at anchor in the harbour, and he learned that more were about to join them. A man of short temper and poor judgment, he quarrelled with an equally strong-willed British captain, James Colnett, who had already spent the two previous seasons trading on the coast. The conflict grew heated and Martínez arrested Colnett, seizing his ships, crew, and cargo, and sent them all under a Spanish guard to San Blas. Following the incident, Martínez abandoned his new fort and returned to San Blas for the winter.

Another British trader, John Meares, reported this "Nootka incident" to the British government, which further escalated the matter into a diplomatic confrontation. It almost led to armed conflict between the rival imperial powers, but they defused it in time with a treaty called the Nootka Convention of 1790. Under its terms, two commissioners were to meet at Nootka to settle details of jurisdiction over a piece of land that Meares claimed to be his.

While Martínez had been away from San Blas, two men had taken command in Mexico. They reviewed the incidents at Nootka and Martínez's actions, making decisions about what was to happen next. The first of these men was a new viceroy, the count of Revillagigedo. The other, as the new commandant of the District of San Blas, was Captain Juan Francisco de la Bodega y Quadra. The latter had first come to the base in 1768 with the first cadre of navigation specialists. He had made two heroic voyages of exploration along the coast as far as Alaska and afterward had served with distinction in Spain. Accompanying him on this posting were six other officers to further strengthen the naval force at San Blas.

Revillagigedo and Bodega y Quadra agreed that Martínez's withdrawal from Nootka in 1789 had been a strategic error. So, when they mounted a major expedition to Nootka early the following year, they gave command of a three-ship flotilla to seasoned naval officer Francisco de Eliza, and ensured he was well supplied with materials and arms. Eliza was to re-establish the fort and change its name to Santa Cruz de Nuca, to show that Nootka was a permanent outpost of Spain, occupied and defended.

Accompanying the expedition was a company of Mexican militia under the command of soldier Captain Pedro de Alberni. Alberni was a skilled horticulturist and had brought with him live-stock and a selection of seeds for an experimental farm, in what appears to have been the first deliberate introduction of extraneous species to Vancouver Island by Europeans. Unfortunately, the ships also brought Norwegian rats, which came ashore, multiplied, and impeded Alberni's efforts at farming.

As well as rebuilding the fort and outbuildings, Eliza was commissioned to explore the vicinity north and south, guided by several skilled pilots who were part of his complement. In addition to charting the area, Eliza was to examine "the nature and character of the country, the quadrupeds, insects, birds, fish, metals precious stones, plants vegetables, and fruits, and the character and number of Indians and strangers."[11]

How he was meant to fulfill this requirement was unclear, since no one trained in natural sciences accompanied the exped-

ition. Eliza was also to start trading for sea otter pelts and he carried sheets of Mexican copper to pay for them.

ELIZA'S EXPLORATIONS INTO JUAN DE FUCA, 1790 AND 1791

Soon after arriving, Eliza dispatched two exploring parties. Ensign Manuel Quimper took *Princesa Real*—the renamed sloop seized from the English captain James Colnett—with 40 men, including the experienced pilot Gonzalo López de Haro. They headed south from Nootka into Clayoquot Sound, then into the entrance that Barkley had found and named the Strait of Juan de Fuca. They explored the length of the strait, noting at the eastern end some arms that led in different directions, but time did not permit further investigation. Because of unfavourable tides and winds, they had great difficulty leaving the strait and could not get back to Nootka, so Quimper opted to return to their Mexican base in San Blas.

There, Quimper and López de Haro prepared a chart and report on their exploring mission, including some notes on the wildlife they observed:

> The mountains of north side are suggestive of some fertility, and of being traversed along their summits . . . [on the south] high pines and other trees can be seen. Buffalo, stags, deer, wild goats, bears, leopards, foxes, hares, and rabbits feed on their luxuriant pastures, and uncommonly large partridges, quail and other unknown kinds of little birds on their seeds. . . .
>
> Fish and shellfish are not at all abundant but the land is fertile and produces rich salmon and black berries, strawberries and other wild fruit of very good taste. . . .
>
> Fish [at today's Dungeness Bay] are most plentiful, particularly large salmon, rayfish, flounder, sea-bass, red snapper, codfish, *mojarras*,[12] and anchovies. There are also . . . geese, cranes and three kinds of ducks.[13]

One of the new group of junior officers, Jacinto Caamaño, accompanied Eliza on the 1790 expedition and remained at Nootka for a few months. He kept a journal titled "Vegetation and Classes of every Species which is known." In it, he included the following, under the heading "Flying Animals":

> During our sojourn we saw eagles with white heads and white tail feathers, all the rest of their body being black, a great number of crows, Sparrow hawks [Pearse suspected these to be American kestrel], geese, sea gulls, ducks of several species, wild pigeons, cranes, blackbirds or thrushes, and some tiny birds, even smaller than sparrows which sang quite well.[14]

In the first few months of 1791 a flurry of crossed reports and instructions passed between San Blas and Nootka. But in the end, Eliza, with a team of pilots, followed up on Quimper's exploration by penetrating deep into Juan de Fuca and beyond. A smaller party investigated what they termed the Canal de Rosario,[15] today's Strait of Georgia. Except for a description of killing an elk, which fed them for three days, Eliza's report makes no mention of wildlife. Moreover, Narváez's log of the exploring party is lost. Fortunately, one of the other participants did record some useful observations—the very experienced Juan Pantoja.[16]

Pantoja had arrived as navigator aboard *San Carlos* in late March, and the exploring party departed in early May, but during that short period, he noted at the place he called Puerto de San Lorenzo de Noca (today's Nootka):

> Here there are two kinds of rich salmon, white and red, large and small sole, *mojarras*, red and grey red-snapper, herring and sardines, the last being so plentiful that when they come to spawn the sea is white with it.[17]

Pantoja described the locals' methods of fishing and their technique of killing whales, and continued:

> The fruits found here are yellow and violet bramble berries, very agreeable to the palate, strawberries and others of different kinds which I do not mention as I do not know their names. There are peas, chick-peas, celery, amaranth, and roses, all wild, as well as a great abundance of chamomile, thistles and elder trees. . . . In the very rough forests bears are found, deer, wolves, coyotes, buffalo, and a small animal something like the ferret of Spain, which, before it was known that there was such an animal, made great havoc among the chickens the commanders had on shore. One night they killed sixty, large and small.
>
> There are eagles of regular size with a white head and tail, hawks, doves, geese, ducks, crows, gulls, woodpeckers, and sparrows. In the summer for a short time swallows and swifts are seen and there are plenty of cranes and bees.[18]

Pantoja noted that "the country [at Nootka] is very mountainous and covered with thick and leafy pines of various kinds but none which produces pine nuts. Most of them are of extraordinary thickness and length." But later, once he entered the Strait of Georgia, he noted a change in the terrain:

> On both coasts particularly on the shores, different kinds of pasture are very common on which feed buffalo, stags, deer, wild goats, hares and rabbits. On the seeds and abundant fruits, some of which are agreeable to the palate, two kinds of dove feed, one of the color and shape of our domestic pigeon, different unknown little birds and a kind of the colour and shape of a chicken, with golden feathers and swift flight like that of a partridge. So great is the abundance of these that I have killed some of them. Their flesh does not differ from that of our chicken.[19]

It may also be noted that among the herbiage at the edges of the beach I have seen whole thickets of rose bushes with innumerable roses of red colour and of five petals, and an incredible quantity of tame bees. . . . Most of them are of a dark yellow colour rather than black.

Once inside the Strait of Georgia, the exploration party (which did not include Pantoja) reported:

> The tides in it do not keep any regularity but that the currents and whirlpools are very much greater than usual. We have also seen there a great number of gulls, tunny fish and immense whales. As we have observed but very few of these in the whole strait [of Juan de Fuca] they either breed in the Canal de Rosario or enter by some other way.

The map compiled by the exploring party was called *Carta que comprehende los interiores y veril de la Costa* [. . .] *1791*.[20] On it, at the northwesterly limit of their sortie, they noted three place names linked to natural history. In the distance the party saw a land feature they recorded as "Ya Campo Alange" (Alange Field Island), plotted in the vicinity of today's Cape Mudge, the southern tip of Quadra Island. "Alange" seems to relate to the dogwood tree.[21] Almost certainly, Narváez and his companions could not have identified tree species on the distant feature, so their reason for giving it that name remains a mystery. At the location of today's French Creek they marked a feature, Rº de las Grullas—River of the Cranes. Some authorities have suggested that these were not sandhill cranes, but great blue herons, still seen there in large numbers. Nearby, the chart shows two Islas de Ballenas—Islands of Whales, marking an encounter with a pod of killer whales.

Pantoja remained with *San Carlos* at anchor in the bay he

called *Puerto Quadra*, later named Port Discovery by George Vancouver. While there he noted:

> Among [these hills] the sailors and troops saw bears, leopards [probably cougars], coyotes [a puzzle, since they are not found in the coastal area], wolves, deer, hares, and rabbits and two kinds of doves and chickens. They killed more than fifty of these birds and a few of the four first-named species, which served us all as moderate refreshment, since we were in great need. To this is to be added the great abundance of a special thick bramble which at the end of July began to ripen.

After the boat party rejoined Eliza, the three most experienced pilots, Narváez, Pantoja, and López de Haro, worked on their composite chart aboard *San Carlos*. For the return to Nootka, apprentice navigator Carrasco took command of *Santa Saturnina*. On leaving the Strait of Juan de Fuca, Eliza—as have many sailors—encountered northwesterly winds and currents, making a journey toward Nootka extremely difficult. Failing to make any headway, *Santa Saturnina* turned south to Monterey. As *San Carlos* struggled to approach the entrance to Nootka Sound, Eliza spied in the distance two large vessels leaving the harbour.

FIG. 4-6 *Rosa Nutkana*. The Nootka rose, noted by many who came to Vancouver Island, and beloved by residents. Watercolour by Sophie Pemberton in later life. *Image pdp00985 courtesy of the Royal BC Museum and Archives [image edited].*

FIG. 5-0 A bed of California mussels and gooseneck barnacles, both important food species for Indigenous Peoples. Mussel shells were also used as cutting tools. *Photo © courtesy of James Holkko.*

CHAPTER FIVE

THE MALASPINA EXPEDITION VISITS NOOTKA

"Natural history in all its branches . . ."

I N 1788 CAPTAIN ALESSANDRO MALASPINA, having just completed a circumnavigation of the globe, was a rising star of the Spanish navy. Together with Captain José de Bustamante y Guerra, he submitted a proposal for an ambitious voyage of scientific investigation to the Americas and the Pacific. It was a time of Spain's interest and concern over competition for "her" Vatican-endorsed[1] dominance of the New World.[2] The British and French had already made such voyages into the Pacific, and Spanish authorities had heard rumours of Russian plans to establish a base somewhere along the coast of Alta California, perhaps at Nootka, a place visited by Cook and Pérouse. The officers' proposal reached receptive ears.

The expedition fitted well with strategic goals of scientific and political advancement related to the Age of Enlightenment. It also matched a personal enthusiasm of King Carlos III, who had allocated ample funding to pursue such initiatives. In mid-October the king swiftly granted his approval—just two months before his death. But the momentum continued; two new corvettes, *Descubierta* and *Atrevida*, were purpose-designed, built, and fitted out for the exploring expedition ahead.

Malaspina chose most of the personnel, both service and civilian, for the expedition. These included two brothers, both army officers. The elder, Antonio Pineda, took overall responsibility for "natural history in all its branches"; his brother, Arcadio, for organizing the scientific records. A keen amateur naturalist, Antonio had made a study of the bird collection at the national Museum of Natural Science.

Among key naval officers were Antonio de Tova y Arredondo, first officer of *Atrevida*; Dionisio Alcalá Galiano, a specialist in astronomy; the young cartographer Felipe Bauzá y Cañas; and Cayetano Valdés, nephew to the minister of marine and a skilled hydrographer.

The expedition's contingent of civilian scientists included botanist Luis Née from the Royal Pharmacy garden. A respected Austrian academic recommended another distinguished naturalist for the expedition, Bohemian Tadeo (Tadeáš, Thaddeus) Haenke. Haenke not only had a doctorate in mathematics and astronomy from the University of Prague, but had studied medicine, mineralogy, and botany at the University of Vienna. He spoke six languages, including Spanish, and had travelled in Syria, Greece, and the Tyrol. This 29-year-old polymath even played the harpsichord.

At first, the Austrian emperor Joseph II was reluctant to allow Haenke to leave. On reconsideration, he relented, even providing funds for the journey and granting the scientist official status as an imperial emissary. Haenke prepared a comprehensive scientific field kit and library, and set off to meet the Spanish king before joining the expedition. Spanish royal preference at the time was for their own nationals to represent their country's scientific prowess. Despite this, and at the last moment, Carlos IV granted exception for this scholar.

Two official artists, José del Pozo and José Guio, would support the scientists by drawing botanical and zoological specimens, landscapes, portraits, and illustrations of mission events. Guio, in addition to having drawing skills, was a taxidermist. Neither of these men, however, proved his worth to the team, and both were replaced during the voyage.

THE MISSION, AS PLANNED

Three objectives formed the rationale for the expedition. The first was to gain a better knowledge of the enormous, largely undefended coastlines of Spain's American possessions—to survey and chart them accurately, and to prepare sailing directions for future expeditions. The second was to assess the political, strategic, and economic condition of Spain's poorly protected empire and its peoples. The third was to document and acquire specimens in the natural sciences for the national collections.

Explicitly stated, the expedition, which was expected to take three years, would follow the example set by the voyages of Cook and Pérouse. Malaspina received some additional secret orders: to investigate Russian and British settlements and pos-

FIG. 5-1 The young polymath from Bohemia, Thaddeus Peregrinus (Tadeo) Haenke, was seconded to the Malaspina expedition by the Austrian emperor Joseph II. *From an 1829 portrait by V.R. Grüner, Prague.*

sible encroachment into California, and to verify recent reports of a transcontinental, navigable waterway.

The voyage left the Spanish port of Cadiz on July 1, 1789, with an ambitious plan to chart the Pacific coastline as far as San Blas in New Spain and make scientific studies within Mexico. Then they were to chart the coastline north from San Blas as far as the Bering Sea, some 3,500 miles (5,600 kilometres), before exploring the South Pacific and surveying the coast of New Zealand. This was expected to take them back to Cadiz by May 1793. This was a mission impossible to fulfill, even without the delays needed for science. They reduced the scope, but the voyage would last more than five years.

TADEO HAENKE'S HEROIC EFFORTS TO JOIN THE EXPEDITION

As well as being an eminent, all-round man of science, Haenke proved himself to be resolute and resourceful. As soon as his participation was approved, he hastened from Vienna to Madrid, passing through Paris on the eve of the French Revolution. King Carlos IV received him warmly, assured him of financial reward, and provided written credentials as a *teniente de la Marina* (naval lieutenant). Haenke then hurried to join the expedition at Cadiz but arrived to find it had sailed just two hours earlier. Not wanting to miss the opportunity for such a voyage, he sailed on the next vessel destined for Montevideo, in current-day Uruguay, hoping to catch Malaspina there.

A storm arose just before they were due to arrive, and in darkness, Haenke's ship foundered on rocks close to shore. Securing his two sets of credentials within his stout bed-cap, he swam for it. He was rescued but had lost his precious library, clothes, and equipment left on board. Safely ashore, he learned that the expedition's corvettes had sailed a week previously. Although he then was ill for three weeks, his intent to be part of the expedition didn't waver.

Haenke's credentials gained him swift access, first to the local governor and then to the viceroy in Buenos Aires, the senior Spanish imperial authority in the region, who treated him well. With funding, documents, and an escort all authorized by His Excellency, Haenke set out again. He crossed the vast pampas on horseback over the Andean high cordillera into Chile, finally meeting up with the expedition in Valparaíso in April 1790. As he travelled, Haenke kept notes on the creatures, plant life, and geological features he observed. Malaspina noted that during his traverse from Buenos Aires, Haenke had collected 1,400 specimens of plants new to science or inadequately described. He was welcomed aboard *Descubierta* and told he would be reporting to Antonio Pineda. He proved himself a great asset to the expedition in many fields of its scientific activity, as well as socially.[3]

OTHER KEY PERSONNEL

Several of *Descubierta*'s officers developed interests in various scientific aspects of the mission, assisting in observing and collecting specimens. One, Antonio de Tova, proved an excellent ethnologist. He met and conversed with Indigenous Peoples, making extensive, insightful notes on their languages, customs, beliefs, and intertribal relationships. One of the cabin boys, José Cardero, demonstrated a talent for drawing, which the officers recognized and encouraged. His talents came to the fore when one of the official artists, del Pozo, left the expedition in Peru. With some guidance from Guio, the remaining artist, Cardero drew views, people, birds, and fish for the mission's record, and enjoyed the title of *dibuxante*—an illustrator without formal training—but no extra pay. His skills developed with practice, and the results, if short on artistic flair, showed detail and accuracy.

While in Lima, Malaspina, concerned at the shortage of skilled and motivated artists needed to keep up with the scientific collectors, sent a message to Valdés in Madrid asking for two more. These were recruited and dispatched to join him at Acapulco at the close of 1791. They were Italians Fernando Brambila and Juan Francisco Ravenet of Parma.

The two vessels separated in Panama, to meet up later in Acapulco. *Atrevida* arrived first, in February 1791, and the botanist Née and the younger Pineda revelled in the abundance of new plants they found in the vicinity. While they awaited *Descubierta*, a young man presented himself to Captain Bustamante bearing a note from Viceroy Revillagigedo. He was Tomás de Suría, reporting as a temporary artist in response to Malaspina's request for the viceroy to find him replacements for del Pozo, who had remained in Lima, and Guio, who was often incapacitated by fever.

Suría, a Spaniard, had studied at the Academía de Bellas Artes in Madrid, under the world-famous typographer and engraver Jerónimo Gil. When Gil became director of the Mexican college of engraving in 1778, Suría followed, and was employed as an engraver at the Mexican mint. Gil nominated his former student after getting the viceroy's request to identify a suitable artist. There being no room aboard *Atrevida*, Suría had to await the arrival of the sister ship. In the meantime, he worked under Pineda, drawing "various fish, birds, quadrupeds, and the anatomy of animals"[4] and some scenes around Acapulco.

THE PLAN CHANGES

In March 1791 *Descubierta* arrived in Acapulco to join *Atrevida*, and Malaspina paused to reflect on their progress to date. Malaspina rode to Mexico City to consult with Viceroy Revillagigedo. Aware that the new king, Carlos IV, differed from his father in his approach to science and the expedition, the commander was anxious to know how this might affect their mission. He was still in the capital when an urgent message arrived from Valdés; they were to proceed immediately to Alaska. They were to verify a report, from two centuries earlier, that a navigable passage across the continent existed that emerged into the Pacific at latitude 60° north. A recently published French map had depicted such a route.

Dubious about the veracity of this story, Malaspina nonetheless knew that he must obey the order. So, leaving most of the scientists to continue work in Mexico in his absence, he took only Haenke as naturalist, and Suría and Cardero as artists. Advised by the local pilots, they headed westward out into the Pacific, then turning north and making landfall at 56°. It was midsummer but still horribly cold compared with tropical Acapulco. They continued north as far as 59°15' where they found, as he had suspected, the story of a waterway to be fictitious.

Malaspina and all his crew were disappointed. However, he had complied with the order, and their stay of nine days in Alaska, at Yakutat, provided Haenke with the opportunity to botanize and observe the Tlingit culture, the artists to portray local people and scenes, and the navigators to observe the longitude. The expedition ships then headed southward again to visit, as planned, the outpost of San Lorenzo at Nootka Sound. They arrived there on August 13, 1791, having survived a week-long, ferocious storm off Haida Gwaii. To their relief, they saw the Spanish flag flying above the small battery of San Miguel as they entered the harbour and anchored.

HAENKE'S SOJOURN AT NOOTKA

Pedro de Alberni—captain of the small garrison and acting commander of the base—and Lieutenant Manuel Saavedra greeted the visitors. They informed Malaspina that their superior, Francisco de Eliza, was currently away exploring deep into the Strait of Juan de Fuca. The newcomers noted huts of wooden planks, built and kept in good order, as were the bakery and the vegetable gardens. Malaspina was impressed with the discipline of the men and the abilities of the officers. He also noted that they had suffered greatly from scurvy and fevers over the preceding harsh winter: 9 men had died, and 32 sick had been sent to Monterey. He also learned that their crops and livestock had been ravaged by rats (mostly brought by visiting ships) and wild animals.

The geographer Bauzá immediately set up an observatory. He and Haenke began to fix the local longitude to compare it with Cook's calculation and take bearings to significant points of land and nearby peaks. On the second day, a secondary chief of the Mowachaht, Tlupana, nervously came aboard *Atrevida*. He explained that his people, who earlier had been badly treated by Esteban Martínez, were understandably concerned at this sudden, fourfold increase in Spanish forces in their harbour. Malaspina wanted to meet the head chief, Maquinna, to discuss the latter's concerns, but when Cayetano Valdés and Bauzá went to deliver the invitation to Maquinna at his other village at Tahsis, they found it deserted. All had fled into the forest.

Malaspina and Bauzá knew that Nootka Sound included many inlets and side channels not yet properly charted. Keen to know if any of them connected with Juan de Fuca, they sent out two well-supplied, fully armed boats with both a pilot and an interpreter from the garrison. In the process, they discovered that Friendly Cove was on an island—Mazarredo.

Meanwhile, the rest of the company kept occupied cutting firewood and replacement spars for those damaged in the storm, as well as improving conditions at the garrison. Ship surgeon Francisco Flores prepared a quantity of antiscorbutic beer from molasses and pine needles to demonstrate the process to Alberni, a precaution against another severe winter. (Flores had earlier ordered that all the expedition's officers and men take

lemon juice to keep the ravages of scurvy at bay.) In addition, the expedition's blacksmiths and armourers provided help and equipment to repair or replace the garrison's weapons and farm implements, already badly deteriorated. They also provided instruments and supplies for the sick bay, food, clothing, and four casks of wine. Alberni reciprocated with much of the produce then available from his farm.

Gradually, and with the generous distribution of presents, the locals regained confidence and visited in growing numbers, including, eventually, Maquinna. Finally, he and the Mowachaht arrived in ceremonial war canoes to perform a dance of welcome on the beach—good relations had been re-established. Malaspina noted: "From that moment on, our peaceful intentions were thoroughly understood and lasting friendship established with much close bonds between us."[5]

Malaspina had secured Maquinna's confirmation that the Spanish establishment at Nootka had his full consent and could remain. Eventually, this would prove a key element in treaty negotiations with the British over dominion in this region.

Again, Antonio de Tova was active in conversing with the local people, particularly with Natzapé, a young Mowachaht chief, discussing their customs, beliefs, traditions, and the community's relationships with neighbouring groups. He kept a detailed and insightful record of his findings. One interesting piece of information obtained from Natzapé was that a trading route, or "grease trail," led from Tahsis northward via lakes and rivers to a village of the Nuchimases (Nimpkish or 'Namgis), of the Kwakwa̱ka'wakw Peoples. Natzapé was also a chief of that group through marriage, and he often led trading parties between the two.[6]

The natural history record of the Malaspina expedition's two weeks at Nootka is not extensive. Haenke was the only natural scientist aboard. Nonetheless, he was just as assiduous

FIG. 5-2   One of Haenke's scientific notebooks wrapped in vellum for protection from insects. *Museo Naval, Madrid [image edited]*.

at Nootka as throughout his participation in the expedition. He made full use of the limited duration of their visit.

The multilingual Haenke unfortunately wrote his copious notes on botany, geology, zoology, ethnology, and probably much more in several different languages, often within the same description—difficult for anyone else to transcribe. He left all his notes with the expedition when he separated from it at Lima on the return journey. His plan, agreed by Malaspina, was to make a second crossing of the Andes and pampas and rejoin the expedition at Buenos Aires. But he became engrossed with what he found in Peru and Bolivia and remained there for the remainder of his life.[7]

The specimens that Haenke collected at Yakutat and Nootka were included in the huge inventory shipped to Spain from Acapulco. Many of these were also destined for Prague, in accordance with the permission granted by Joseph II. During storage, and the turmoil of the Napoleonic conquest of Spain, the specimens became separated from the corresponding notes. His records, along with all those of the expedition, were locked away and forgotten. Publication of the reports was further confused by political intrigue involving Malaspina and Prime Minister Manuel Godoy—an influential schemer and favourite of the queen, who had by then become powerful. Inevitably, Malaspina lost this fight. Justified recognition for the achievements of his expedition would take decades to emerge.

Fortunately for scientific posterity, Haenke did prepare a short essay in Latin, finally published in 1987.[8] It summarized the physical character of the Nootka area, and noted that the kitchen gardens of the local garrison grew radishes and lettuce just as tasty as those in Europe. It then listed the wildlife he had observed.

> The number of birds is few. At least in August. *Corvus* major and minor [raven and northwestern crow], very common in all Europe;

Ardea grus [great blue heron]. *Picus pileatus* [pileated woodpecker]. *Motacilla regulus* [kinglet] *Falco columbarius* [merlin] and *Mergus* [merganser].

> The number of fish were abundant and included all kinds of perch like *Perca rubens*, *P. pallens*, and *P. squamosa*, two species of *Pleuronectiformes* [flatfishes] called Lenguado [sole, flounder] and a species of Róbalo [sea bass]. The *Salmo salar* was very tasty, delicate, not yellowish, more so than at Port Mulgrave. *Sic Clupea sardina*, two kinds of *Sparus* [called mojarra]. The *Scorpanae* [rockfishes] and the *Coti* [sculpins] were plentiful and finally, there were *Squalus armatus* [skate] and many fishes of a peculiar aspect with fins in the form of ample wings and long and isolated genitals with a greasy sunken head [ratfish]. They were of brilliant silver colour, but even so, not good eating.... On the marine rocks, everywhere, there are mussels and abundant edible crustaceans.

> Sea-stars of various colours such as violet, reddish, and yellow.

> We rarely saw insects, mostly butterflies and small beetles.

As for the vegetable kingdom, he noted many examples under a temperate, soft sky:

> The woods are composed of four distinct types of pines: *Pinus sylvestris* [Scots pine—not present at Nootka], *P. abies* [Norway spruce—not present], *P. Canadiensis* [not identified], and *P. balsamus* [not identified], together with *Cupressus thyoide* [white cedar—not present].

It seems that the reference works for trees available to Haenke did not help with what he saw. He listed several fruit-bearing bushes, 10 medicinal plants, including some antiscorbutics, and 25 other identified plants, and then noted: "This brief catalogue shows that

FIG. 5-3 Type specimen of *Heuchera micrantha* (small-flowered alumroot) in Prague National Herbarium. Haenke collected this plant at Nootka and it was sent to Prague as part of the agreement for his participation in Malaspina's expedition. It is the type specimen for this species. *Presl, K.B., Reliquiae Haenkeana, Prague: 1831.*

very few of these species live in Europe (or the Alps) but are abundant in North America. They are natives of Canada and Virginia."

In the Prague Průhonice Park Herbarium, which holds the largest collection of Haenke's botanical specimens, 829 in all, 28 species are listed as originating from Nootka.[9] The scientific names do not correspond with those mentioned in his essay.

Saavedra and Alberni had been most cooperative with Haenke and Malaspina's officers, passing on their experience, hard won over the two previous years. Another of Malaspina's Nootka reports probably derived from such knowledge. It recorded the various types of timber found there, evaluated for ship building and repair:

For masts and yards of all vessels.

1. Pine with very thin smooth white bark and .6 cm thick. It has few knots and the largest ones are 3.2 cm in diameter and it was from this tree that a mast was made. It is light, flexible, and gives off an aromatic white pitch. [western white pine or yellow cedar]

2. Fir tree. It has dark and somewhat rough bark which is not very thick. It has some knots but not very large. It has little sapwood. It is light, flexible and somewhat streaked and gives off pitch the colour of egg yolk. From this tree a topmast was made. [Sitka spruce or lodgepole pine]

3. Pine of a thick black bark with white streaks, very rough and with many large knots. It has much sapwood and is heavy. It is good for heavy planks and canoes because it is thicker than the other kinds. Its branches can be used for knees and seizing, and for charcoal. [Douglas-fir]

4. Easily split pine. It has not very thick, rough dark coloured bark. The leaf is wider than that of the rest and of it beer is made. It

is very fissile. It gives off much pitch which the natives make use of for their wounds. At the end it has many knots. It is good for planking and from its roots various futtocks and knees can be made for vessels up to 200 tons. [Sitka spruce, western hemlock, or lodgepole pine]

5. Cypress pine. It has dark, thick bark and the natives make use of it to manufacture their clothing and ropes. It is weak wood and fissile, but very light. From it the natives make planks by splitting it with wedges along the grain of the tree, and they press them to make them straight. [western red cedar]

Under these trees is found in abundance a type of short grass that is found in these high latitudes which they call moss. It grows in the shade and on the rocks. With this they caulk the clinker-built vessels in Galicia. After it is dry, it is placed between various boards and once it enters the water it expands so as to make it as tight as if done with oakum and of greater duration. They also weave with it [sphagnum].[10]

SURÍA AND CARDERO RECORD THEIR IMPRESSIONS

Tomás de Suría, during probably his first experience of life aboard a working ship, kept a remarkably detailed and frank journal for his trip. This was not as easy as he would have wished. The cabin he shared with the second officer was so tiny that

while stretched in my bed with my feet against the side of the ship and my head against the bulkhead . . . the distance is only three inches from my breast to the deck, which was my roof. This confined position does not allow me to move in my bed and I am forced to make a roll of cloth to cover my head, and, although this suffocates me, it is lesser evil than being attacked by thousands of cockroaches.[11]

FIG. 5-4 *Berberis aquifolium.* The tall Oregon grape is abundant on southern Vancouver Island in open, rocky sites. Painting by botanical artist Emily Sartain (see chapter 16). *Courtesy of the Sisters of Saint Ann.*

Most regrettably, Suría's record is incomplete. The only volume known to have survived is marked "Primer Cuaderno" (first notebook) and even that is missing pages at the end, which would have covered his last few days in Nootka. He did include a note: "A small fruit like a black grape, bittersweet, which the botanist [Haenke] called bear-grape [probably the locally abundant Oregon grape]."

He continued:

> The botanist, Don Tadeo Haenke . . . made a collection of plants but very meagre because he could not find in port other plants distinct from those in Europe. He did, however, find many anti-scorbutic plants classifying these as well as the pines of which there were many different species.[12]

Suría had made several sketches of scenes and people at Port Mulgrave and at Nootka. These included depictions of the ceremonial arrival of Maquinna's canoes, the dance on the beach at Friendly Cove, a group of people in a flotilla of canoes fishing for sardines, and portraits of Maquinna, his wife, and other Mowachaht characters.

Cardero also sketched scenes and portraits at Mulgrave and Nootka, and painted some birds, including a "Picus" (flicker) and a "Gracula" (red-winged blackbird), both of which he could have seen at Nootka. The portfolio also contains some others that could not have been seen there, including a "Gaviota atricilla" (laughing gull), an "Ave passeriforme" (thrasher), a "Tetrao (*Regio-montanus*)" (California quail), a "Golondrina del mar" (noddy tern), and a "Tetrao (*Lagopus Americano*)" (female rock ptarmigan).

On the evening of August 28, taking advantage of outflow winds, Malaspina's corvettes cleared the reefs at the entrance to *Cala de Amigos* (Friendly Cove, now Yuquot), making for the open Pacific for their return to continue the planned voyage. They had not seen *San Carlos* approaching from the south, and so missed meeting Eliza by just two days. Knowing that the latter was already exploring the interior of Juan de Fuca, Malaspina considered it prudent to keep well offshore as they made their way south to Monterey. Two weeks later they arrived to a welcome by the commander of the *Presidio* and an abundance of fresh, local produce.

After they had been there a few days, another Spanish vessel entered the harbour to anchor nearby. It was *Santa Saturnina*, under apprentice pilot Carrasco, arriving from Juan de Fuca. Malaspina was frustrated that Carrasco was unable to provide much detail about the latest discoveries made by Eliza and his subordinates, since he had remained with Eliza in *San Carlos*. The other pilots were still working on the logs and charts. The commander did learn enough, however, to convince him that the entrances seen at the eastern end of the strait held good potential. They could lead to the long-sought waterway to the North Sea (as Spaniards called the Atlantic). He felt that his expedition should be the one to investigate it further.

At San Blas, Malaspina learned that his friend, Francisco Mourelle, who knew the coast well, was scheduled to make an exploratory voyage on *Mexicana*, a newly built goleta (a small, shallow-draft schooner). The viceroy and Bodega y Quadra intended Malaspina to follow up on the findings of the Quimper expedition of 1790. They were still unaware that Eliza had already done so.

Interesting news from Madrid awaited Malaspina in Acapulco. The naval authorities expressed satisfaction with the progress of the expedition, confirmed promotions for key officers, and awarded a substantial bonus to be shared among all deserving members. Also, the dispute with Britain relating to the events at Nootka in 1789 had been largely resolved. A meeting between national representatives was to take place at Nootka in the next year. Bodega y Quadra would lead the Spanish delegation, termed the *Expedición de Límites*. The viceroy also confirmed that Mourelle, with Carrasco, would take *Mexicana* exploring into Juan de Fuca.

Malaspina respectfully suggested a possibly better plan. It would be safer to take two goletas rather than a single, vulnerable craft. And instead of Mourelle, who was debilitated by relapsing fever, two of his best officers should undertake the mission. Both officers, now frigate-captains, were trained exploration hydrographers. The contributions to New Spain already made by expedition scientists Pineda, Née, and especially Galiano had impressed the viceroy, so he concurred. He ordered that a second, identical goleta be constructed, to be named *Sutil*. He also appointed Mourelle as his special secretary, with responsibility for compiling an archive of all documents related to the exploration of the coast of Alta California, and to the north.

Having gained the viceroy's agreement, Malaspina appointed Dionisio Alcalá Galiano and Cayetano Valdés as co-leaders for the mission. Two of his other officers, with reliable crew, all volunteers, would support them. They were to form a special detachment to explore the channels at the eastern end of Juan de Fuca. At the specific request of the two leaders, their ex-steward José Cardero, now a capable artist, would join them, and at an appropriate pay scale. No other naturalist would form part of the team. Malaspina gave the explicit priority for the mission: "exploring all the internal channels of the strait of Fuca . . . to decide once and for all . . . questions of the communication or proximity of the Pacific Ocean and the Atlantic in this parallel [of latitude]." As for natural history:

> All other objectives of botany, zoology, and lithology you will regard as fortunate accessories which cost neither the slightest risk or sacrifice of your own safety, nor the slightest loss of time on the part of the commission.[13]

Fortunately, Cayetano Valdés was among those naval officers of the main expedition who had shown interest and assisted in the activities of the naturalists, so some observations about wildlife and vegetation were included in the journal.

Once the expedition reached Acapulco, Suría, with an excellent commendation from Malaspina, returned to the Academy of Art in the capital to complete his drawings, as did Guio. Soon afterward, the two new Italian artists, Brambila and Ravenet, joined the expedition. Eight months later, Suría went back to his post in the *Casa Real de la Moneda*, the Royal Mint, and Guio, a sick man, returned to Spain.

Late in December, after the goletas detachment had been arranged, *San Carlos* arrived back in San Blas carrying Eliza's report to the viceroy on his explorations. A new chart, *Carta que comprehende los interiores y veril de la Costa* [. . .] *1791*, compiled by his trio of pilots, accompanied the report. Eliza gave his opinion that "the passage to the [Atlantic] Ocean, which foreign nations have searched for with such diligence, cannot if there is one, be anywhere but in this great inlet."[14]

Malaspina had left before the contents of Eliza's package had reached the viceroy. When Bodega y Quadra studied the chart it contained, he noted that, in addition to the intriguing news about the Canal de Rosario, Eliza had been unsuccessful in his earlier attempt to explore farther north from Nootka. The chart of the coastline Bodega y Quadra was compiling still lacked information for that sector, where, yet another rumour had it, an entrance leading east had been found.

On December 20, 1791, *Atrevida* and *Descubierta* had left Acapulco bound for Guam and the Philippines. Before departing, Malaspina had entrusted 40 cases to royal officials for onward dispatch to His Majesty. They contained botanical, zoological, and geological specimens, cultural artifacts, and supporting documents such as logbooks, reports, drawings, maps, charts, and perspective views for all the various sorties. The boxes were all sealed with whale fat to preserve perishable material.[15]

As a result of court treachery soon after his return, Malaspina, previously considered a national hero, suffered several years' incarceration in the fortress of La Coruña. The records of his expedition remained impounded and neglected for a century. His fellow officers, however, were not treated as badly; eight of them reached flag rank (rear admiral or above). In more recent years, in Spain and internationally, Alessandro Malaspina's name, reputation, and legacy have been vindicated, and he is now recognized as an outstanding leader, explorer, and philosopher of the Spanish Enlightenment.

Despite Malaspina's instruction to the captains of the goletas sortie that they were only to note matters of natural history as a secondary objective, the expedition did record some new and interesting information. The talented artist José Cardero drew some excellent likenesses of birds he had seen. The contribution of the first trained naturalist to visit the Nootka region, Tadeo Haenke, would have been significant, but unfortunately his notes, correspondence, and specimens were unavailable for later researchers until collated and translated into Spanish in 1987.[16]

FIG. 5-5 *Grácula*. Painting by José Cardero, an officer's servant with an aptitude for art. He saw and painted this red-winged blackbird at Nootka. *Museo Naval, Madrid, ms. 1725 (85)*.

VISTA DE LA BAHÍA DE NUTCA, DESDE LA PLAYA DEL ESTABLECIMIENTO ESPAÑOL.

FIG. 6-0 *Vista de la Bahía de Nutka desde la playa del establecimiento español*, by José Cardero. In the spring of 1792 seven Spanish naval vessels crowded into the tiny cove at Nootka. Three naturalists aboard had come to investigate the local flora, fauna, and peoples. *Archivo General del Ministerio de Asuntos Exteriores y de Cooperación, Madrid, ms. 146, lám. 5.*

CHAPTER SIX

THE SPANISH EXPEDITIONS OF 1792

S PANISH INVESTIGATIONS IN THE VICINITY of Vancouver Island and the mainland inlets of British Columbia intensified and combined in the year 1792. Multiple threads of royal interest in the region interwove to form a complex and unique fabric of enquiry. They included geographic, scientific, strategic, and commercial strands. While primarily focused on the tiny harbour of San Lorenzo de Nutka,[1] together they covered a much wider area.

Toward the end of the previous year, Viceroy Revillagigedo received new directives from Madrid through the first minister, Count Floridablanca, orders strongly influenced by the court. People close to King Carlos IV had questioned the continuing investment in Martín de Sessé's botanical activities in New Spain. They had turned down his request for additional funding to enable José Moziño, José Maldonado, and Atanasio Echeverría to continue participating in the research. Madrid directed that Manuel Quimper's discoveries in Fuca must be followed up by further exploration, and endorsed the plan to detach part of Alessandro Malaspina's team to explore in vessels supplied by the viceroy.

An outcome of the newly signed Nootka Treaty was that the viceroy was required to designate a senior officer to meet with a British counterpart at Nootka, where they were to agree on the boundary between their two territories. Relations between the two imperial powers were currently amicable, so the negotiations were to be courteous, while safeguarding Spain's overall interests.

In San Blas, Viceroy Revillagigedo nominated his most trusted officer, Juan Francisco de la Bodega y Quadra, to represent Spain and instructed him to make ready for the mission. Additional vessels would be needed to support Bodega y Quadra's new mission. The goletas *Mexicana* and *Sutil* had been allocated to the Fuca detachment, leaving insufficient ships at San Blas. A warship, *Santa Gertrudis*, was transferred temporarily from Lima, and a new 12-gun brigantine, *Activa*, was ordered built; both were assigned to the mission. An important reason for including *Gertrudis* was to uphold Spain's naval image when the British representative arrived for the negotiation.

Bodega y Quadra took charge of the extensive collection of documents assembled by Francisco Mourelle. These related to the complete history of exploration by all parties of the coast and included the journals of Cook, Pérouse, and Dixon. He also had his own files from when he had reviewed the Nootka Incident and Martínez's actions.

He called his mission Expedición de Límites (Expedition of the Limits to the North of California). It would have, at his own request, a natural history element in addition to its hydrographic and diplomatic purposes. He had noted the benefit that scientists had brought to the Cook, Pérouse, and Malaspina expeditions. This concept fitted well with the viceroy's dilemma over how to continue the work of the botanical expedition. Redeployed as part of the Límites expedition and funded from that budget, the three members of Sessé's team—Moziño, Maldonado, and Echeverría—could continue their work. Sessé notified the three that they were to report immediately to Bodega y Quadra at San Blas and that they should take all necessary technical gear and supplies for an indefinite period on the north coast.

Spain had an urgent and vital interest in controlling the entrance to the intercontinental waterway, when and if it were discovered. Also, it was proving difficult to operate out of Nootka under the all-too-frequent poor weather and sailing conditions. Combined, these factors created the need to identify and establish an alternative base within Fuca. Manuel Quimper's report had indicated a suitable site—the harbour of Núñez Gaona (Neah Bay), just inside the entrance on the southern side. Bodega y Quadra assigned one of the San Blas officers, Salvador Fidalgo, to take his ship *Princesa* and install the new outpost there.

JACINTO CAAMAÑO

Lieutenant Jacinto Caamaño had been part of the group reinforcing San Blas in 1789. The following year, he joined Francisco de Eliza at Nootka. Caamaño had not participated in the explorations into Fuca, nor had he been given responsibility in the upcoming missions. He felt badly treated and made a personal entreaty to the viceroy to be given opportunity to prove his worth.

Revillagigedo assigned Caamaño to the Límites expedition as commander of the frigate *Aránzazu*. He was to take his ship to Nootka with the rest of the squadron, and then carry out the exploration of the coast north as far as Bucareli Bay at latitude 55°23'. The ship was old and clumsy, far from ideal for venturing solo into uncharted waters, but it would carry a boat for the actual explorations.

Tomás de Suría had lamented the lack of personal space aboard *Descubierta*, but the goletas being built at San Blas were a great deal smaller and far more cramped. Narrow of beam and shallow of draft, they were designed to operate in protected waters, close inshore; they were totally unfit for the open ocean. Much of the space in the hold was taken up with ballast, needed to keep them upright in a wind. There was barely room under cover for the two officers; the rest—22 sailors and marines in each 15-metre-long vessel—would have to squeeze into the holds somehow. In semi-finished condition, the goletas sailed to Acapulco for completion of the fitting out.

They arrived too late for this work to be undertaken by the senior carpenters of Malaspina's team. It was left to the crew of the goletas with whatever local help they could muster and material they could scrounge; there was precious little of either. The goletas finally managed to put to sea on March 8, bound for Fuca. The journey proved horrendous; five weeks out and well offshore, *Mexicana*'s mainmast snapped. They carried no materials to repair it. The wind intensified, and they needed to reaffix the rigging to prevent further, possibly fatal damage. The only carpenter in the party was aboard *Sutil*. Somehow, by lashing the ship's oars to the stump of the mast as supports, the crew managed to jury-rig a mainsail, and limp along for another four weeks until they would reach Nootka.

BODEGA Y QUADRA'S EXPEDICIÓN DE LÍMITES

Once Bodega y Quadra and his team had arrived at Nootka, Eliza and his men—who had by then served two years there—would return to San Blas, leaving Bodega y Quadra, now referred to as the "governor," in direct charge of the outpost. His second-in-command would be sub-lieutenant Félix Cepeda. He, too, had been among the 1789 group, and he spoke French and English, potentially valuable skills for the diplomatic task ahead.

The squadron, as planned, would consist of four vessels: the impressive frigate *Santa Gertrudis*, the new brig *Activa*, the aging *Princesa*, and another veteran frigate, *Aránzazu*, usually occupied in ferrying people and supplies from San Blas to the garrisons of Monterey, San Francisco, and San Lorenzo. After a series of setbacks, Bodega y Quadra was forced to sail for Nootka with just *Santa Gertrudis*. A hurricane-force squall blew in just as they were approaching Nootka but eased enough for them to enter on April 29. Maquinna and an entourage of village chiefs immediately came to welcome him and, to his relief, assured him of their friendship.

The condition of the buildings at the garrison impressed Bodega y Quadra, as did the kitchen garden. He was also pleased to note the fitness and good morale of the men, and their amicable relationship with the Mowachaht. He gave full credit to the skills of Eliza and Pedro de Alberni, who he knew had endured a testing two years. The governor could see that the main house, which consisted of two storeys, needed further work to bring it to a condition suitable for entertaining the British delegation when it arrived. Eventually, six Spanish vessels managed to struggle into San Lorenzo de Nutka and all needed extensive repairs from the damage they had suffered while getting there.

Bodega y Quadra recognized that Moziño, in addition to being a botanist, was a qualified physician, an enormous benefit to an isolated community. Maldonado's knowledge of medicinal plants, too, would be useful. These were members of the team who merited special treatment.

Their accommodation on land was as comfortable as could be expected in a military outpost at the extreme edge of the Spanish empire. The three naturalists began what turned into a four-month-long study of the area and its inhabitants. They were, however, limited in the scope of botany and zoology work they could perform:

> It is almost impossible for even the most resolute person to penetrate the interior [of the island], because it contains a multitude of deep gorges and thick underbrush common to all forests. The natives inhabit only the beaches, and the mountains are reserved for the bears, lynxes, raccoons, weasels, squirrels, deer, and so forth.[2]

Alberni's men had cleared the forest immediately around the garrison for horticulture. Other than in that tiny area, Moziño's observing and collecting were confined to the shorelines of the cove and nearby inlets. Even there, "on going ashore one finds nothing anywhere except small, sandy beaches, brambles, thickets, precipices, large sharp rocks, and huge craggy masses in disorderly array, covered in pines and cypresses."[3]

It is understandable that Moziño would devote much of his time at Nootka to the study of the Mowachaht people—their language, lifestyle, customs, and beliefs. While he did note their diet, a curious omission in his notes is any local knowledge of the curative powers of plants. It seems odd that he, a botanist and physician, would not have investigated such matters.[4]

During the month that the goletas waited in San Lorenzo, they underwent as extensive refits as local conditions allowed. They were then in a far better condition for their mission than when they had left Acapulco. The governor made sure that they had all the latest charts and reports, including that of the Eliza / Narváez expedition of the previous year.

The goletas finally got away on June 5, bearing messages for Fidalgo, who, a month earlier, had arrived in *Princesa* at Núñez Gaona to set up the new fort.[5] They found that the work was well underway, with stockades, livestock pens, and a garden plot already in place. Fidalgo was wary of the locals, the Makah,[6] who had a reputation for attacking shore parties and even ships. But Galiano and Valdés did meet one chief, called Tetacus, and struck up a friendship with this confident, inquisitive, and knowledgeable man.[7] The Spaniards noted that the prow of his canoe carried a stylized bird, which Tetacus called *suayuk*, an eagle with horns, the mythical thunderbird, powerful enough to carry off a whale.

Tetacus travelled aboard *Mexicana*, guiding the ships to his home, the place marked on Quimper's chart as Puerto de Cordova, today's Esquimalt Harbour. Here the visitors recorded:

> The forest is thick, and the vegetation the same as at Nutca, but with wild roses in more abundance. Some gulls, ducks, kingfishers, and other small birds were also seen. It is noteworthy that we saw waterfowl only near the land, and not out in the inlet.[8]

The goletas continued their exploration into the Canal de Rosario and had reached Point Roberts when they encountered a British naval expedition on a similar mission. This was led by Captain George Vancouver, whose vessels were HMS *Discovery* and HMS *Chatham*. The two groups quickly established a com-radely relationship, exchanging results of their explorations, and sailing together for a few days. Having reached Teakerne Arm, near Desolation Sound, the four ships anchored together and explored the nearby inlets, sharing observations.

Vancouver's officers, in ship's boats, noticed a change in the tidal flows. They deduced that to the north, there must be a second inflow from the Pacific, and therefore, the land to their west must be an island, or islands. Vancouver communicated the finding and deduction to his new Spanish friends. They agreed to continue separately, taking different routes, and meet up at Nootka.

Those in the goletas discovered that the route through the islands required transiting several hazardous narrows with strong tidal surges, whirlpools, and rapids. In one of these, which they named Angostura de los Comandantes (Arran Rapids, north of Stuart Island), they noted:

> It is no exaggeration to say that the current . . . has a velocity of twelve [knots]. The sight is most strange and picturesque: the waters flow as if they were falling from a cascade; a great number of fish are constantly rising in them, and flocks of gulls perch on the surface at the entrance to the channel, allowing its rapid flow to carry them along, and when they have reached its end, they fly back to their original position and repeat the experience. This not only amused us, but it also supplied us with a means by which to gauge accurately the force of the current.[9] [Theed Pearse identified these gulls as "probably the Mew and Bonaparte."][10]

The goletas returned to Nootka on August 31, after some 12 weeks. They had made the first recorded circumnavigation of Vancouver Island. Vancouver's three ships, *Discovery*, *Chatham*, and the resupply ship HMS *Daedalus*, already lay at anchor, and he was in discussions with Bodega y Quadra. After careening

FIG. 6-1 The decorated front of a chief's house at Quatsino Sound depicts the mythical thunderbird carrying off a whale. The story of this epic struggle has been linked to the "orphan tsunami" of 1700. See *Scientific American*, January 6, 2015. *From a postcard in author's collection.*

the goletas and exchanging cartographic data with the British navigators, they departed for Monterey and San Blas.

Galiano wrote and signed the final report on the expedition, but most likely the other three officers and Cardero helped compile it, and it was later edited. The report included some notes on Nootka, the Mowachaht, and local natural history. These notes seem to be based on discussions with Moziño, Alberni, and others with longer residence at the outpost.

> The natives only inhabit the coasts, leaving the mountains to bears, deer, lynx, wolves, beavers, badgers, otters, squirrels, moles, and rats. . . . The land birds found in the district of Nootka are sparrows with a curved beak [Pearse: Bewick's wren], woodpeckers, canaries [goldfinch or yellow warbler], grey pigeons [band-tailed], herons, eagles with white heads and necks, crows and humming birds. The aquatic birds are not numerous, and there are found only some fresh- and salt-water ducks, diving birds, curlew [whimbrel] and gulls. Among reptiles, snakes and vipers have been seen. Of insects, those which are most troublesome are the mosquitoes, which are very plentiful.
>
> The sea which washes the shores of Nootka is richer, since it produces excellent salmon, ling, cod, eels, trout, soles, ray, sardines, herrings, etc. But of its diverse and valuable products, the Indians chiefly value two, the [grey] whale and the [sea] otter, the former because it provides them food for much of the time, and the latter because with its skin they cover themselves and protect themselves, while it is also the only money or medium of exchange of which they make use of in carrying on trade.[11]

The chapter concludes with a long description of the sea otter, its characteristics, and the trade in its pelts.

The four officers handed back their goletas at San Blas and returned to Spain. There, Galiano and Valdés managed

FIG. 6-2 *Anas Coronata.* Atanasio Echeverría's painting of a male surf scoter. *Biological Illustrations #6331.0287, Torner Collection of Sessé and Mociño, Hunt Institute for Biological Documentation, Pittsburgh, PA.*

to establish that their expedition was distinct from that of Malaspina, who was by then out of favour and in prison. Their report, complete with a set of new charts, Cardero's depictions of places, events, artifacts, and people, and the brief notes on wildlife, was accepted and published, and their achievement heralded as a contribution to national prestige.[12]

CAAMAÑO'S NORTHERN SORTIE

Soon after the goletas expedition had left Nootka for Juan de Fuca, the governor was able to turn his attention to getting Caamaño's northern reconnaissance underway. The aging frigate *Aránzazu*, essentially a freighter with a draft of 13 feet (4 metres), was slow and ill-fitted for such a task, but no other vessels were available, and the need to survey that sector of the coast was crucial. His men repaired and modified the frigate's launch to prepare it for exploring. Supplies sufficient for two months were boarded. Two experienced pilots, Juan Pantoja and Juan Martínez, would support Caamaño. In addition, two of the scientific team, botanist Maldonado and artist Echeverría, were to accompany the expedition.

Bodega y Quadra briefed Caamaño on the objectives: he was to explore and chart the complex of channels around Bucareli Bay on Prince of Wales Island, then head south into Hecate Strait. There, he was to investigate a possible strait, first reported by the (fictitious) Admiral Bartolome de Fonte about latitude 53°. At that same latitude, Caamaño was to explore an entrance that had been more recently reported to Eliza by the Englishman James Colnett; Eliza called it Nepean Sound.[13]

Caamaño accomplished his assigned tasks, visiting several islands and channels already well known to fur traders (though not to the Spaniards), including the entrance mentioned by Colnett. Caamaño sent Martínez away in the launch to investigate it. He returned, having ascended 18 leagues (100 kilometres) and finding it to be closed. That inlet was later called the Douglas Channel. *Aránzazu* returned to Nootka, discovering and passing outside Triangle Island, and anchored on September 7, having been out three months.

Maldonado provided Caamaño with a list of the wildlife and plants he had noted for inclusion in the latter's report. The area they had explored was one of steep-sided, heavily forested fjords and islands. It seems probable that nowhere did they venture inland, but they did, however, visit a few Indigenous coastal villages.

Maldonado's list of quadrupeds, probably based on skins he had seen being worn by the local people, included black bear, elk, red deer, wild goat, coyotes, weasels, stoats, wolves, seals, and sea otters. W.A. Newcombe, the co-editor of Wagner's article, commented, incorrectly, that the elk (moose) and wild goat do not inhabit the places visited. The botanist included another mammal, the "Grampus—in great numbers" (killer whales) but listed them under fish.

The birds listed at Bucareli Bay were "falcons (or sparrow hawks), stormy petrels, sandpipers, oyster catchers, gulls, a new variety of woodpecker, snipes, linnets, crows." Pearse considered that the falcon would have been the peregrine, the petrels the fork-tailed or Leach's, and the linnet the pine siskin.

Maldonado was impressed with the fish they encountered: "various kinds of salmon, halibut of huge size, sardines in great numbers, *mojarras* [brown rockfish], cod, red bream, and dog fish. The shellfish noted were limpets, cockles, mussels (small), and crabs of various sizes."

Curiously, for one prepared by a botanist, the list of plants was not further divided; trees are mixed in among shrubs, creepers, herbs, ground cover, and even fungi and lichen. The trees listed were "Canadian pine, spruce, cypress (evergreen), Canadian cork tree, sandalwood, berry pear [perhaps salal],

FIG. 6-3 Ling cod, a species from the kelp forest highly appreciated by Indigenous people and incomers. *Plate 5 from* Fishes of the Pacific Coast of Canada, *Fisheries Research Board of Canada, 1961.*

common sloe (also blackthorn), strawberry tree [Newcombe guessed salmonberry],[14] service tree [*Pyrus sorbus* or perhaps saskatoon berry], and apple [both could be crabapple]." He listed 56 other plants, some identified by scientific names, others by their common Spanish names translated into English for the article by a retired naval captain, Harold Grenfell.

Two weeks after returning to Nootka, Caamaño was placed in temporary charge of the establishment until Fidalgo could arrive to take over. By this time, the governor's negotiations with Vancouver had come to an impasse, and they agreed to refer the matter to higher authorities. Bodega y Quadra had already issued orders for Fidalgo to withdraw all men, equipment, and stores from Núñez Gaona and take command at San Lorenzo de Nutka. He sailed in *Activa* bound for Monterey, taking with him Moziño, Maldonado, and Echeverría.

JOSÉ MOZIÑO'S SCIENTIFIC REPORTS FROM NOOTKA

The scientists spent the next three months at Monterey working on their collections of specimens and compiling their notes. Moziño produced a book-length manuscript, *Noticias de Nutka*, consisting of 16 articles chiefly concerning the ethnology of the Mowachaht Peoples. Having gained a good command of their language, he was able to record and describe their lives, beliefs, customs, ceremonies, and methods of hunting, fishing, and gathering vegetable foodstuffs. He began with a general geographic description of their territories, and later included a summary of the history of their contacts with Europeans. Moziño was the first trained scientist to have recorded such details for any Indigenous Peoples of the north Pacific coast. He did so at a time when the group memory and oral traditions remained intact and strong.

Moziño appended two lists to his text, both highly detailed and significant. The first, a "Brief Dictionary . . . of the Language of the Natives of Nootka," contained 220 entries. Included were the words for sea otter, bear, deer, squirrel, rat, dog, seal, eagle, crow (two kinds), goose, seagull, sparrow, fish, whale, salmon, herring, mojarra (brown rockfish), sardine, and octopus. While he recorded the words for various parts of plants, he did not list any species. In his text, however, he did mention several food plants. The second appendix was a "Catalogue of animals and plants . . . examined and classified according to the system of Linnaeus."[15]

Moziño's catalogue presents several problems in attempting to match the names he lists with their present-day ones. The Eurocentric nature of existing lists meant that Moziño and Maldonado had to correlate their sightings and specimens with Old World equivalents, if they existed. This was not always possible. A further complication is that Moziño and Maldonado did not record the location seen or collected. The list apparently contains species from beyond Nootka, including from Bucareli Bay, Nepean Sound, and even Monterey. Moreover, the distribution of species in 1792 is not known. Current distribution maps may not be valid.

The translator-editor of the most available version of Moziño's account was Iris Wilson (Engstrand). She called upon several experts in botany and zoology to help identify the modern names for the species on Moziño's list, but some doubts remain. For example, the list includes several Eurasian birds—the skylark, pheasant, starling, and yellow wagtail—none of which could have been seen there at that time. It also includes some southern species—the frigate bird and tropic bird—which would have been seen at San Blas but not at Nootka. Echeverría did not list locations, but his drawings help identification.

The list of almost 400 entries covers quadrupeds, birds, fish, insects, crabs, "worms," crustaceans, and 230 plants. As an

DIOMEDEA EXULANS

FIG. 6-4 Moziño misidentified Mendoza's copy of Echeverría's accurate watercolour of a marbled murrelet as *Diomedea exulans*, a wandering albatross. *Archivo General del Ministerio de Asuntos Exteriores y de Cooperación, Madrid, ms. 146, lám. 41.*

early listing of the results of a scientific expedition that included Vancouver Island, it is of considerable interest. Unfortunately, the lack of location data and the extraneous species limit its value for the natural history record of just the island.

In addition to Moziño's appended list of species, he includes within the articles of text several references to local plants and wildlife that he encountered while at Nootka. In Article 1, describing the geography, he records:

> I realized that birds were scarce because of the small number I was able to arouse. I was barely able to see a woodpecker, a hooked-bill sparrow, two hummingbirds, and two larks. The rest of the birds only inhabit the seashore, because it is their source of food but even here, the number of species is not abundant nor is the incidence great of the few species that do exist. Here are white-headed falcon, yellow-speckled falcon, sparrow hawks, crows, herons, geese, seagulls, and so forth.[16]

Some of these birds do not appear in the appended list. The white-headed falcon (*Falco leucocephalus*) was probably the bald eagle, but a bird painted by Echeverría and titled *Falco albiventris* (white-bellied falcon) was evidently the osprey, which could well have been seen at Nootka. The yellow-speckled falcon was the American kestrel, and the sparrow hawk, either a sharp-shinned or a Cooper's hawk. While Pearse thought that the hooked-bill sparrow might have been a Bewick's wren, Echeverría also painted a more likely possibility, the red crossbill.

In Article 2, describing the Mowachaht diet, Moziño observed:

> Another condiment ... is whale oil, or that of sardines, which they mix according to their taste in their dishes of roasted or boiled foods. They also use deer meat, I presume they scorn that of the

LOXIA CURVIROSTRA.

FIG. 6-5 *Loxia Curvirostra*. Echeverría's drawing of a red crossbill. *Archivo General del Ministerio de Asuntos Exteriores y de Cooperación, Madrid, ms. 146, lám. 40.*

bear or sea otter. They like geese and seagulls and other aquatic birds, but I have not been able to learn whether they use eagles for the same purpose, or whether they hunt them only to use their feathers. . . .

I counted up to thirty-six [dishes served at a feast], a number I judge comes from the several kinds of fish, birds, and animals on which they ordinarily subsist. Also, they do not fail to eat the vegetables that grow wild during the summer. For them the juicy berries of the *Andromeda* [bog rosemary] are the most delicate fruit. They also consume with pleasure the three species of blackberries that grow among their forests; the *vaccinium* [huckleberry or blueberry], crabapples and wild pears, madrone [arbutus] berries, currants, and strawberries. The flowers and fruit of the wild rose haw, the silver weed [cinquefoil, *Potentilla*], the tender stalks of the angelica, the leaves of the lithosperm, the roots of the trailing clover, and the scaly onionlike bulb of the Kamchatka lily [rice root] are the vegetables which providence appears to have provided them in order to correct the alkaline imbalance caused by the continuous use of fish and seafood toward which these islanders are inclined. I doubt they like garlic because, it annoyed them greatly to see it on our tables.[17]

Early in 1793, Moziño delivered his *Noticias de Nutka* manuscript to the viceroy, who ordered several manuscript copies or versions to be made. He then rejoined Sessé. Echeverría placed his drawings with artist friends at the Royal Art Academy in Mexico, for making multiple copies by hand. The illustrious German naturalist Baron Alexander von Humboldt, visiting the Royal Botanical Garden in Mexico City, admired Moziño's work, and thought its description of the ethnology of the northwest coast people deserved to be published in French. It was not, nor even printed in Spanish until 1913. The version used for this edition did not include any of Echeverría's illustrations.[18]

While at Nootka, and again at Monterey, Moziño had opportunity to compare notes and even make field excursions with a fellow physician-botanist. This was Archibald Menzies, who accompanied George Vancouver on his three-season survey of Vancouver Island and the nearby mainland coast.

FIG. 6-6 *Medeola Notkana.* Echeverría's sketch of the northern rice root—or Kamchatka, black, or chocolate lily—whose bulbs were an important food for many northwest coast peoples. *Biological Illustrations #6331.1967, Torner Collection of Sessé and Mociño, Hunt Institute for Biological Documentation, Pittsburgh, PA [image edited].*

FIG. 7-0   Archibald Menzies was the first scientist to record, and name, the rhinoceros auklet. *From* Audubon's Birds of America *[image edited]*.

CHAPTER SEVEN

ARCHIBALD MENZIES

*"Promote the interest of science,
and contribute to the increase of human knowledge . . ."*

BOTANY WAS IN ARCHIBALD MENZIES's blood: he was the second son of a family that by tradition was responsible for the gardens and forests at Castle Menzies, the clan seat in Perthshire, Scotland. In 1768 Dr. John Hope, professor of botany and keeper of what became the Royal Botanic Garden, University of Edinburgh, accepted the lad as a student gardener.

A few years later, Hope recommended him for further training at the university's medical school as an apothecary and surgeon, and he qualified in 1778. Menzies briefly assisted a surgeon in north Wales before joining the Royal Navy as an assistant surgeon. He served, including under battle conditions, on the east coast of the Americas and for a few years on land at the Halifax naval station. Whenever possible, Menzies studied the local flora and collected seeds and dried plants from Nova Scotia and the Caribbean. Following an introduction by Hope, he sent consignments of seeds to Joseph Banks for germination at Kew Gardens, as well as to Hope and to the gardens of Castle Menzies.

MENZIES VISITS NOOTKA WITH COLNETT

In 1786, Menzies returned to Britain with gifts of plant specimens for the herbaria of both of his influential fellow collectors, Hope and Banks. He hoped they might help him secure a position as surgeon for a long voyage to distant lands. He learned that English captain James Colnett had retired from the Royal Navy and was planning a commercial fur-trading venture, taking two ships. The voyage was to exploit the sea otter opportunity found during James Cook's last voyage. Menzies planned to apply, but first he solicited Banks's support, writing: "It will at least gratify one of my greatest earthly Ambitions & afford one of the best opportunity of collecting Seeds & other objects of Natural History for you & the rest of my friends."[1]

Banks's endorsement helped secure the success of Menzies's application to Richard Cadman Etches, the financial backer of the voyage. Not only would Menzies serve as surgeon aboard *Prince of Wales* but, as he wrote to Banks:

[Etches] was kind enough to promise me every indulgence the situation of the voyage would permit . . . for the West coast of N. America presents to me a new & an extensive field for Botanical researches as well as other branches of natural history; & I can assure you that I shall loose [sic] no opportunity for collecting whatever is new and rare, or useful, in my branch of natural knowledge.[2]

Etches had granted a special favour. The general rule for individuals on fur-trading missions was that they not barter with locals on their own account for fear of disrupting the primary negotiation and affecting prices.

Before departing, Menzies spent time with Banks studying the botanical collection from Nootka and Oonalaska (Aleutian Islands) that was brought back at the close of Cook's last, and fatal, voyage. Menzies discovered that a friend and former shipmate, James Johnstone, was to be first mate on *Prince of Wales*, an added attraction. The second ship on the expedition would be *Princess Royal*.

After setting sail in September 1786, the two ships rounded the Horn and visited Nootka, Nasparti, Haida Gwaii, and Banks Island[3] to acquire pelts and, in Menzies's case, collect botanical material. They spent the winter cruising through the Hawaiian archipelago, before *Prince of Wales* went on to collect more Alaskan peltry during the 1788 season. Meanwhile *Princess Royal* returned to Nootka, Haida Gwaii, and the Strait of Juan de Fuca. The two vessels reunited at Hawaii in September before sailing for Macau and Canton in China. They carried about 2,000 sea otter pelts and 65 "cloaks" made up from pelts, valued in total at 80,000 Spanish dollars, equivalent to $4 million Canadian today.[4]

The syndicate, which now included John Meares, invited Colnett to take *Argonaut* and three other ships back to Nootka for more pelts. He accepted and sailed, to clash on arrival with Esteban Martínez in what became known as the Nootka Incident of 1789. *Prince of Wales*, with Menzies still aboard, but under the command of James Johnstone, was not in the flotilla returning to Nootka but completed the circumnavigation. Menzies returned to London in July 1789, having been gone three years. He distributed the seeds and plants collected during the voyage among his influential patrons.

WITH GEORGE VANCOUVER TO THE NORTH PACIFIC COAST

His appetite for distant travel still not sated, Menzies immediately sought out another such voyage. While he had been gone, the Admiralty had been planning an expedition to find, or positively refute, the existence of a western portal to the Northwest Passage. The north Pacific mainland coast between latitudes 40° and 60° had still not been properly charted, and two vessels were assigned to the task: *Discovery*[5] and, as tender, *Chatham*. The voyage had already been postponed for about a year because of possible conflict with Spain, but now Lieutenant George Vancouver, RN, had been given command.

Menzies dearly hoped for the post of surgeon on that expedition and again asked Banks to help secure it. Banks, by now a most influential figure, also wanted Menzies's participation so he, Banks, would have preferential access to any new botanical material discovered. He pressed the matter with the Admiralty, but the surgeon's berth had already been filled by an Alexander Cranstoun. Banks, not to be thwarted, arranged that Menzies be listed as a supernumerary botanist, accommodated but having to pay for his own food. His contract provided a salary of £150, and he was allowed a servant, the seaman John Ewins, to help tend the plants.

To Vancouver's annoyance, Banks also persuaded the Admiralty to authorize construction of a large, lidded, and windowed "plant hutch," to be positioned on *Discovery*'s quarterdeck. This was for Menzies to nurture live plants to bring back to Kew. It proved a great inconvenience to Vancouver and the other officers, and an ongoing source of friction.[6]

The home secretary, Lord William Grenville, was to provide instructions for Menzies detailing what was required of him on the voyage. Grenville not only delegated to Banks the drafting of those instructions but also had him sign the document and issue it from Banks's personal address. The concluding paragraph read:

> You are to keep a regular journal of all occurrences that happen in the execution of the several duties you are entrusted to perform, and enter in it all observations you shall make on every subject you are employed to investigate; which journal, together with a complete collection of specimens of the animals, vegetables and minerals you shall have obtained, as well as such curious Articles of the Cloths, Arms, implements and manufactures of the Indians as you shall deem worthy of particular notice, you are on return to deliver to His Majesty's Secretary of State for the Home Department, or to such person as he shall appoint to receive them from you.[7]

For Menzies, these orders clearly established that his line of reporting was to Banks, rather than to Vancouver. The normal requirement for naval officers to keep journals during voyages and to submit them at the close to the captain seemed to have been overridden in this case. Menzies would not be considered a ship's officer, but rather a representative of another branch of government. This would have later ramifications.

Vancouver's two ships set sail from Falmouth, Devon, on April 1, 1791. To Menzies's delight, they took a very different route to the Pacific north coast of America from his earlier voyage. Colnett, intent on getting to the source of sea otter

FIG. 7-1 A replica of the "plant hutch" constructed on *Discovery*'s quarterdeck on display at VanDusen Botanical Garden, Vancouver, BC. *Image CVA 1502-314 courtesy of City of Vancouver Archives [image edited].*

pelts as fast as possible, had headed westabout. They had made only two stops on their way: the Cape Verde Islands and Staten Island in Patagonia. Vancouver, given some intermediate charting duties, went eastabout, stopping sometimes for weeks at a time at Tenerife, the Cape of Good Hope, New Holland (the southwest tip of Australia), New Zealand, Tahiti, and Hawaii. At each place, Menzies was able to go ashore and explore the local flora. The ships, guided by American fur trader Robert Gray, rounded Cape Flattery on May 1, 1792, to enter the Strait of Juan de Fuca more than a year after setting out.

THE STRAIT OF JUAN DE FUCA

Vancouver had strict orders to trace and chart only the mainland coast, ignoring islands or water entrances that did not offer navigability to ocean-going vessels. Accordingly, he kept to the southern shore of the strait, stopping briefly at the new Spanish outpost of Núñez Gaona at Neah Bay. Vancouver's survey method, once inside Juan de Fuca, was to anchor the ships in a protected place and establish an encampment on land nearby. Boat parties of surveyors would then disperse for a few days at a time to chart stretches of the coastline, returning to consolidate their results onto the master chart. At the camp, specialists would set up an astronomy tent for the several nights of observation required to determine the accurate coordinates for that location.

The first of the encampments was named Port Discovery (now Discovery Bay near Sequim, Washington). There, the party found trees recently felled with steel axes, a sign of prior European presence. They later learned that the same place had been used the previous year by the Eliza expedition, which had named it Puerto Quadra.

These encampments gave Menzies ample opportunity to investigate the botany of the surrounding area and collect seeds

FIG. 7-2 *Band-tailed doves.* Audubon depicts them in the branches of a western flowering dogwood, now the provincial tree of British Columbia, and first documented by Menzies. *From* Audubon's Birds of America *[image edited].*

ERIC GROVES'S RESEARCHES

Eric Groves's career was associated with the Natural History Museum at South Kensington in London. He devoted much effort to the botanical record of Menzies's voyages. In the early years, he worked on restoring the museum's water-damaged specimens following incendiary bombing during the Second World War. Latterly, he identified and built a consolidated record of currently known specimens. He searched the herbaria of the British Museum, the Royal Botanic Gardens at Kew and Edinburgh, and the botanists' Linnean Society, also in London.

Groves presented several papers on his research, adding significantly to current understanding of Vancouver and Menzies's important voyage of scientific discovery.

In one of those papers, he pointed out that Menzies went ashore collecting at many more places, on four continents, than are recorded in his journal, and commented that

> Menzies used every opportunity to search for and collect good representative material at each of the habitats he visited. . . . He collected not only flowering plants but also ferns, mosses, hepatics [liverworts], algae and lichens.[8]

Groves speculated how Menzies collected plant specimens in the field:

> He probably carried a small plant press similar to that used by Banks of Cook's voyage, made of wooden slats enclosing the drying papers and secured round with a thick leather strap. . . . To carry his press, a quantity of paper, sketch materials and probably notebook would have required some sort of holdall to keep them dry, apart from preventing loss when getting in and out of boats on survey journeys. . . . Menzies would have got the sailmaker to sew up some canvas. . . . Painted with boat-paint it would have kept the contents dry and together.[9]

FIG. 7-3 *Caltha leptosepala*. Menzies collected this holotype, or type specimen, of the alpine white marsh marigold at Prince William Sound. Also found on Vancouver Island, it is one of the specimens restored and collated by Eric Groves. *Image © Trustees of the Natural History Museum, London.*

Viverra putorius.

FIG. 7-4 *Viverra putorius* by A. Echeverría. A midshipman from *Discovery* threw a stone at a cat-sized animal at Port Discovery. He discovered that the striped skunk had effective defences. *Biological Illustrations #6331.1248, Torner Collection of Sessé and Mociño, Hunt Institute for Biological Documentation, Pittsburgh, PA [image edited].*

and specimens to dry or to attempt to grow in the plant hutch. He also participated in the boat forays, but his time for botanizing was more restricted while with them. Menzies's orders had specified that his task

> [is] of an extensive nature as it includes an investigation of the whole of Natural History of the countries you are to visit, as well as an enquiry into the present state & comparative degree of civilization of the inhabitants you will meet . . . to enumerate all of the Trees, Shrubs, Grasses Fens, and Mosses . . . to note what sort of Beasts, Birds and Fishes likely to prove useful either for food or commerce . . . and always to act as you judge most likely to promote the interest of Science, and contribute to the increase of human knowledge.[10]

The scope of these instructions far exceeded the ability of any one man plus assistant, as Banks well knew. Indeed, Banks had planned to bring an 18-strong entourage for Cook's second voyage. Nonetheless, Menzies made a valiant effort, even after Cranstoun, the official surgeon, fell sick early in the voyage, leaving Menzies to cover his duties as well as those of botanist.

Menzies's experience up to that time fitted him well for the botanical task he was about to face. He not only had spent two seasons on this coast, with opportunities to botanize, but also had spent a few years in Nova Scotia on the eastern seaboard and so was already familiar with North American genera and species.

Menzies's journal, though long delayed in completion, provided a detailed and valuable record of events for most of the voyage. It is especially significant for its notes on ethnology, second only to those on plants. Much to the frustration of subsequent botanists, however, it was not a full annotation of the botanical discoveries made on the expedition. Menzies would certainly have kept detailed, technical descriptions of the plants he found. Researchers W. Kaye Lamb[11] and Eric Groves both believed that Menzies kept a separate botanical record, which was subsequently lost.[12]

While Menzies assiduously collected botanical specimens, time did not permit much work on other aspects of natural history. His journal, however, mentions a few times officers, or "our sportsmen," shot birds for the pot. This was before the advent of shotguns, but some of the party had brought muzzle-loading, flintlock "fowling pieces" with them for just such opportunities. Otherwise, Menzies's journal contains only a few records of fauna related to Vancouver Island. On one of the excursions from Port Discovery,

> in strolling about the Beach one of the gentlemen knockd down an animal about the size of a Cat with a stone & as he was going to pick it up it ejected a fluid of the most offensive smell & impregnated the air that no one could remain any time within some distance of where it fell. I satisfied myself however that it was a Skunk (*Viverra Putorius*).[13]

At Refuge Cove, Desolation Sound,

> we here killed some large Grouse which on starting perchd in the Pine Trees [Pearse: "obviously Blue Grouse"], & we saw some Deer but did not get near enough to have a shoot at them; it is surprising how fond these Animals are of insulate situations to which probably they are driven by being chaced or harassed by other animals such as Wolves, Foxes &c.[14]

In that same archipelago he found sea mammals.

Tho these channels are a considerable distance removed from the Ocean yet we found them frequented by Whales, Seals and Porpusses, but we saw very few sea Otters, which shews that these Animals are not fond of penetrating far into the inland branches tho the Channels are deep & spacious abounding with insulated Rocks & Caverns that form commodious recesses for such Animals.[15]

And he marvelled at wasp nest architecture.

Some Wasp nests suspended to Trees of a curious & extra-ordinary structure. . . . Its figure was globular, about 4 inches in diameter, & perforated underneath with a small hole of the size sufficient to admit one of the Wasps in or out at a time. The outer covering was composd of a paper like substance of a light ash colour & made up by several folds overlapping one another here and there like the Tiles of a house to throw off the wet. . . . This exterior covering was evidently made up of bleached minute fibres of rotten & decayed wood, bleached by long exposure to the weather, which had been collected & agglutinated together by some waxen matter into its present form & appearance by the indefatigable labour of these wonderful & curious Mechanics.[16]

Later, amid the Mill Group of islands in Queen Charlotte Sound, where both *Discovery* and *Chatham* had already run aground, Menzies and Master Joseph Whidbey were in the pinnace, scouting ahead for the best channel, when Menzies observed:

We came to a small barren Island on which we landed to take some bearing & here I saw a vast abundance of a new species of *Lepas* [goose barnacle] adhering to the Rocks in large Clusters, together with a large species of Mussel which was likewise new. A

great number of Sea Otters which we disturbed & frightened off the Rock when we landed, continued swimming about it while we staid & afterwards followed us some way in the Boat, sometimes approaching very near.[17]

Menzies's mentions of fish were even more sparse. It was standard practice for members of the crew to deploy a seine net whenever they set up camp, to provide fresh seafood. The naturalist kept an interested eye on the hauls. At Port Discovery, he noted:

We seldom obtained a sufficient supply for all hands, the fish generally caught were Bream of two or three kinds, Salmon Trout & two kinds of flat fish, one of which was a new species of *Pleuronectes* [flounder], with [Dungeness] Crabs which were found very good and palatable & we seldom failed in hauling on shore a number of Elephant Fish (*Chimœra Callorrhynchus*) and Scolpings (*Cuttus scorpius*) but the very appearance of these was sufficient to deter the use of them, they therefore generally remained on the Beach. [The elephant fish is now known as the spotted ratfish, and the scolping, the sea scorpion sculpin.][18]

A few weeks later, in a small lagoon near Deception Pass, they caught

a peculiar variety of Trout I had not seen before with a vermillion spot near the lower angle of the Gills but differing in no other respect from the common fresh water Trout [now known as cutthroat trout].[19]

He mentioned only a few bird sightings. Again, while at Port Discovery, he noted:

While dinner was getting ready . . . with one of the Gentlemen [I] strolled over an extensive lawn, where solitude and rich pasture prevaild . . . where the Plough might enter at once without the least obstruction . . . or herds of Cattle might here wander at their ease over extensive fields of fine pasture though the only possessors of it we saw at this time were a few gigantic [sandhill] Cranes of between three & four feet high who strided over the Lawn with a lordly step.[20]

And later, at the same place,

silence & solitude seemd to prevail over this fine & extensive country, even the featherd race as if unable to endure the stillness that pervaded every where had in great measure abandoned it & were therefore very scarce—A few large Cranes that inhabit the inland pastures, some white headed eagles that hoverd over the Arms & perchd in the trees on both sides watching for fish seemingly their only prey, a few Ducks that were seen in two or three places on the ponds behind the point and a kind of small Blackbird with red Shoulders (*Oriolus phœnicius*) that hopped amongst the Bullrushes with a few crows that seemed to accompany the Indians comprehended our ornithological list of this extensive tract.[21]

Near Marrowstone Point, Port Townshend, Vancouver and Broughton were taking a boat to a small island for some observations. Menzies accompanied them

to examine it, at the same time for plants. . . . About the Rocks were a number of black Sea pies [black oystercatchers] of which we shot several & found them good eating. . . . On our return . . . the vessels had been visited by a few Natives who had nothing to dispose of but a few Water Fowls particularly a blackish coulourd

8249

FIG. 7-6 (LEFT) "A peculiar ornament to the forest" was how Menzies recorded the oriental strawberry tree, named scientifically *Arbutus menziesii* in his honour. *From* Curtis's Botanical Magazine, *vol. 5, fourth series, 1909, plate 8249.*

FIG. 7-7 (ABOVE) Prickly-pear cactus on Mitlenatch Island in the Gulf of Georgia, currently the northernmost limit of the species. *Photo by author.*

VANCOUVER'S ROUTE AROUND VANCOUVER ISLAND

After leaving Port Discovery, George Vancouver's route led him to explore the intricacies of Admiralty Inlet and Puget Sound, leading to dead ends. Then he followed the coastline north to Point Roberts where he encountered the Spanish expedition. The two teams, on similar missions and both with orders to be cooperative, exchanged charts. They sailed together up the Strait of Georgia (although giving it different toponyms) and into Desolation Sound, where they anchored together for a few days. Agreeing to continue northward separately and with different routes, they parted on friendly terms. Vancouver's ships chose the route through Discovery Passage. Before transiting Seymour Narrows, they paused to await slack water in a protected cove, which Vancouver named Menzies Bay.

By this time, they had realized that a changed tidal pattern meant that to their west lay a large island, with Nootka on its far side. At Cheslakees village, at the mouth of the Nimpkish River, they found a group who traded with the Mowachaht via an overland trail. Crossing Queen Charlotte Sound to regain the mainland shore, they continued charting north to the close of the season, when they made their way to Nootka. Vancouver had a pre-arranged meeting with his diplomatic counterpart, Juan Francisco de la Bodega y Quadra, which took a month, but they were unable to resolve the issue.

Notwithstanding the impasse, the two officers formed a strong bond of friendship and agreed that the island the two teams had revealed should be called Quadra and Vancouver's. Vancouver so named it on his first published charts, but regrettably, his superiors ordered that the Spaniard's name be omitted thereafter.

species of Auk with a hornlike excrescence rising from the ridge of its Bill, & as it appeared to be a new species I named it *Alca Rhinoceros* & described it.[22]

MENZIES'S INCIDENTAL BOTANICAL NOTES

Menzies found and mentioned some interesting plants in his journal:

Besides a variety of Pines [at a deserted village in Port Discovery] we saw the Sycamore Maple, the American Alder, a species of wild Crab [apple] & the Oriental Strawberry Tree, this last grows to a small Tree & was it this time [early May] a peculiar ornament to the Forest by its large clusters of whitish flowers & ever green leaves, but its peculiar smooth bark of a reddish brown colour will at all times attract the Notice of the most superficial observer.[23] We met with some other Plants which were new to me & which shall be the subject of particular description hereafter.[24]

As Captain Vancouver was going to land on [Protection Island] to take some bearing I went with him to have another short stroll on that delightful spot & among other Plants I collected I was not a little surprizd to meet with the *Cactus opunta* [prickly pear] thus far northward, it grew plentifully but in a very dwarf state on the Eastern point of the Island which is low flat & dry sandy soil.[25]

As Menzies left Admiralty Inlet, he summarized the trees he had noted:[26]

The Woods here were chiefly composed of the Silver Fir, White Spruce, Norway Spruce & Hemlock Spruce together with the American Abor Vitae [Groves: western red cedar] & Common Yew: & besides these we saw a variety of hard wood scattered along the banks of the Arms, such as Oak, the Sycamore or great Maple, Mountain Maple & Pensylvanian Maple, the Tacamahac [Groves: balsam poplar] & Canadian Poplars [Groves: black cottonwood?], the American Ash, common Hazel, American Alder, Common Willow & the Oriental Arbute, but none of their hardwood Trees were in great abundance or acquired sufficient size to be of any great utility, except the Oak in some particular places. . . .

We also met here pretty frequent in the Wood with that beautiful Native of the Levant the Purple Rhododendron, together with the great flowered Dog-wood, the Carolina Rose & Dog Rose [Groves: Nootka rose], but most part of the Shrubs and Underwood were new & undescribed, several of them I named. . . . Others from particular circumstances were doubtful & could not be ascertained till they are hereafter compared with more extensive description &c. on my return to England.[27]

FRIENDLY COVE REVISITED

While negotiations between the Spanish and British captains proceeded, Menzies renewed his acquaintance with the Mowachaht, and particularly one of his two companions on botanical walks from his visit five years earlier. Known as the *Taisa*, she was the wife of Maquinna's brother. When they recognized each other, "I emptied my pockets of all the little Trinkets they contained in her lap & begged her to come on board the Vessel with her father[28] who she told me was still alive, that I might have an opportunity of renewing our friendship by some gratifying present."[29]

TAISA DE NUTCA.

FIG. 7-8 *Taisa de Nutca*. The young Mowachaht woman who had earlier accompanied Menzies at Friendly Cove was, by the time of his second visit, a *Taisa*, a chief's wife. She has gathered a basket of medicinal plants. *Archivo General del Ministerio de Asuntos Exteriores y de Cooperación, Madrid, ms. 146, lám. 33.*

He also met the Spanish botanists Moziño, Maldonado, and Echeverría, and compared notes. He recorded:

> One of them had been in the *Aranzazu* to the Northward & had made a considerable collection of plants from different places they touched at, the other whose name was Don José Moziño remained at Nootka with Sʳ Quadra together with an excellent draughtsman Sʳ Escheverea a Native of Mexico, who as a Natural History Painter has great merit.[30]

By the time they had reached Nootka, Surgeon Cranstoun's condition had deteriorated, and he was sent back to England with the supply ship *Daedalus*. Vancouver pressured Menzies to formally agree to take the position of surgeon.[31]

At the time, the relationship between the two men had improved, so Menzies agreed. An added inducement was that he would get a second cabin for his collections. In the event, formalizing the arrangement would turn out badly for Menzies.

THE JOURNEY HOME

After the collapse of the negotiations, both delegations departed from Nootka, bound for San Francisco. The Spaniards were again extremely hospitable to the British mission, resupplying the ships with food and declining any payment. The luxuriant flora Menzies found there and at Monterey most impressed him. Again able to compare notes with Moziño and his companion botanists, Menzies wrote to Banks:

> There are two Botanists here [San Francisco] which have been with Don Quadra to the Northward all Summer, they tell me they are part of a Society which have been of late years at the expense of his Catholic Majesty in examining Mexico and New Spain, and collecting material for a *Flora Mexicana* which they say will be published before our return to England; and they have promised me a copy of it. . . . I cannot help envying them the assistance they have in being accompanied by an excellent draughtsman [Echeverría].[32]

Vancouver wintered over in Hawaii and returned to the coast in the next two seasons to complete his survey of the mainland coastline. In the process, he and his team disproved all rumours of any entrance to a transcontinental, navigable waterway.

Mission accomplished, in August 1794 Vancouver and his men started the long journey home. They called in at Nootka, San Francisco, and Monterey, as had been their custom, and briefly paused in the Galapagos Islands, before heading for Valparaíso, Chile, still a Spanish colony. They were invited to visit the capital, Santiago, and the governor, Ambrosio Bernardo O'Higgins (an Irish soldier of fortune), entertained them with a banquet. Legend has it that some strange nuts were served as one of the courses, and that Menzies pocketed a few, to plant in the hutch on *Discovery*'s quarterdeck. The nuts survived the passage round the Horn and made it to Kew, where five flourished as distinctive trees. They are well known today as *Araucaria imbricata*—Chilean monkey puzzle trees.

After rounding the Horn, the ships struggled to reach St. Helena, where Vancouver learned that war with France had been declared. He captured a Dutch ship, an ally of France, as a prize and sent it home with some of his crew. Soon afterward, a storm hit, *Discovery*'s plant hutch was swamped, and Menzies's precious live specimens were lost. This caused a serious rupture between the botanist-now-medical-officer and his captain. To further widen the breach, Menzies declined to submit his scientific journals to the captain at the end of the voyage, considering that they should be given to his sponsor,

FIG. 7-9 A mature araucaria in Ross Bay Cemetery. Menzies took nuts served at a Chilean banquet and had them propagated at Kew. They grew into the spectacular monkey puzzle tree. *Photo by author.*

Banks. Tempers cooled by the time they reached Deptford in the Thames estuary. Menzies apologized, and Vancouver accepted and dropped charges.

AFTERMATH OF THE VOYAGE

After a momentous voyage lasting four and a half years, circumnavigating and visiting four continents, the officers and crew were paid off on September 13, 1795. Menzies, who had been contracted only for this commission, was now without income. Banks tried to have Menzies's rate continued while he completed his journal, since he had been obliged to do double duty on the voyage, but without success. Lacking private means, Menzies asked for assignment to another ship, while promising Banks that he would continue producing a fair copy of his notes.

Banks had ambitions to release Menzies's journal before Vancouver could arrange for his own to be published, but this did not prove possible. Even by early 1798, Banks had received only three out of four volumes of Menzies's clean manuscript, and the final one never appeared. This would have covered the last phases of the voyage, from Chile to London, including the row over the damage to the plants in the flooded frame.

Menzies had been kept busy as surgeon on the Admiralty yacht, during which time he received an honorary doctor of medicine degree from Aberdeen University. Banks, understandably, grew frustrated with Menzies's failure to complete his narrative. Even today, a full version of his journal is yet to be published but is understood to have been, at long last, commissioned by the Hakluyt Society.

During a posting as squadron physician on a voyage to Jamaica, Menzies developed asthma and was eventually released from the service on half pay. He married and set up in private practice in London, where he continued successfully for the next 23 years. He had been elected a member of the Linnean Society in 1790 and remained an active participant for the rest of his life. Younger botanists, such as John Scouler and David Douglas, consulted him before they went to the American west coast, the latter to collect for the Royal Horticultural Society.

Menzies's collection of several hundred species[33] as dried specimens is to be found dispersed through several institutions. Menzies worked with staff at Banks's herbarium to classify the plant material he had found. They also prepared multiple sets of them. The first, and most complete, was given to the herbarium and is currently at the Natural History Museum in London.

Unfortunately, taxonomic recording of his findings did not come until after later expeditions, resulting in many instances where credit for discovering new species rightly his (or perhaps Haenke's or Moziño's) was given to others. Included in this list are such well-known plants as Garry oak, Douglas-fir, bigleaf maple, ocean spray, skunk cabbage, salmonberry, Oregon grape, and Pacific rhododendron. The late Eric Groves worked assiduously to redress this injustice.[34] However, the arbutus, or Pacific madrone, which Menzies first saw at Port Discovery, was later named *A. menziesii*, in his honour.

Researcher, naturalist, and historian Jerry Gorsline has produced a list of 235 species of ferns and flowering plants, including trees.[35] These species are known to have been (or could have been) collected by Menzies in the northern lowlands of the Olympic Peninsula, Washington, a rainshadow ecosystem comparable to that of the southern end of Vancouver Island.

FIG. 8-0 *Phyllospadix scouleri*, a newly described genus of flowering surfgrass, collected by Scouler and named after him by Hooker. The brown split kelp is also present. *Photo © courtesy of Courtnay Janiak. www.ebbandflow.photography.*

CHAPTER EIGHT

NATURALISTS IN THE HUDSON'S BAY COMPANY ERA, PART I

Scouler and Douglas

IN JUNE 1824 TWO EMINENT British naturalists, both distinguished in the scientific aspects of exploring distant lands, discussed a new opportunity. Both strongly advocated that trained scientists should accompany all British expeditions, naval and commercial, and both knew Sir Joseph Banks, who shared that view. The Hudson's Bay Company (HBC) had invited them to suggest a suitable candidate to participate in a voyage to the northwest coast of America.

The first of these advisers was Dr. John Richardson, who had accompanied Sir John Franklin as surgeon and naturalist on two major expeditions into the Arctic and subsequently led the search for the missing explorer. At the time residing in Edinburgh, Richardson was working on a major government publication, *Fauna Boreali-Americana*,[1] preparing the sections on quadrupeds and fishes and assisting William Swainson with the birds.

The second was William Jackson Hooker, Regius Professor[2] of Botany at the University of Glasgow. Encouraged by Banks, he had earlier undertaken botanical expeditions to Iceland and the Alps and had recently published *Flora Scotica*. He was also working on the botanical material from the Franklin expeditions for eventual inclusion in *Flora Boreali-Americana*.

The opportunity the two men discussed related to an upcoming voyage of the HBC supply vessel the *William and Ann*, to the company's Fort George near the mouth of the Columbia River.[3] The purpose of the voyage would also include investigating the trade in sea otter pelts along the north Pacific coast, particularly at Sitka, before returning to London. The anticipated duration was two years. The position of ship's surgeon, which also entailed carrying out other scientific research throughout the voyage, was yet to be filled.

Hooker had the ideal candidate: John Scouler, "a young man every way qualified for such a situation . . . unquestionably one of our ablest botanical students."[4] Scouler was born in 1804, the second son of a calico printer, in a village southwest of Glasgow. After a standard elementary education plus some tutoring by a local clergyman, at the age of about 13 he enrolled in a logic class at the University of Glasgow. He continued studies intended for the medical profession, including botany and other natural sciences, as well as human anatomy and surgery. In September 1824 he travelled to Paris to further his studies for a few months at the renowned Jardin des Plantes.

Immediately upon Scouler's return, Hooker put forward his name to the HBC, which accepted the suggestion. Notwithstanding Scouler's lack of practical experience or formal certification, the Royal College of Physicians and Surgeons of Glasgow swiftly granted him status as their licentiate.

In London, before joining the ship, Scouler visited both Dr. Richardson, who advised him on the preparation of zoological specimens, and Dr. Archibald Menzies, by then aged 70. Three decades earlier, he had sailed those same waters with George Vancouver. Menzies instructed the 20-year-old in collecting and preserving botanical specimens. Both men showed their personal collections to the young traveller about to embark on his own journey of discovery.

It happened that another of Hooker's protegés, David Douglas, would also sail aboard the *William and Ann* but would disembark at Fort Vancouver. Funded by the Horticultural Society of London,[5] Douglas would collect botanical specimens from the region around the fort, the basin of the Columbia River, and more generally throughout the interior of the Columbia district.

After a cursory elementary education in rural central Scotland, Douglas had apprenticed, then qualified, as a gardener at two grand estates. The second of these, Sir Robert Preston's Valleyfield, was renowned both for its splendid collection of exotic plants and for an extensive botanical library. Douglas seized the unique opportunity of studying these. He then joined Hooker's newly established Glasgow Royal Botanic Garden, where he became the star student, and was soon promoted to head gardener.

FIG. 8-1 The venerable botanist Archibald Menzies was consulted by John Scouler and David Douglas prior to their voyage to Fort Vancouver. *Image © The Royal Botanic Gardens, Kew.*

Vancouver Island's non-Indigenous society initially took its cultural style and character from the structured, mainly Scottish, ethos of the Hudson's Bay Company. Most of the earliest settlers were retired company men and their mixed-race families. In the late 1850s this social structure underwent a radical upheaval from the flood of rootless prospectors and associated support train of the gold rush.

There followed a period of more orderly settlement by economically comfortable people from England buying land[7] to farm. Among them was the class known as remittance men.[8] A third contingent of later arrivals was retired colonial officers, on a pension but reluctant to return to life in the smoky suburbs of London.[9] Together, they attempted to create a fanciful, idealized replica of the genteel Home Counties, a style "more English than the English." The style persisted as governance of the colony passed from the company to direct rule from London, to continue after 1871 when the united colony elected to join the dominion, and afterward.

One of the features of this style, as in England, was a wide interest in natural history. Many of the arrivals brought with them avocations and pastimes related to the natural world.[10] The impetus for social approval of such activity by both men and women came primarily from the several learned societies established in London.

The first of these, and the oldest extant natural history society in the world, was the Linnean Society, founded in 1788 and granted a Royal Charter in 1802.[11] Based on the acquisition of Linnaeus's notes and collections, it continues his work on evolution and taxonomy. There followed the Horticultural Society (1804 and 1861), the Geological Society (1807 and 1825), the Zoological Society (1826 and 1829), the Geographical Society (1830 and 1859), and the Entomological Society (1833 and 1885). A separate Botanical Society was founded in 1839 and lasted 20 years, but it has all but vanished from the record.[12]

The half-century between 1820 and 1870 has been described as the "Heyday of Natural History." To be an amateur during those years was no disadvantage socially.[13] In 1851 the Great Exhibition, the grand scientific and promotional initiative of Prince Albert, gave rise to the great museums of South Kensington. Currently, there are over 200 learned societies in the United Kingdom,[14] many of which have members around the world.

At the outset, the clubs drew their members from the elevated ranks of society at large: the peerage and landed gentry, naval and military officers, clergy, the judiciary and bar, the City and its guilds, ship owners, physicians, politicians, Westminster mandarins and colonial administrators, as well as scholars and gentlemen amateurs. They met over formal dinners, for lectures followed by discussion. They recorded these meetings in published proceedings, transactions, journals, or annals that today comprise invaluable records of developing knowledge in the fields of their interests. Distinguished citizens proudly appended initials, indicating fellowship of the societies, to their calling cards.

The participation of such high-status figures made a gentleman's avocation for various and esoteric aspects of the natural sciences a social accolade. It became perfectly respectable for grown men to study newts or collect butterflies, birds' eggs,[15] beetles, fungi, or mosses. Ladies too showed interest in nature, especially botany.[16] Even middle-class residences nurtured gardens, their conservatories filled with lovingly tended exotic foliage and tropical orchids. Aspidistras embellished many front windows. Daughters' accomplishments in painting floral and botanical subjects earned proud praise. In England during the late 19th century, collecting crazes developed for seaweeds, seashells, and particularly ferns.[17]

2843.

r. J.H.

Pub. by S. Curtis Walworth

FIG. 8-2 *Gaultheria shallon,* salal, a fruiting shrub growing densely along the north Pacific coast. Indigenous Peoples favour the plant for its sweet berries and for the medicinal properties of its leaves. *From* Curtis's Botanical Magazine, *plate 2843.*

Hooker, having seen Douglas's abilities on field excursions, felt that the young man was ready for a greater challenge. So in 1823 he recommended him to the Horticultural Society of London for a botanical collecting expedition to the northeastern United States and Upper Canada. Following Douglas's success on this mission, the society arranged with the HBC that he travel to Fort Vancouver[18] to collect material from their western districts. By this time he was just 25 years old. Before departing, he too consulted with Richardson and Menzies.

As Scouler and Douglas boarded the *William and Ann,* they discovered to their mutual surprise and pleasure that they were to be companions for the voyage, the former as a senior member of the crew, the latter as a passenger. They had known each other from Hooker's lectures, and both took delight in having a kindred spirit to share in the grand adventure.

The six-year-old *William and Ann,* a 140-ton register, single-deck snow[19] owned by the HBC, had been refurbished for the voyage with a full copper bottom and iron cables. Scouler recorded that they

left Gravesend with every thing necessary for the preservation of plants and animals. Every article, either of medicine or food which could in any degree contribute to our comfort, or assist in preventing scurvy was liberally provided.

Under Captain Henry Hanwell Jr., the ship carried a complement of 14. This was Hanwell's first command as skipper, and his performance would prove below expectation. At one o'clock, July 27, 1824, under heavy rain, they weighed anchor and left the Thames estuary. They made stops at Madeira and on both sides of South America, including the Galapagos Archipelago, giving the two young men opportunities to study exotic botany and wildlife. They were not the first naturalists to visit the islands; in

1795 Menzies himself had called there as Vancouver's expedition returned to Britain.

In the Galapagos, Douglas collected 45 birds of 19 genera, and 145 plant specimens, all of which he knew would be of great interest in England. Unfortunately, the continuous rain and high temperatures of the equatorial region, including a hurricane, resulted in most of them rotting before they could be preserved. Scouler noted:

> [Collecting here] is an extensive labour, & would require a more extensive knowledge of the island than can be acquired in a transient visit of two days, to give an account of the natural productions.[20]

After a voyage of eight and a half months, which Douglas described as "long and tedious," *William and Ann* arrived at the estuary of the Columbia River. Despite heavy rains and thick fog, Captain Hanwell managed to cross the treacherous sandbars and anchor on the north shore of the river. While awaiting a pilot from Fort George, the naturalists explored. Douglas immediately identified a plant he had seen in Menzies's collection. "On stepping on the shore Gaultheria Shallon [salal] was the first plant I took in my hands. So pleased was I that I could scarcely see anything but it."[21] It grew exactly as Menzies had noted.

Douglas also recorded seeing for the first time the tree that would become linked to his name: "The ground on the south side of the river is low, covered thickly with wood, chiefly *Pinus canadiensis*, *P. balsamea* and a species which may prove to be *P. taxifolia*." These will have been western hemlock, balsam fir, and Douglas-fir, none of which are now considered to be of the genus *Pinus*. Although Menzies had brought back his description of the tree and some twig samples, he had not acquired any cones or seeds. This would be Douglas's task, among many others.

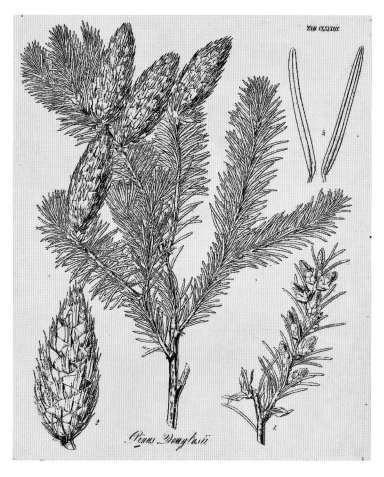

FIG. 8-3 *Pinus douglasii*, the fir renamed for David Douglas but first reported by Archibald Menzies. *From* Flora Boreali-Americana, *plate 183.*

Repairs needed to the vessel delayed the voyage for the next two months. The botanists were able to make good use of this time, travelling by canoe, together and separately, between Forts George and Vancouver, collecting and recording plants, as many then were in full bloom. Douglas noted that during that time he had increased his plant collection by 75 species. Douglas intended to remain on shore, based at Fort Vancouver, while Scouler continued as ship's surgeon when the voyage resumed. Alexander Mackenzie, an experienced fur trader who knew the local Indigenous Peoples, would take Douglas's berth. A local interpreter was also hired.

SCOULER'S SORTIE TO THE NORTH

Early in June, *William and Ann* again navigated the Columbia's sandbars, left the river, and headed north. The plan was to visit Nootka Sound, but adverse winds deterred the cautious Hanwell from risking his first command of a ship. Instead, they continued northbound outside Vancouver Island, noting many albatrosses, as far as the southern tip of Haida Gwaii. Transiting Hecate Strait and Dixon Entrance, Scouler obtained a few specimens of kelp, and recorded that they "contained several smaller species, & to abound in marine animals, as *Sertulariae, Crustaceae*; we also found a *Holothurian* & a sp. of *Patella*."[22] These were hydroids or "sea ferns," crustaceans, a sea cucumber, and a limpet.

The ship reached Dundas Island at the mouth of the Portland Canal, close to latitude 54°40', which would become the maritime boundary between British Columbia and Alaska. Becalmed here for a few days, Scouler had a chance to get ashore to botanize. Among the plants he collected were a saxifrage, a potentilla, and what he termed *Xanthium spinosum*, which was probably devil's club. He also collected an intertidal flowering surfgrass of a new genus, which Hooker later named *Phyllospadix scouleri*.

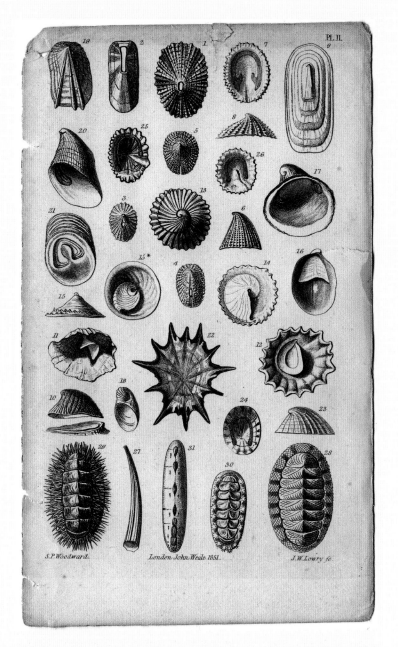

FIG. 8-4 A plate of woodcut illustrations of shells, including (#1, top row, centre) a limpet similar to that collected by Scouler, attached to a kelp plant. Note also the dentalium (#27, bottom row) like those harvested by the Mowachaht and widely traded with tribes of the interior. *S.P. Woodward's 1851* Manual of the Mollusca, *plate 11.*

EXTIRPATION OF THE SEA OTTERS

Sea otters are key denizens of the coastal kelp-forest ecosystem from Hokkaido, Japan, to central Baja California. Before the late 1770s, they numbered in the hundreds of thousands. Relentless hunting of these populations to satisfy the Chinese market for their fur brought them to virtual extirpation within less than a century. This was the first Vancouver Island species to feel the devastating effects of the new commercial culture upon one of harmonious relationship with the natural world.

The Indigenous Peoples of this coast knew and appreciated the beauty of the pelts of these animals and the warmth they could provide. For millennia, hunters prized them as clothing reserved for their chiefs, and considered them as prime goods for vigorous intercommunity trading and alliance building, and for Potlatch ceremonies. They also ate the meat. While this pre-contact predation was significant, it posed no threat to the creature's survival as a species. That all changed after Cook's few weeks in Nootka Sound in 1778. His men discovered that the 1,500 prime pelts they could acquire for broken belt buckles or a pewter plate would fetch a fortune in China.

Over the next few years, 27 vessels, British and American, arrived to exploit this business opportunity, quickly exhausting the available stock of pelts from the Mowachaht of Nootka and the neighbouring inlets. In fierce competition, they explored northward, discovering new stocks and of better quality as the latitude increased.[23] Russians, based at Sitka, also participated in the depredation but had limited access to the Chinese market. During the 10 seasons between 1804/05 and 1814/15, Bostonmen (American fur traders) alone traded over 103,000 sea otter pelts in Canton, with a peak volume of 16,647 pelts in 1808. Twenty years later, although the price for sea otter pelts remained high, the number had dwindled to an average of 500 a season, and in 1841 the trade was abandoned.[24]

In 1825 Captain Henry Hanwell Jr., in *William and Ann*, sailed to Portland Inlet seeking—without success—sea otters for the Hudson's Bay Company. That same season, the nine vessels of the Boston fleet had acquired only 2,250 pelts among them to take to Canton.

On the brink of extinction, the sea otter—with fewer than 2,000 individuals left in the wild—was declared a protected species in 1911. In 1969 and '70, the Pacific Biological Station started work to re-establish colonies on the west coast of Vancouver Island. They caught 89 animals in the Aleutians and Prince William Sound for relocation in Checleset Bay, near the Brooks Peninsula. Five years after the release, biologists spotted 35 individuals at that location, with another 15 off Nootka Island. The transplants flourished and spread, with colonies found from Ucluelet to the Scott Islands and around to Port Hardy, and on the nearby mainland coast. In 2013, researchers counted 5,600 sea otters off the coast of Vancouver Island. The population has continued to expand annually at a rate of about 8 per cent.[25]

FIG. 8-5 Evidence of population recovery. A raft of female sea otters, some with pups, off the coast of Calvert Island. *Drone photo by Keith Holmes, Hakai Institute.*

Hanwell and the trader Mackenzie spent much of the month of July attempting to obtain beaver and sea otter pelts from villages in the Portland Inlet and Canal and from Vancouver's Observatory Inlet, largely without success. The weather was atrocious, tides fast and unpredictable, shores rocky, anchorages poor, and mooring places hard to find. By this time, Bostonmen (American fur traders) had virtually exhausted the supply of otters.

Because the ship's boats needed to land to replenish water supplies, Scouler managed to get ashore and collect specimens. At Observatory Inlet alone, Hooker listed 36 species of plants found by Scouler, many of which were new to science, including a new moss that Hooker named *Scouleria aquatica*.

They were still in Salmon Cove when they witnessed a remarkable event: the mass arrival of "Hunchback salmon" heading upstream to spawn. Hanwell's log recorded that they "speared about 50 of them they were not good fish but were useful to us in being fresh food: sent a party to get as many as possible."[26] Scouler reported and preserved a specimen, which eventually reached Richardson. The dramatic shape of the spawning male's jaws appeared in Richardson's *Fauna Boreali-Americana* named as *Salmo scouleri*.

Abandoning the hope of bartering for furs, and without investigating trading opportunities at Sitka, Hanwell left the Portland region to head south. After waiting a few days for the fog to clear, *William and Ann* managed to pass through the Nootka entrance, but was unable to turn into Friendly Cove (Yuquot) so anchored in Marvinas Bay, a few miles inside the sound.

IN NOOTKA SOUND AND THE STRAITS OF JUAN DE FUCA AND OF GEORGIA

At the end of July, an elderly Chief Maquinna, who had known Vancouver, paid a visit to that explorer's "sons," pleased that the

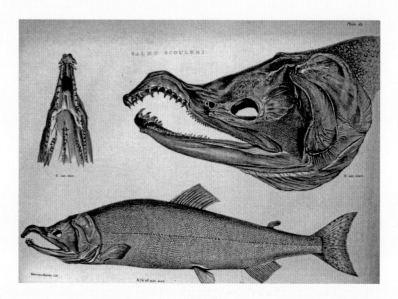

FIG. 8-6 *Salmo scouleri*. Scouler's drawings of the remarkable head of a male spawning pink salmon, which he described as "Hunchback salmon." *From John Richardson's* Fauna Boreali-Americana, *fig. 31, in Charles Nelson's biography of Scouler [image edited].*

vessel was British. Scouler noted that the local people, now neglected by Madrid and London, were in a state of poverty. Since supplies of sea otter had long since disappeared from the area, Maquinna and his people were seldom visited by foreigners.[27]

A crowd of locals in 25 canoes brought fish, salal berries, bulbs Scouler identified as *Allium* (onion), and *Phalangium esculentum* (camas lily), a local staple. He incorrectly assigned Atlantic names to the fish species. Onshore, Scouler collected specimens of silver burweed, pearly everlasting, Smith's fairy-bells, gumweed, and a few more seaweeds.

It took the ship a week from leaving Nootka Sound to enter Juan de Fuca. On August 8, on the south shore, they passed the village of the Makah people, and 15 canoes came out to greet them, bringing fish. Many of the paddlers recognized Mackenzie as a friend, as he had traded with them for furs. Scouler noted a large pack of white dogs running free on one of the nearby islets. He learned that they were fed regularly and their "wool" harvested. Combined with cedar fibres the wool made hard-wearing blankets. The weavers also managed to incorporate coloured stripes in good imitation of the HBC trade blankets.

Three days later, *William and Ann* anchored in Port Discovery, farther down the southern shore of the strait. This was the same haven used earlier by the Eliza, Vancouver, and Galiano expeditions. Canoes of friendly Clallum people arrived, bringing "fishes, ducks & all the vegetables their country afforded," and greeted Mackenzie warmly. Clearly, relations with the trading establishment on the Columbia seemed excellent. Captain Hanwell, however, remained nervous, noting

> some of the canoes here are very large, nearly the length of the vessel; on some were twenty stout Indians, they had plenty of guns with them.... Several of the Canoes are decorated with hair taken from their Enemies.[28]

Scouler, far more comfortable, wanted to land, but Hanwell would not allow a boat ashore. The doctor found another solution by bartering for a dead mouse he saw in one of the canoes. Before setting out, he had anticipated adding new rodents to the record. The locals quickly understood the concept and brought him three species of mice, pigeon guillemots, and grebes. Unfortunately, most of these were too putrid to preserve.

Also at Port Discovery, Scouler noted:

> In the vicinity of their village are many of the those poles so well represented by Captain Vancouver's voyage. We found it difficult to ascertain the use of this curious apparatus, but was told by some of the Indians they were for catching birds.[29]

He also noted that the coast between Tatooch (Neah Bay) and Port Discovery was densely populated, which

> is not to be wondered at when we consider the abundant means of support the country affords. The sea yields an abundant supply of excellent fishes of the most agreeable kind, every rivulet teeming with myriads of salmon; and the land affords an endless variety of berries and esculent [edible] roots.[30]

He learned that the locals abandon the coast between October and March and retreat into the interior to hunt "birds, especially of the duck tribe, & beaver, otters & elks" for food, clothing, and trade.

> Soon after leaving Port Discovery, "two canoes came to us from the Nootka side. In one of them was a famous chief named Waskalatchy, who had wandered more over the NW coast than any Indian upon it."[31]

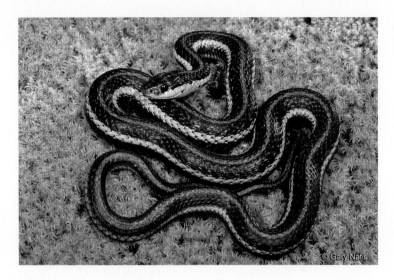

FIG. 8-7 Among piles of driftwood near Point Roberts, Scouler found "a mass of serpents." They were harmless northwestern garter snakes, known locally as "red racers." *Photo © courtesy of Gary Nafis, CaliforniaHerps.com.*

Waskalatchy was a Coast Salish man from Snohomish, known to the HBC as "the Frenchman." He guided them to a safe anchorage at Strawberry Cove on Cypress Island in the San Juan Archipelago. The vessel next stopped at a village on Lummi Island, where Scouler landed and collected rushes and sedges, California aster, and a "beautifull" mugwort.

From Lummi, continuing northward into the Strait of Georgia, they stopped briefly at a village of the "Sangtch" at the foot of a cliff, just south of Birch Bay. At their next anchorage, near Point Roberts, poor weather prevented anyone landing. The next morning their friends from Lummi and Sangtch came to warn them that canoes of "two very powerful & dangerous tribes, the Cowitchen & Yakultax" were headed their way. By this time, the mariners knew about intertribal hostility and had heard similar dire warnings about rivals. The advice did not unduly worry them.

When, soon afterward, the notorious Cowichans arrived, they proved "as friendly and peaceable" as had all their previous contacts. One of them showed signs of having had smallpox, the only example Scouler saw on the coast, but he recorded that the locals were in dread of contagion from contact with people of the interior.

Ashore, Scouler found accumulated driftwood, which over the years had been partly covered by peaty sand dunes, and behind which was an impenetrable salt marsh covered in tule (bulrushes) six or seven feet high. He collected specimens of a spirea bush, two species of balsamroot, an evening primrose, and other common plants such as cleavers, knotweed, bedstraw, and wild licorice. Among the piles of driftwood, he saw a host of garter snakes. He noted that "they are perfectly harmless & the ground seamed a mass of serpents. One could not turn over any piece of old wood without dislodging from 18 to 20 of them."[32]

While the doctor gathered plants at Point Roberts, Hanwell sent the longboat to investigate the source of fresh water they had noticed to the north, possibly a major river. The crew reported that there was a river (the south arm of the Fraser), but many sandbanks blocked its mouth. With only six feet of water, the river could not be accessed by ships. Hanwell decided that his mission was therefore completed, and he would return to the Columbia.

Hanwell retraced their route, stopping again at Lummi village—where Scouler found a new variety of *Sanicula*—and Neah Bay. On September 1, they arrived at the headland at the mouth of the Columbia. A few days later they anchored near the now-abandoned Fort George, and Mackenzie hired a local canoe to take Scouler and himself to Fort Vancouver. He carried a note from Hanwell for the governor, that *William and Ann* was now "ready to receive homeward bound Cargo."

Scouler and David Douglas spent a week together comparing notes and preparing specimens before the former returned by canoe to rejoin the ship. Douglas asked Scouler to take letters, journals, and several boxes of specimens back to the Horticultural Society of London for him. He would also have letters for Hooker, Menzies, and his brother. Scouler had to wait almost a month before the ship departed. It rained most of that time, so he remained aboard working on specimens of birds brought by the local people in exchange for tobacco.

Because he had become interested in ethnology, Scouler prepared vocabulary lists of Chinook Jargon and other languages he had picked up. He also made notes on local customs, including burial practices and traditional skull deformation in childhood.[33] During the night before sailing, he went ashore to a local burial ground and removed two skulls and the "well-preserved mummy" of a child. The local Chinook community[34] knew of this act and were understandably incensed, as Douglas later reported to Hooker.

Douglas had intended to go to the ship to watch over his precious boxes being loaded, but an injury to his knee from a nail became infected, delaying this plan. He arrived to learn that *William and Ann* had crossed the bar only an hour earlier. But his collection to date was in safe hands and was delivered in good condition. He remained behind to continue collecting, as planned.

Hanwell did not stop anywhere on the return voyage, but they did pass close to Galapagos again, as well as Easter Island, the Falklands, and the Azores. Off these islands, Scouler saw frigate birds, storm petrels, boobies, and tropic birds, some of which he managed to shoot and add to his collection. The crew often caught sharks and swordfish for food, and the scientist made notes and dissected their organs, such as eyes. On April 13, 1826, *William and Ann* anchored in the Thames estuary, and two days later Scouler disembarked at Gravesend, having been away just over 20 months. To the doctor's credit, there had not been a single case of scurvy during the voyage.

After a brief meeting with Menzies, Scouler reported, with his collection, to his mentor Hooker. The latter incorporated many of the plants into his monumental *Flora Boreali-Americana*. Hooker named one genus and twenty species *"scouleri"* after the collector, including Scouler's willow and Scouler's surfgrass. The book was instrumental in Hooker's appointment soon afterward as director of the Royal Botanic Gardens, Kew.[35] Scouler devoted much of the ensuing year to documenting his collection, editing his diary, and writing papers for scientific journals. In April 1827, the University of Glasgow awarded him a doctorate in medicine.

Scouler immediately embarked on a second voyage as ship's surgeon. He sailed aboard *Clyde*, on charter to the East India Company, bound for Madras and Calcutta, and returning in June 1828. Little is known of Scouler's second voyage except that he collected some plants while stopping for a few days in Cape Town. On his return, he took the post of professor of mineralogy and natural history at the Andersonian (now

FIG. 8-8 (LEFT) The beautiful Scouler's corydalis or fumewort has been found on Vancouver Island only on the Nitinat River, but is more common in Washington and Oregon. *Photo © courtesy of Hans Roemer, Victoria.*

FIG. 8-9 (RIGHT) *Silene scouleri.* Scouler's catchfly is a native species of the introduced, and now more common, bladder campion. *Photo © courtesy of Matt Fairbarns, Aruncus Consulting.*

Strathclyde) University in Glasgow. He was also curator of the university's museum. From 1834 for 20 years, he was professor of mineralogy of the Royal Dublin Society. He died in 1871 in Glasgow. Scouler's own collection of botanical specimens from western North America is now in the herbarium of the New York Botanical Garden.

DOUGLAS'S EXPLORATIONS AND DEMISE

Following *William and Ann*'s sortie to the north, David Douglas remained based at Fort Vancouver. He went on to make an enormous individual contribution to the botanical knowledge about western North America. Dr. John McLoughlin and other local officers of the HBC fully supported him. He explored a vast territory from northern California to the Columbia basin and out to Hawaii. As he progressed, he collected botanical and zoological specimens. He also made meteorological, magnetic, lunar, and astronomic observations, as well as field sketches.

In 1827, he accompanied the annual fur brigade from Fort Vancouver across the mountains to York Factory in Manitoba. From there he returned briefly to Britain with a collection that threatened to overwhelm the capacity of the Horticultural Society. The London and Scottish scientific establishments lauded his collecting and his meticulous record-keeping in many disciplines.

Two years later, despite failing eyesight, he made a second expedition to the Pacific coast, again sponsored by the Horticultural Society and the HBC. This time he covered the country between Puget Sound and Santa Barbara, up the Fraser Valley to Fort Alexandria and Stuart Lake. On his return, his canoe overturned in a cataract outside Fort George (Prince George, not the one on the Columbia River). He lost his botanical notes and specimens for 400 species, as well as his precious diary, his clothes, and food. He wrote to Hooker, "This disas-trous occurrence has much broken my strength and spirits."[36] He struggled back to Fort Vancouver on the brink of exhaustion and starvation.

During a short recuperation, he learned that two young Scottish doctors, William Fraser Tolmie and Meredith Gairdner, had recently arrived. Both were disciples of Hooker, interested in botany, and keen mountaineers. The presence of such fellow scientists pleased Douglas and reassured him that his unfinished work would be continued.

He then went, for the third time, to study the volcanoes in the Sandwich Islands (Hawaii). From there, he planned to take a ship to return to Britain. A few months later, alone on a mountain trail, he fell into a pitfall trap intended for feral cattle. An angry bullock, already in there, gored and trampled the 35-year-old botanist to death. Amid controversy, his mutilated body was brought to Honolulu, examined by four physicians, and respectfully interred.

While David Douglas never visited Vancouver Island, his contribution to the natural history knowledge of this region was immense. He had collected and sent back some 7,000 species, many new to science. He has been justly described as "one of our greatest and most successful exploring Botanists, to whom the world is deeply indebted."[37] The British Museum, Kew, and the University of Cambridge now house his botanical collections. His zoological specimens are with the Universities of Glasgow and Strathclyde, the Royal Scottish Museum, Edinburgh, and the Zoological Society of London.

FIG. 9-0 A splendid specimen of the western flowering dogwood in full bloom in a suburban garden near Cadboro Bay, Saanich. *Photo courtesy of David Leeming [image edited].*

CHAPTER NINE

NATURALISTS IN THE HUDSON'S BAY COMPANY ERA, PART II

Gairdner, Tolmie, Grant, and Jeffrey

TWO SCOTTISH DOCTORS

In the early 1830s, an epidemic of malaria beset the Hudson's Bay Company (HBC) trading territory around the lower reaches of the Columbia River. The epidemic severely affected the local Indigenous communities, ravaging whole villages. People at Fort Vancouver, including the only doctor for the entire region, suffered as well. The company once more sought Professor Hooker's help in recruiting two additional physicians. Because the need was urgent, they offered attractive salaries. Hooker, recognizing an opportunity for continuing Scouler's fieldwork, nominated two botany-oriented, qualified candidates.

Meredith Gairdner, born in 1809 in London and son of a Scottish physician father, had earned his degree in medicine at the University of Edinburgh. He had also shown interest in meteorology, geology, zoology, and botany. After a period of study in Germany, he published a paper in a scientific journal on microscopic life within hot springs. He was now keen for further experience in distant lands.[1]

The other candidate, William Fraser Tolmie, was less quali-fied. Like John Scouler, he was a licentiate of the Royal College. Three years junior to Gairdner, he was born into a middle-class, Presbyterian family in Inverness. He had had a grammar school education in Perth, and then an uncle funded his two years of medical studies at Glasgow, leading to a diploma in 1831. Tolmie's keen interest in botany drew him to the attention of Hooker, and he also met John Scouler, by then on the faculty at the Andersonian. Like Scouler and Gairdner, Tolmie had a great thirst for knowledge—across a wide spectrum of intellectual disciplines and languages—which he retained throughout his long life.

During nearly four decades of service to the HBC, Tolmie would prove worthy in many roles. He was a conscientious company man, an astute fur trader empathetic with local peoples, a highly competent farm manager, and an able scientist. Tolmie retired from the HBC with the rank of chief factor. Later, as a respected legislator, a substantial landowner, and the devout, sober, and upright patriarch of a large family, he was a pillar of the Victoria community during its tempestuous early years.

At Hooker's suggestion, Gairdner and Tolmie had called on Dr. Richardson in London before boarding ship. Among Richardson's tips for collecting natural history specimens was one for protecting the skins of birds from insects: to wrap them in paper oiled with terebinth (turpentine from the Levant). They both assembled sets of instruments, chemicals, and materials for botanical and zoological work, as well as their surgical and medical equipment. Gairdner had a rifle, and Tolmie, a gun and a pair of pistols.

In September 1832, the two recruits boarded the company's supply ship *Ganymede* at Gravesend, for the eight-month voyage around the Horn bound for Fort Vancouver, with a stop along the way at the Sandwich Isles, today's Hawaii, and, at the time, very friendly with Britain. Despite the cramped conditions aboard ship, Tolmie welcomed the chance to continue his studies from the case of books he had brought with him, and from the birds and fish—even a turtle—that found their way on board. He kept a detailed journal of his investigations, readings, and conversations with fellow passengers.[2]

As *Ganymede* traversed the southern latitudes, Tolmie interspersed his reading with attempts to shoot or catch specimens from an increasing flock of albatrosses and related seabirds that surrounded the ship. He attempted to preserve the skins and skeletons and to dissect various organs, keeping detailed notes. The crew would harpoon the occasional porpoise or shark to add to the food supply but allowed the scientists access to the parts that interested them.

In early May 1833 the two medical men arrived at Fort Vancouver to a welcome by "the governor," Chief Factor Dr. John McLoughlin. The malaria epidemic still raged. McLoughlin had been the only doctor for the whole district and had himself fallen victim. According to Tolmie's readings, medical opinion of the day considered that intermittent fever, as malaria was known, was transmitted by contagion or marsh gases. No sooner had they arrived than

> in traversing pine wood the Govr. pointed out to me a tall slender tree having a profusion of large syngenesious [united by the anthers] flowers called here Devil's Wood [western flowering, or Pacific, dogwood]. Having being informed that the root was employed in the U.S. for the care of the Intermittents, Mr. Mc L. used it here last season in doses of 3½ drm of dried root in powder & succeeded in subduing diseases without cinchona [a botanical source of quinine found in the Andes] &c.[3]

The company had engaged both Tolmie and Gairdner for dual roles: those of surgeon and junior clerk. They could expect to take on duties such as trading and general administration, as well as those of medical officers. McLoughlin assigned Gairdner to take charge of the hospital at Fort Vancouver, while Tolmie would go to the new outpost of Nisqually, at the southern end of Puget's Sound, and then move to Fort McLoughlin on Campbell Island on the central coast, near today's Bella Bella.

Gairdner, at Fort Vancouver, endured a difficult time with the fever epidemic. He was handling up to 300 cases, including McLoughlin's, as well as performing extra duties as a clerk and filling in for stricken officers. This allowed no time for pursuing his scientific research, as he had been promised, nor for reading. In the spring of 1836, he developed tuberculosis and was sent, without pay, to convalesce in Hawaii. He died there, six months later.

Gairdner's name was associated with four species: two plants—a penstemon and a caraway—a bird, the downy woodpecker, and a fish, the steelhead trout.[4]

FIG. 9-1　The anadromous steelhead, a subspecies of the rainbow trout; both keenly sought by fly-fishers. *Illustration by E.B.S. Logier in* Trout and Other Game Fishes of BC, *Department of Fisheries, Ottawa, 1932 [image edited].*

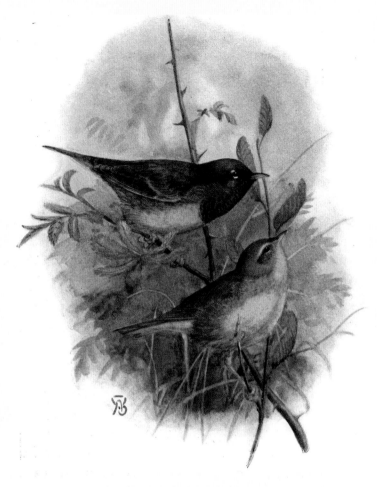

FIG. 9-2 Allan Brooks's painting of Tolmie's warbler. The bird was so named by Townsend, but Audubon renamed it after his colleague MacGillivray (who had no connection with the species). *W.L. Dawson's* Birds of Washington, *1909 [image edited].*

WILLIAM TOLMIE AT NISQUALLY AND FORT MCLOUGHLIN

For the first few months after arriving at Nisqually in 1833, Tolmie helped to establish the new trading post and learned the technicalities of fur trading and some of the various local dialects of the Coast Salish people bringing furs and meat to the post. His companions were mostly men referred to as "Canadians" (mixed race) and "Kanakas" (Hawaiians). He also spent useful time improving his marksmanship and getting company hunters to fine-tune his gun. He could muzzle-load a single ball capable of felling an elk or bear, or a range of different-sized shot for smaller game. He was able to extend his collection of small mammals and of birdskins, including even tiny kinglets. During the fall migration, he observed enormous flocks of geese, ducks, and cranes resting in the extensive local wetlands.

He also continued collecting botanical specimens and his educational reading. Despite the long delays of mailing by sea, he sent reports and specimens to Hooker and Scouler, and letters to his friends and family back home. For this, he experimented with flight feathers from various birds to make quill pens.

Tolmie spent much of the next 10 years in various company outposts, gaining experience and seniority as a trader. While there in 1834 he met and helped a visiting American ornithologist, John Kirk Townsend, who named a new species in his honour, Tolmie's warbler. Through a miscommunication the artist and cataloguer John James Audubon renamed it, after a colleague, MacGillivray's warbler, but it retained the scientific name *Oporornis tolmiei*.[5]

In 1842, while Tolmie was on a year's leave in Europe, Douglas selected the site of Fort Victoria to replace Fort Vancouver as the company's primary west coast depot. The following spring Douglas returned to begin building the new fort.[6]

As that was happening, Tolmie arrived to take up his new responsibilities for the Puget's Sound Agricultural Company, an HBC subsidiary at Fort Nisqually. During the next 15 turbulent years, he oversaw flocks that grew to over 8,000 sheep, more than 3,000 cattle, and 300 horses. One year, they shipped over 15,000 bushels of grain to Sitka.[7] Tolmie made a point of employing many of the local Indigenous people as herders and farmhands, which he considered to be a way to help compensate them for the loss of their camas fields to the new agriculture and pastures.[8]

In February 1849, 37-year-old William Tolmie relocated to Fort Victoria and married Jane, the daughter of John Work, his close friend and colleague, and they began creation of a brood of 12 children. That same year, London declared Vancouver Island to be a British colony under a charter to the HBC for colonization.

One of the provisions of the charter was for the company to manage the recruitment of British settlers, including organizing a legal system for property ownership. The company also needed to address the complete lack of maps or information about the interior of the island. Such specialized tasks required an experienced surveyor. Officials in London first appointed a well-born young Scot, Walter Colquhoun Grant, who had recently resigned his military commission and had applied to settle in the new colony. Grant, who claimed to be a surveyor, seemed the ideal solution to the need. He arrived in September 1849, to be the first settler of the colony.

WALTER COLQUHOUN GRANT

It quickly became apparent that Grant was unqualified for either surveying or mapmaking.[9] Out of his depth, he resigned after only a year. Grant went on to try his fortune in the goldfields of California, where he did well. Returning to the island in a small chartered schooner, he explored and traded a little before leaving for good in 1853.

Grant left two legacies of his brief presence in the area. The first resulted from a side trip to Hawaii, where brilliant yellow blooms on shrubs in the consul's garden reminded him of his highland home. He collected seeds from these Scotch broom plants for his farmstead at Sooke. Three of them germinated and went on to become an extensively invasive and toxic pest, displacing native species. Grant's second legacy, while more benign, was also contentious. In 1857 he presented a paper to the Royal Geographical Society of London entitled "Description of Vancouver Island, by Its First Colonist."

By then, Grant was back in the army in India and already a lieutenant colonel. A dashing cavalry officer, but without any training or apparent interest in the natural world while on the island, and having seen only limited parts of it, he nevertheless felt entitled to include a four-page section on "Vegetable productions and natural history." It began: "The Flora of Vancouver Island is poor, and no new varieties of plants have been discovered in the country."[10]

He went on to briefly discuss camas, salal, *uva-ursi* (kinnikinnick or bearberry), horsetail, berries, and crabapple. He noted that "the potato[11] is almost universally cultivated . . . eight or nine varieties, generally of a larger size than that is attained by any potatoes in Europe," and speculated that the roots had been introduced by traders some time previously. He claimed, incorrectly, that the local people did little hunting, but "during winter, they capture in nets and shoot great quantities of wild-fowl."

According to Grant, "the particulars given [in the report] are all the result of personal observation," but that claim seems dubious. During his short stay in Victoria, Grant made friends among the HBC officers, and he maintained contact with some of them after he left. Much of the information in his report probably derived from these connections. From the sprinkling of scientific names, at least one of his correspondents was knowledgeable about natural history.

Referring to birds, Grant mentioned the *Tetrao obscurus* and the *T. richardsonii* (now considered two subspecies of the blue grouse) and a "drum partridge" (probably the ruffed grouse) as of interest to the sportsman. He continued:

> Of small birds, there is the Mexican woodpecker [possibly the flicker], and a large, misshapen species of bulfinch—note [song] it has none [probably the red crossbill]; and indeed *aves vocales* may generally speaking be said never to be met with on the west coast of America. . . .
>
> Of aquatic birds there is a vast variety. They have the Scaup duck, the *Anser Canadiensis*, the Golden eye, the common mallard, the teal, the crested grebe and numerous others. They completely cover the lakes and inland salt-water lochs in winter, but altogether leave the country in summer. There is also a large species of crane which frequents the marshes and open ground and furnishes "material" for capital soup if you can bag him; they are, however, very shy.[12]

As for quadrupeds, Grant wrote:

> Two species of bear are found on the island, the black and the brown; such of the natives as have muskets occasionally kill them, and bring their skins for barter to the Hudson's Bay Company; they are numerous in most parts of Vancouver Island. . . .
>
> Of deer three species are met with: the *Cervus elaphus*, or elk, the *Lencurus*, or large, white-tailed deer, and a smaller species of black-tailed deer. . . .
>
> Black and white wolves infest the thick woods as also a small species of panther, but none of these are very numerous. Squirrels and minxes are found everywhere in great numbers,

and both land and sea otters are occasionally to be met with; the latter is only found on the north coast of the island; the animal is generally from 4 to 8 feet long, reaching however sometimes to a length of 12 feet,[13] and its fur is very soft and delicate, being by far the most valuable of any animal found on the north-west coast; it is generally of a jet black colour though sometimes it has a brownish tinge. Signs of the beaver have occasionally been seen by old trappers on Vancouver Island, but the animal has never actually been met with. Altogether there are few animals producing valuable furs on Vancouver Island, and I should conceive the value of furs actually trapped and traded on the island cannot exceed 40£ per annum.[14]

A surprising omission in the report, especially for a man from the Scottish gentry, was any discussion of salmon and other fisheries. His only mention was a passing reference to the local people's diet.

Grant, who had brought machinery for a sawmill with him, went into considerable detail about the timber resources:

> There are several varieties of fir in the woods. There are the *Douglasii* (*breve braccata*) and the *Grandis* which are the most common. The former furnishes material for excellent spars. . . . The *Canadensis*, the *Mitis* and the *Alba* which flourish well wherever there is any depth of soil. . . . There is also the large red cedar of America, which grows into a noble tree; the *Abies*, *Nobilis* and the *Cupressus thyoides*.[15]
>
> The largest and most picturesque tree of the fir tribe in Vancouver Island is the *Nobilis*. . . . This tree sometimes reaches a height of 250 feet, with a circumference of 42 feet at the butt; the bark is from 8 to 14 inches thick. The white maple grows in all the low woodlands, and is abundant, but never reaches any great size. Wherever there is any open prairie two kinds of oak *Quercus*

suber clavigata[16] and another similar species somewhat darker in the bark and harder in the quality of the wood, are found. . . .

A large species of Arbutus grows on the sea-coast and on the banks of rivers; it grows to a height of from 30 to 40 feet, the bark is smooth and of a bright red colour, the wood is hard and white and takes an excellent polish. Only one kind of pine had yet been found on the island: the *Monticola*.[17]. . .

To the spectator from the sea-board, the island appears one mass of wood; by far the greater portion, however, of that wood which so pleases the distant eye is utterly worthless, from its nature as from its position . . . owing to the singularly broken face of the country, the [trees] may wave defiance to attempts of any the engineer to dislodge them.[18]

That he considered the forest "utterly worthless" and impossible to harvest shows Grant's failure to acknowledge Indigenous uses of local resources. Where his report covers the Indigenous population, it is from an uninformed and imperialistic viewpoint. But the Royal Geographical Society felt it merited his award of their gold medal. Joseph Despard Pemberton, the trained and sophisticated surveyor who replaced Grant, was scathing about the information in Grant's report when he published his own book, *Facts and Figures Relating to Vancouver Island and British Columbia*, a few years later.

TOLMIE IN VICTORIA

In 1851 Pemberton arrived in Victoria, well qualified and prepared to tackle the cartographic and cadastral tasks that the new colony urgently needed. He mapped the areas surrounding the fort and began to register property titles. Initially, apart from Grant's parcel at Sooke, the only takers for the colonial settlement scheme were officers of the HBC. Among the first were two old friends, Dr. Tolmie and John Work, who acquired adjacent acreages, which they called Cloverdale and Hillside.

FIG. 9-3   Dr. William Fraser Tolmie in about 1860, as he was settling into Cloverdale, his house and farm near Victoria. *Image I-61857 courtesy of the Royal BC Museum and Archives [image edited].*

Over the next few years, Tolmie added adjoining parcels until, by 1859, his land holdings had reached 1,100 acres. By then he had completed construction of his fine house, the first stone private residence in British Columbia. He devoted his attention to making Cloverdale an exemplary farming operation. He also continued to serve the company as chief factor on its regional boards of management and in Vancouver Island's House of Assembly. Tolmie represented Victoria in the provincial legislature from 1871—when the united colony joined the Canadian Confederation—until he retired from public life in 1878.

Tolmie maintained contact with Dr. Hooker when the latter became director of the Royal Botanic Gardens at Kew, London. Several plants were associated with Tolmie's name, including a genus, *Tolmiea* (*T. menziesii,* the piggyback plant, is popular as indoor vegetation), a sedge, *Carex tolmiei*, and a saxifrage. He introduced dahlias and acacia trees to Victoria. In 1866, from a trip to buy pedigree cattle stock in San Francisco, he brought back some live California quail. These he reared in a compound at Cloverdale until they numbered about 200; then he released them, to survive to this day. He tried to do the same with mountain quail from San Juan Island, with less success.

Tolmie retained a lifelong interest in Indigenous culture and languages, including names for plants and animals. He contributed vocabularies to Scouler's 1841 paper to the Royal Geographical Society: "Observations on the Indigenous Tribes of the N.W. Coast of America." In 1884, with Dr. George Dawson of the Geological Survey of Canada,[19] he co-wrote "Comparative vocabularies of the Indian tribes of British Columbia with a map illustrating distribution." Dr. William Fraser Tolmie died two years later and is buried in Ross Bay Cemetery in Victoria.

JOHN JEFFREY[20]

In Edinburgh, a group of botanists, academics, and gentlemen landowners were impressed by the accounts of David Douglas's expedition to the western slopes of the Rocky Mountains. In late 1849, they decided to jointly fund a follow-up expedition to the same region to collect seeds, particularly conifers, that they could propagate in Scotland. They formed a committee—led by George Patton and Professor J.H. Balfour, director of the Royal Botanic Garden, Edinburgh—to pursue the idea and solicit funding by participants. Their formal association, usually called the Oregon Expedition,[21] quickly raised over £600, considered sufficient to proceed, and they sought someone suitable to undertake the mission.

The group found the ideal candidate in John Jeffrey, a 23-year-old gardener at Edinburgh's Royal Botanic Garden. By a strange coincidence, Jeffrey had been born in a village only a few miles from the birthplaces of both Archibald Menzies and David Douglas in Perthshire, the same county as Patton's estate. Jeffrey had recently won a prize for the best collection of dried plants from the Edinburgh area.

The eminent status of members of the association, including many from the Scottish gentry, ensured a favourable response from the HBC to a request for support. The HBC agreed to convey Jeffrey and his "outfit"—camp gear and supplies, surveying instruments, collecting equipment, and a technical library—from London by their ship *Prince of Wales* via Orkney to York Factory.[22] They would provide accommodation for him at their various forts along his journey to the west coast, and one of their officers to escort him between posts. They would supply all his needs while in their territory and advance him money if he were to go outside it (i.e., to the United States).

Jeffrey signed a three-year contract undertaking to keep a diary of his journey, and in early June 1850 he went to London, where he met with experts, including Dr. Hooker, before sailing. In mid-August, he arrived at York Factory, a settlement and HBC trading post on the southwestern shore of Hudson Bay. He realized that if he waited until the next annual brigade left for Fort Vancouver in July, he would lose a full collecting season. He opted instead to join the far more arduous "winter packet" headed west, leaving the bulk of his equipment to be brought to Fort Vancouver by the brigade.

In the company of Chief Factor John Lee Lewes,[23] he set out for Cumberland House on the Saskatchewan River, arriving in early October. There he was to await the next winter express, due to start for Jasper House in the new year and to arrive no sooner than late March. Once again, Jeffrey decided not to delay, but to push ahead:

> All the distance I walked on snow shoes. . . . The distance from Cumberland to Jasper House is 1200 miles [1,931 kilometres]. During this journey I slept with no other covering than that found under the friendly pine, for the space of 47 nights, on several occasions, the thermometer standing from 30° to 40° below zero [Fahrenheit, equal to -34° to -40° Celsius].[24]

After a month at Jasper, instead of waiting for the winter express, he set out with another escort, Robert Clouston, each bearing a backpack and rifle. They travelled on horseback until deep snow made it impossible, then continued on snowshoes. Their itinerary after Jasper is unclear, since Jeffrey's diary never reached Edinburgh, if indeed he kept one. There are only a few HBC station logs and Jeffrey's location notes associated with the specimens he collected.

In early October 1851, he presented his credentials to the governor in Fort Victoria and spent the next few months based there making collecting forays. On some of these he had a keen young companion, James R. Anderson,[25] a lad of 11 years, who was attending school in the fort. On one of their jaunts, Jeffrey shot a woodpecker in a Douglas-fir on Beacon Hill. The lad remembered the incident and 76 years later Anderson, by then a noted botanist, campaigned to have a commemorative plaque put on the tree. One of the birdskins Jeffrey sent home was a northern flicker, perhaps the bird collected with the boy on that day.

Other birds included in his box number 3 were three species of grouse—the ruffed, sharp-tailed, and black—a pine grosbeak, and a black-billed magpie.

His specimens would have been preserved in the scientific form: all meat removed, but skin, beak, feathers, with lower legs, feet, and wings attached, preserved with arsenical soap and roughly stuffed with cotton wadding.

On another occasion, Jeffrey visited Mullachard, the home of Captain W.C. Grant near Sooke, where he collected seeds of the checker mallow, or marsh hollyhock. Aboard ss *Beaver*, he made brief visits to Fort Rupert, at the northern end of Vancouver Island, and across Haro Strait to the company salmon fishery on Belle View (San Juan) Island. Somewhere on Vancouver Island he found two species new to science: the western hemlock and the red-flowered gooseberry, both of which were successfully propagated at the Royal Botanic Garden in Edinburgh. On Trial Island, Jeffrey found a species endemic to the southeastern tip of Vancouver Island, Macoun's meadowfoam, now protected as endangered.

In all, 48 species of the more than 400 plants he collected on that journey carried the location identifier of "Vancouver Island." A further four were marked from "Belle View." Notable among the former were the yellow glacier lily, the twinflower (*Linnaea borealis*, said to be the great man's favourite), and the yellow sand verbena, on whose record he noted, "This is the finest plant

FIG. 9-4 (LEFT) Allan Brooks's painting of a red-shafted flicker, now called the northern flicker. Jeffrey collected a specimen during an outing to Beacon Hill Park accompanied by a boy, James R. Anderson. *W.L. Dawson's* Birds of Washington, *1909 [image edited].*

FIG. 9-5 (RIGHT) *Magpie.* This was one of the birds seen by Cook's officers in King George's Sound (Nootka) and which they recognized from Britain. *Gouache painting, signed F.L. Beebe, 1938. From author's collection [image edited].*

that I have seen on Vancouver Island."[26] Jeffrey prepared a box of specimens, including many packets of seeds and complete cones, together with his botanical notes, and a few beetles and birdskins. Somehow, he obtained and included samples of gold from the Queen Charlotte Islands, where a gold rush had begun. In early December he wintered over in Victoria, where he collated, packed, and dispatched his collections to Edinburgh in five packages via different routes. Three of these never arrived.

In April 1853, drawing $500 from the company, he set out once more for Umpqua in Oregon and Mount Shasta in California, and on to the Sierra Nevada. By early October he had reached San Francisco, where he sent off his last, and very small, consignment of specimens to the association. It seems that by this time both his health and morale were poor. He had arranged for his mail to be forwarded to the British Consulate in that city but did not call in to collect it. There was no further contact with him, and various rumours had him joining an expedition to Fort Yuma in New Mexico to explore the Gila and Colorado Rivers, murdered by renegades for his mule and modest kit, "killed when trading with the Indians,"[27] or perished from thirst in the desert. This was the lawless era following the California gold rush, when any of these scenarios was plausible.

Some members of the association seemed oblivious to the dedication Jeffrey had shown under the most arduous conditions. They expressed dissatisfaction with his later efforts and opposed renewal of his contract. All reports from people who had encountered him in the field praised his energy, dedication, temperance, and steadiness. The map of Vancouver Island records Jeffrey's name as a mountain north of Victoria, whose shoulder forms the summit of the Malahat Drive. While the location of the Douglas-fir recalled by James Anderson is unclear, there is today a splendid, introduced specimen of Jeffrey's pine (*Pinus jeffreyi*) near the summit of Mount Tolmie in Victoria.

FIG. 9-6 *Pinus jeffreyi*. Jeffrey's pine near the summit of Mount Tolmie in Victoria. It is not native to Vancouver Island, but has been introduced. *Photo by author.*

FIG. 10-0 Blue camas in bloom on the park-like slopes of Beacon Hill in Victoria. Universally admired by the earliest British arrivals. *Photo by author.*

CHAPTER TEN

NATURALISTS WITH NAVAL AND MILITARY EXPEDITIONS, PART I

Notes from the Wilkes, Kellett and Prevost Visits

THE WILKES EXPEDITION

In early May 1841 two vessels flying the standard of the US Navy entered the Strait of Juan de Fuca, 49 years after George Vancouver had done the same. They were the sloop of war USS *Vincennes* and the brig USS *Porpoise*, part of the six-vessel United States Exploring Expedition led by Lieutenant (and self-styled "Captain") Charles Wilkes.[1] The ships cruised eastward along the southern shore of the strait to Port Discovery. During a few days' respite, Wilkes recorded: "There are few places where the variety and beauty of the flora are so great as there are here . . . in such profusion, as to excite both admiration and astonishment."[2] He also noted the nearby tall poles, reported by Vancouver. He learned from the locals that they were to support nets for catching geese at night as they came to graze on the lush meadows.

The ships then entered Admiralty Inlet to make their way down Puget Sound and anchor off the large ranch and farm of the HBC's subsidiary Puget's Sound Agricultural Company, at Fort Nisqually. Wilkes just missed meeting Dr. William Tolmie, who had departed overland on his year's furlough, but Alexander Caulfield Anderson welcomed them. Captain William Henry McNeill was also there, with the HBC's sidewheeler SS *Beaver* laid up for repair. The company men were hospitable and supportive to the visitors, who, nonetheless, ostentatiously hoisted the American flag on a 60-foot pole outside their observatory tent.

The "US Ex. Ex.," as the expedition became known, had left New York almost three years earlier, after a decade of political quarrelling, to survey and scientifically study islands and lands surrounding the Pacific Ocean. The intention was to demonstrate the new nation's status alongside the traditional imperial powers. Cook, Vancouver, and Ross had made such voyages of exploration for Britain; Bougainville and Pérouse for France; Malaspina for Spain; and Bering, Chirikov, and Kruzenshtern for Russia.

The 40-year-old Wilkes, while a competent hydrographic surveyor and geodesist, lacked both the experience and gravitas required to command such a squadron for such an extended and high-profile mission. His modest seniority created problems in nominating subordinate commanders and in maintaining their

FIG. 10-1 Land snails found and reported by the US Exploring Expedition, under Lieutenant Charles Wilkes, USN. *From author's collection.*

respect during the four-year voyage. Many conflicts occurred between the expedition and people of the Pacific islands, with fatalities on both sides. Wilkes, court-martialled at the conclusion of the mission but cleared of most of the charges, concluded his career with the rank of rear admiral.

The expedition included a corps of seven scientists from varied disciplines plus a taxidermist, an interpreter, and two engraver-illustrators. Notable among the first were the geologist James Dwight Dana and the naturalists Titian Ramsay Peale and Charles Pickering.[3]

By the time they had reached Nisqually, the fleet had already visited Madeira, several ports in South America, Tahiti, Samoa, Fiji, Australia, the Antarctic continent,[4] New Zealand, and Hawaii. While based at Nisqually for two months, survey parties fanned out overland. Ship's boats explored and added soundings to Vancouver's charts of Puget Sound, Hood Canal, and the mainland coast as far as the mouth of the Fraser River, and renamed many places.

Wilkes intended that *Porpoise* continue up the Strait of Georgia and circumnavigate Vancouver Island. They had just begun charting the San Juan Archipelago when the news of the loss of his second-largest ship, USS *Peacock*, reached Wilkes. He called off further work, including the circumnavigation, to consolidate the squadron at Astoria. Records of the San Juan survey work somehow disappeared in the confusion. Before leaving Juan de Fuca, boats from *Vincennes* surveyed Neah Bay while *Porpoise* examined Port San Juan on the opposite shore, the only work accomplished on Vancouver Island.

The strategic value of Admiralty Inlet, Puget Sound, and the San Juan Islands much impressed Wilkes. The loss of the *Peacock* to the treacherous currents and shoals of the Columbia River bar emphasized the significance of the safe haven offered by the sound. He strongly advised his superiors to incorporate them into the US claims during border negotiations over the Oregon Territory. A few years after his report, they did just this during discussions to resolve the boundary outlined in the Treaty of Washington of 1846.

THE NEW ESTABLISHMENT

The British government in London was aware of the growing American activity in what they termed the Pacific Northwest. The US Ex. Ex. under Wilkes confirmed this encroachment. Settlers had begun to travel across the mountains to the southern part of the Oregon Territory, supposedly under joint jurisdiction. Politicians were becoming bellicose. Another war loomed unless they could agree on the border west of the Rockies.

The HBC felt that its exclusive trading licence provided more scope than it actually did. The company requested a greater, and visible, imperial presence in the region to protect its perceived rights. As a backup, however, it developed an alternative strategy. In case Fort Vancouver should become victim to the onrushing American flood, the HBC would seek a new base of regional operations on the southeastern corner of Vancouver Island.

In 1842 James Douglas came to evaluate a short list of five sites for the new "establishment." He recommended the one at "Camosack," and the following year received instructions to proceed with the construction of what was to be Fort Victoria. Meanwhile, officials in London considered whether British interests in the region would be worth the effort and expense of protecting them. To resolve the question, they needed opinions of the situation more independent than that of the HBC. The question of the border was pressing, and they needed greater intelligence on which to base their negotiating position. Accordingly, they dispatched two missions to evaluate and report. The British Army would cover the defensive aspects of the forts, termed an "appreciation of the situation," while the Royal Navy would inspect the harbours and other maritime considerations.

In 1845, the commander-in-chief of the Pacific Station, Rear Admiral George Seymour, sent Captain the Hon. George Gordon, RN, to evaluate from the naval perspective. Gordon, although politically well connected, turned out to be an inept, disobedient naval officer, and an irresponsible commentator. In the armed frigate HMS *America*, he stayed barely a month and dismissed the entire region for trivial, personal reasons. He sneered that the local deer, when hunted on horseback, behaved differently from Scottish stags on a highland moor. Also, the local salmon provided poor sport for the fly fisherman.[5]

That same year, two young military officers arrived, having travelled overland from Halifax and being supported on their way by HBC officials. An infantryman, Henry Warre, and Mervin Vavasour of the Royal Engineers travelled in the guise of sportsmen on a jaunt. They first came to Fort Vancouver, thence by canoe to Nisqually and Port Discovery, where *America* lay at anchor. One of the ship's boats conveyed them, in a storm, to the new Fort Victoria, where they remained a few days.

Their report, in marked contrast to that of Gordon, was thorough, to the point, and largely positive. Warre and Vavasour noted that the neighbouring harbour of "Squimal" (Esquimalt) was far more secure and "affords anchorage and protection for ships of any tonnage." They also made some observations of natural history interest:

> The fisheries (salmon and sturgeon) are inexhaustible, and game of all descriptions is said to abound. The timber is extremely luxuriant, and increases in value as you reach a more northern latitude.... Pine, spruce, red and white oak, ash, cedar, arbutus, poplar, maple, willow and yew.... The cedar and pine become of immense size.[6]

By the time their report reached London, the Treaty of Washington had already been agreed.

THE VISIT OF *HERALD* AND *PANDORA*

Gordon's performance and conduct dissatisfied his superiors. On his return, he faced a court martial for disobedience, was severely reprimanded, and "retired." But the Admiralty still needed better maritime intelligence for the area. It called for second opinions on the harbours of Juan de Fuca and Vancouver Island. In the summer of 1846, four more vessels of the Royal Navy entered the Strait of Juan de Fuca. They were there both to "show the flag" and for charting activities. Among them were two ships charged with a hydrographic survey mission to "complete [charting] the Pacific coast from Guayaquil up to the Arctic Ocean."[7] They were HMS *Herald*, under the command of Captain Henry Kellett, RN, supported by HMS *Pandora*, Lieutenant James Wood, RN.

Kellett would have known of the growing requirement to expand the range of research to cover aspects of natural history during survey operations. Later in the voyage, three civilian scientists did participate, including a German botanist, Berthold Carl Seemann. Sir William J. Hooker, by then, director of the Royal Botanical Gardens at Kew, with whom Seemann had studied, put forward his name to replace another of his protégés as naturalist.

At the conclusion of the six-year voyage, Seemann supervised the publication of the technical reports and wrote the narrative of the voyage. While he and the other scientists had not joined *Herald* until later, Seemann incorporated notes from some of the junior officers who had visited Vancouver Island. From those journals he recorded their first impression of the landscape around Beacon Hill:

FIG. 10-2 *Colymbus Grylle,* pigeon guillemot, painted (and misidentified) by William Ellis on Cook's expedition, and shot for sport by later midshipmen. *Natural History Museum, Watercolour #49,* © *Trustees of the Natural History Museum, London [image edited].*

In 1841, the newly appointed secretary of the Geographical Society of London,[8] Colonel Julian Jackson,[9] published a London version of his book, which had been published in French two decades earlier. The English title was *What to Observe; or the Traveller's Remembrancer.* It provided tips for the uninitiated traveller to remote parts of the globe, and reminders for the more experienced as to what to look out for.

The work attracted the attention and admiration of the Earl of Auckland, the First Lord of the Admiralty. This was at the height of British imperial expansion, and the Royal Navy provided the primary line of early contact and demonstration of authority throughout the less-developed world. Auckland realized that this also created opportunities for gathering scientific, ethnographic, and commercial data. Such work would be consistent with the Victorian thirst for knowledge. Naval officers needed guidance on how best to acquire such information and specimens for scientific specialists to study and evaluate. Auckland felt that Jackson's book did not meet the need.

The Admiralty called for a manual, written for medical officers but for other naval officers as well. This should contain "plain and concise chapters," each devoted to one aspect of science and written by the pre-eminent British specialist in that field. The topics were to be the exact sciences, together with human geography and the social sciences. To emphasize each chapter's credibility, the author should be given explicit credit. The renowned astronomer Sir John Herschel would provide overall coordination and editing.

In 1849, John Murray of London published the first edition of the *Manual of Scientific Enquiry.* In almost 500 pages, 15 chapters covered a wide range of sciences related to physical geography. They included two on natural history: "Zoology" by Richard Owen, FRS, professor at the Royal College of Surgeons of England, and "Botany" by Sir William Hooker, FRS, then director of the Royal Botanic Gardens, Kew. The author of the chapter on geology was Charles Darwin, FRS, FGS. Herschel also provided a long preface, wrote the chapter on meteorology and added appendices to the chapters on astronomy and ethnology. The last of these was a set of rules for transcribing local vocabularies.

Hooker's botany chapter called for the collection of many different aspects of the plant world, both as living specimens for cultivation, and preserved for the herbarium. He gave clear instructions for collecting seeds, bulbs, tubers, cuttings, and rooted individuals, and for their care during long voyages. Some specimens needed to be stored in alcohol or wood vinegar. He also urged the collection of samples of wood and other products that were useful or of economic value—gums, resins, dye stuffs, and medicinal materials such as bark and flowers. He pointed out that there was much botanical work still to be done in all parts of the world. He closed with suggestions for books for the ship's library.

Owen's zoology chapter included "marine species and the lowest forms of animal life," algae, crustaceans, insects, molluscs, vertebrates: fish, reptiles, birds, and mammals. He urged the collection not only of shells, skins, eggs, horns, and similar items favoured by amateur collectors, but also of the internal organs, skeletons, parasites, and pupae, as well as microscopic creatures. He stressed that "all fossils, without exception, may be brought home, in large number and quantity." Owen also wanted detailed information of the humans encountered, for example, their physical condition, culture, diet, diseases, accommodation, domestication of animals, warfare, and weapons. He requested skeletons, or at least skulls, if possible, and if not, plaster casts of head, hands, and feet.

In walking from Ogden Point around to Fort Victoria, a distance little more than a mile, we thought we had never seen a more beautiful country; it quite exceeded our expectation; and yet Vancouver's descriptions made us look for something beyond common scenery. It is a natural park; noble oaks and ferns are seen in the greatest luxuriance, thickets of the hazel and the willow, shrubberies of the poplar and the alder, are dotted about.[10]

One of the midshipmen, thought to be Bedford Pim, published excerpts from his anonymous diary that included this note from his time in and around Victoria:

Squirrel-hunting, puffin-shooting [probably pigeon guillemots], as well as snipe and duck &c., were our principal amusements; and in passing through the wood of Vancouver and smaller islands, we could not but be struck at the lofty and magnificent cedar, pine, oak, and cypress trees, and the blossoms of the yellow laburnum scenting the air; every slope and undulation was a lawn and natural garden, studded with wild plum, gooseberry, currant, strawberry, and wild onion. Long grass and clover intermingled the soil, rich in the extreme, and would grow anything and everything.[11]

Leaving Wood in *Pandora* to complete charting Victoria and Esquimalt Harbours, Kellett crossed the strait in *Herald* to survey the southern shore. Continuous fog impeded their work, but on reaching Port Discovery and New Dungeness, they too, noted the "beacons" first reported by Vancouver:

[T]hey must have been erected with considerable trouble and labour; the upright centre-piece, supported by spurs diagonally placed, was in one instance thirty feet [9 metres], in another twenty-seven feet [8.2 metres] high.[12] Their use, or intention with which they were erected, is still unknown.[13]

Having spent three months in the Juan de Fuca region, the two vessels departed, intending to return. *Pandora* did so, two years later, but *Herald* went to the Bering Sea to join the search for the missing Franklin Expedition. Seemann's highly significant reports on the botany and zoology of the voyage included nothing related to those three months. He, perhaps, considered them only a minor episode in a major expedition of Arctic exploration and scientific discovery.

BRITISH INTEREST IN THE AREA CONFIRMED

By 1849, the government in London had recognized that Vancouver Island was of strategic significance, particularly with the discovery of deposits of good-quality coal at the northern end. At the time, coal-fired steam engines were replacing sail in warships. The combination of the fine harbour at Esquimalt with local access to coal made a convincing case for them to defend the island. The unlimited availability of superb Douglas-fir trees, suitable for masts of even the largest sailing vessels, reinforced such a decision. In that year, they proclaimed Vancouver Island as a British colony, granting the HBC a 10-year lease to manage it on Britain's behalf.

The Treaty of Washington, signed three years earlier, described the new border between British and American territories, west of the crest of the Rocky Mountains, as the 49th parallel as far as the middle of the Gulf of Georgia. The boundary would then follow the middle of the channel between Vancouver Island and the mainland, and then through the middle of the Strait of Juan de Fuca to the Pacific Ocean. This clarified that the whole of Vancouver Island was British. Ambiguity remained over where the boundary line would lie in relation to the San Juan Archipelago. This question proved vexatious and almost led to armed conflict between the parties. The treaty did, however, provide for a joint boundary commission to survey and mark the land portion, and to agree on the maritime sector.

Before that joint commission could start work, however, another factor came into prominence: the discovery of placer gold in the Fraser Valley. At the time James Douglas acted in dual roles as chief factor for the company and as governor of the colony of Vancouver Island. He at once recognized the potential threat to the mainland, north of the new border. Without prior clearance from London, he issued the proclamation of a second British colony on the Pacific coast, and that all gold prospectors and miners in that area would require licences from Victoria.

London ratified his prompt action in declaring the Colony of British Columbia, which proved most timely. In April 1858, a deluge of prospectors and motley hangers-on descended upon Victoria from San Francisco, headed for the diggings. Douglas, now governor of both colonies, increased the volume of his pleas for visible military and naval presence to protect these distant and isolated outposts of the British Empire. London had listened and responded positively.

BRITISH MILITARY AND NAVAL EXPEDITIONS

Four expeditions arrived on Vancouver Island during the years 1857 and '58. Two consisted mainly of Royal Engineers; the others were vessels of the Royal Navy. The first of these to arrive was the steam corvette HMS *Satellite*, Captain James C. Prevost, RN, commanding. His appointment was as the British boundary commissioner. The previous year, he had served on the same station as commander of HMS *Virago*, spending much of the mission defending the newly discovered gold deposits on the Queen Charlotte Islands (now Haida Gwaii).

During the *Satellite* mission, he assembled a collection of birdskins and sent them to a friend, Dr. Acland at Oxford University. Acland, in turn, passed them on to Philip L. Sclater,

the secretary of the Zoological Society of London, for identification. Sclater did so, remarking:

> Though the species are not numerous [35] and are all known, as this is, I believe, the first series of Birds that has been brought to England from a colony which is now attracting so much attention, I have thought that their names would be worthy of record.[14]

Of particular interest in the collection were the inclusion of three specimens of the marbled murrelet, several of the western bluebird, a cinnamon teal, and a mountain quail. This last was probably obtained on San Juan Island, the only local occurrence at that time, although it was later introduced several times into the Victoria region, usually without success.

The second naval expedition was by the survey vessel HMS *Plumper*, with the highly experienced Captain George Henry Richards, RN, in command. There were two elements to his mission: the first was to support Prevost as deputy commissioner for the contentious maritime boundary. The other element was a multi-year hydrographic survey of the coasts of Vancouver Island and the adjacent mainland. Richards needed a base ashore for the winter seasons, provided in some newly built huts at Esquimalt.

In the penultimate paragraph of Rear Admiral John Washington's seven-page, handwritten instructions to Richards as he was "about to proceed to Vancouver's Island," Washington had noted:

> You have also on board on the recommendation of Sir William Hooker, the last works on the Botany and Natural History of the region, and the surgeon of the ship Dr. Forbes has a supply of dredges & other material for collecting and preserving objects of Natural History. . . . I need hardly commend these gentlemen to

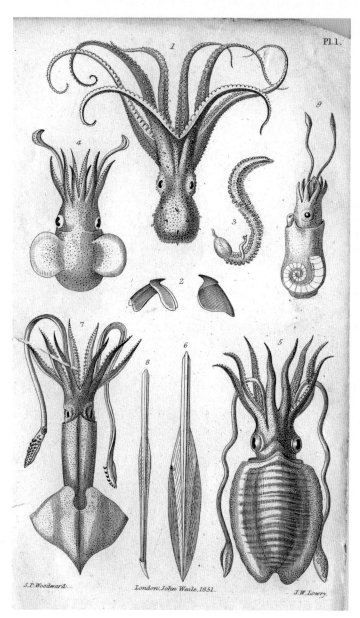

FIG. 10-3 (LEFT) Cephalopods. The British Admiralty required all ships' captains sailing new waters to collect marine invertebrates such as these cephalopods—octopuses, squids and nautiluses. *Plate 1 from S.P. Woodward's* Manual of the Mollusca, *1851. From author's collection.*

FIG. 10-4 (RIGHT) Allan Brooks's painting of a western bluebird. James Prevost collected three of these, and their skins formed part of the first such consignment sent from this coast to Britain for identification and study. *W.L. Dawson's* Birds of Washington, *1909 [image edited].*

your liberal support as I am assured you will afford them boats & facilities for their respective pursuits whenever the more pressing duties of the mission will admit of it. & will encourage them by any means in your powers. Such I may add is their Lordships' express wish and directives.[15]

Most of Richards's officers were surveyors, and two more acquired those skills under his leadership. The surgeon mentioned by Washington was Lieutenant Charles Forbes, MD, MRCS, RN. In addition to membership in the Royal College of Surgeons, he had a substantial knowledge of geology. While in Valparaíso in Chile, Forbes fell sick and returned to Britain. His replacement, at Richards's request, was David Lyall, an old shipmate and highly experienced. After recuperating, Forbes continued his voyage to Vancouver Island aboard the screw frigate HMS *Topaze*. With 51 guns and a crew of over 700, *Topaze* came to defend the new colonies, anchoring in Esquimalt in early March 1860. While here, Forbes would make significant contributions to geographical and scientific knowledge of the latest imperial possessions.

Lieutenant Colonel John S. Hawkins, RE, commanded the first of the military contingents to arrive. He and his team of 6 survey officers and 56 other ranks formed the British element of the land component of the 49th parallel joint Boundary Commission. He too took space in the Esquimalt huts. Since the contingent would be tracing the line from Boundary Bay up over the Cascade Range, across the Columbia Valley, and up to the crest of the Rockies, logistics would be critical. They would require 44 pack horses and 55 mules, which in turn called for a civilian veterinarian to be part of the team. The man selected, John Keast Lord, was also a zoologist, and therefore designated assistant naturalist.

One of the survey technicians, sapper John Buttle, RE, had recently trained in the collection and preservation of botanical specimens, at the Royal Botanic Gardens, Kew, under Hooker. He would assist in this whenever his survey duties permitted. Initially, the team had not included a qualified and experienced botanist, but Hooker believed it should. The team would pass through unexplored territory and unstudied ecosystems ranging from sea level to more than 8,000 feet (2,400 metres). Many plants new to science could well be found. In consultation with Washington, Richards's superior, Hooker arranged that Lyall transfer from Richards's to Hawkins's team. Replacing Lyall as surgeon, Charles Wood arrived to join *Plumper*.[16]

Lieutenant Colonel Richard Clement Moody, RE, commanded the third contingent, a substantial force of Royal Engineers. It was there to provide support for the new Colony of British Columbia. They contributed enormously, and in many ways, to the survival of both colonies, but without advancing the knowledge of local natural history. The other contingents, however, succeeded in just that.

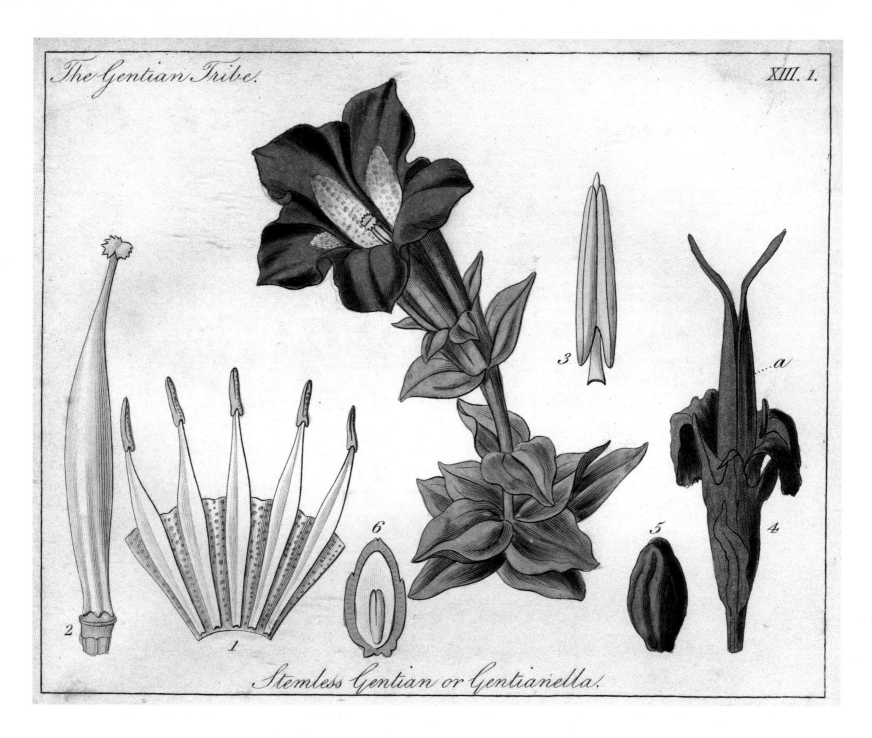

The Gentian Tribe.

XIII. 1.

Stemless Gentian or Gentianella.

FIG. 11-0 *The Gentian Tribe*. Dr. Charles Wood spotted a patch of these plants on his arduous trek across northern Vancouver Island in June 1862. This plate is from a book by Professor John Lindley, Sarah Crease's father, patronizingly intended to simplify botany for ladies (see chapter 16). *Lindley's Ladies' Botany, 1834.*

CHAPTER ELEVEN

NATURALISTS WITH NAVAL AND MILITARY EXPEDITIONS, PART II

Contributions of the Missions' Biologists

BOTANIST DR. CHARLES B. WOOD, RN

To replace David Lyall as surgeon to HMS *Plumper*, Admiral John Washington chose Charles B. Wood. Little is on record of Wood's training and earlier career, but during his time with Captain George Henry Richards, RN, he showed himself to be knowledgeable in natural history and geology. In his role as ship's doctor, he not only provided health care for the crew, but also responded with dedication to a raging smallpox epidemic among the local peoples. He also undertook arduous land explorations with the captain and other surveyors.

On one journey by ship's boat into Jervis Inlet, he reported on the local geology,[1] and then crossed over the steep, forested, 4,000-foot (1,200-metre) high ridge to reach Howe Sound. On another occasion, he made the difficult traverse across the north end of Vancouver Island from Kyuquot Sound to Port McNeill. He and his companion, Lieutenant Phillip Hankin, RN, were short on time to rendezvous with *Hecate*. It was too early in the year; the snows were melting, and several times they had to fight their way up and across rivers in full spate. They fashioned makeshift rafts from logs to navigate a series of lakes. They completed the trek after eight days, completely out of food. Richards noted in his diary that "the Dr. was much knocked up."[2] Wood had intended to collect botanical specimens. Soon, however, he had to abandon both the idea and his equipment because of the terrible conditions, the scarcity of local packers, and the need to travel as lightly as possible.

He wrote a 16-page report to Richards,[3] in which he explained, with disappointment, the reasons for not collecting, and noted midway that "I saw no new trees or shrubs, nor any plant in bloom and I now less regretted my leaving my botanical material behind." The next day, approaching Nimpkish Lake, he added:

> As we descended we passed a large patch of gentian in full and brilliant blossom . . . [and, at the head of the lake,] some of the largest Red Pine trees [western red cedar] I have seen in Vancouver Id. I measured a prostrate one blown down by the wind, some 60ft. [18 metres] from its roots where it had a circumference of 15 ft. [4.6 metres].

FIG. 11-1 (ABOVE) The hill of the Malahat Drive is formed by Mount Jeffrey at the left and Mount Wood at the right-hand end. The two names were chosen by Captain Richards for significant naturalists in Victoria in the early 1860s. *Photo by author.*

FIG. 11-2 (RIGHT) Ruffed grouse, once plentiful on Vancouver Island but easily hunted to its current status of uncommon. *Chromolithograph from a 1909 painting by W.B. Gillette, from author's collection.*

While he did not publish any separate papers, he made significant contributions on natural history to two other important works. He helped David Lyall assemble a large collection of algae, and he wrote detailed sections on zoology and botany for inclusion in a book by his shipmate, Charles Mayne. Richards commemorated Wood's overall contribution by naming geographical features on Vancouver Island after him. Mount Wood, alongside Mount Jeffrey on the Malahat Drive, a cove on Kyuquot Sound, and islets in Clayoquot Sound are all called Wood. His middle name, Bedingfield, is now affixed to a bay in Clayoquot, and a range of hills north of Tofino.

CHARLES MAYNE'S BOOK[4]

Midway through their work on Vancouver Island, the larger and more powerful HMS *Hecate* arrived to replace *Plumper*. Richards, Wood, and most of the other officers transferred to the new vessel. *Hecate*'s first officer, Commander Charles Mayne, RN, had also taken Wood on land sorties into the Comox Valley and Jervis Inlet. He later wrote a book of his experiences in the two new colonies on the Pacific coast of North America and included some notes on the natural history of Vancouver Island. Mayne quoted "my friend Dr. Wood" at length on "the natural history of the two colonies," but with emphasis on Vancouver Island, with which he was better acquainted.

In eight pages,[5] Wood covered the carnivores and other land mammals, cetaceans, and birds.

> "The Willow Grouse, *Lagopus albus* [from the description, this seems to be the ruffed grouse, not the willow ptarmigan], are found on Vancouver Island in immense numbers. . . . These are excellent eating, but are too easily shot to afford much amusement to an English sportsman."

He also covered reptiles, fishes, and flora, describing Hooker's *Flora Boreali-Americana* as "an epitome of the botany of both these colonies." He recorded: "I have seen 'Timothy Grass' grown on the Island 8ft. [2.4 metres] in height."

Wood concluded: "I pass over the Ferns, Mosses, Lichens, the Fungi, and Seaweeds, with the brief remark that they abound everywhere, the first in quantities somewhat troublesome to the agriculturist." In splendid understatement on the grizzly bear, *Ursus (arctos) horribilis*, Wood noted, "[It] is not found on the island. . . . [If you encounter one,] it is wisest to leave him unmolested." He also recorded that, at the time, a sea otter pelt "full-size, undressed and measuring 6 feet, commands the price of thirty blankets—£12–£14."[6]

In addition to Wood's contribution, Mayne's book included an excerpt from an 1862 prize essay written by fellow naval officer Surgeon Lieutenant Charles Forbes, RN, in which he listed, among other things, trees, shrubs, grasses, and leguminous plants. Mayne also quoted Hamilton Moffatt, an experienced HBC trader who knew the interior around the Nimpkish River:

> The zoology is the same as other parts of Vancouver Island, except that the purple marmot [probably the Vancouver Island subspecies] is occasionally found at Koskimo, but not the common grey marmot. The white land-otters, which have at various times been forwarded from here [Fort McNeill], were killed at Kioquettuck [Kyuquot].[7]

He also provided a list of 11 species of local trees from "the woodsmen employed by the [Alberni] Mill" and detailed their qualities and uses. He consulted on the identification of the trees with Dr. Lindley of the Royal Horticultural Society in London, whose daughter, Sarah, then lived in Victoria.[8]

BOTANIST DAVID LYALL

Captain Richards had requested David Lyall as the replacement surgeon for *Plumper*. After earning a licentiate surgeon's diploma from Aberdeen, Lyall immediately served aboard a whaling ship bound for Greenland. He then joined the Royal Navy and sailed on a two-season scientific exploration of Antarctica aboard HMS *Terror* with Sir James Ross. His counterpart aboard their sister ship, HMS *Erebus*, had been Joseph Dalton Hooker, son of Professor William Jackson Hooker, the botanist and director of the Royal Botanic Gardens, Kew.

By 1844, he had sufficient experience to qualify as an MD and served on further scientific voyages. The first took him to New Zealand, and then he served as senior medical officer to Sir Edward Belcher's squadron into the Arctic searching for the missing Franklin Expedition. It was on that voyage that he sailed with and befriended Richards. During all these expeditions he made important botanical collections.[9]

During his time aboard *Plumper* and after transferring to the Boundary Commission, Dr. Lyall corresponded with Hooker at Kew and regularly sent him the results of his collecting. Most of these were dried specimens and seeds. The large collection of fungi he preserved in saline solution did not survive to permit adequate identification and description. Over his four years in the field, he—with the acknowledged assistance of sapper John Buttle, who did much collecting—amassed 6,700 specimens from 1,375 species. These were "not including the Algae, Mosses, *Hepaticae*, or Lichens," which formed other substantial collections.

During the few months at Esquimalt before joining Colonel Hawkins and the boundary contingent, Lyall began a collection of algae. He continued, with some assistance from Wood, during the winter respites when fieldwork in the mountains was impracticable. Together, they amassed a collection of 107 species, 7 of which were freshwater, the rest, marine. Eleven of the latter were new to science. Of particular interest were the Laminariaceae (kelps), which W.H. Harvey[10] described in his report to the Linnean Society, noting that many

> are of such gigantic size that full grown specimens can hardly be expected ever to have been seen in Europe. The *Nereocystis*[11] has a stipes said to attain a length of 300 feet [90 metres]. The *Alariae* [bladderlocks] probably have fronds of 20 to 30 feet [6 to 9 metres] in length—an enormous size for an undivided lamina of cellular tissue.[12] ... [Selecting] such unwieldy objects is no easy task. Dr. Lyall deserves thanks and praise for the manner in which he has performed it, nor less for the great care with which he has preserved all his specimens.[13]

On his return to Britain, and because his collections were of such significance, the Royal Navy granted him a sinecure. This posting ashore on full pay meant that he could work with experts at Kew to classify and arrange the collections and prepare a report[14] for the Linnean Society, of which he was elected a Fellow in 1862.

His report provided general descriptions of the regions the boundary passed through. They ranged from sea level up to summits of the Cascades at 7,500 feet (2,286 metres) and the Rockies at 8,300 feet (2,530 metres), and included two major river valleys, the Fraser and the Columbia. The report then described the vegetation of each region and listed the plants collected. This was pioneering work in the field of bio-climatic zones. A section of his report reviewed the distribution of 17 principal trees along the border strip and their elevation limits. At Esquimalt, he noted finding a blown-down Virginia juniper that was 46 feet (14 metres) long, with a circumference of 5 feet, 4 inches (1.6 metres), measured at 6 feet (1.8 metres) above the ground.

Before transferring to the boundary survey, he was able to experience the flowering glory of the southeastern tip of Vancouver Island and the archipelago in springtime. He noted 13 trees and 11 common shrubs, and observed:

> Amongst the most conspicuous flowering plants met with there in the early part of the season are several species of *Ranunculus*, of *Claytonia*, of *Potentilla*, and of *Saxifraga*, *Plectritis congesta*, *Collomia gracilis*, *Collinsia violacea*, *Dodecatheon Meadia*, *Sisyrinchium grandiflorum*, species of *Fritillaria*, *Camassia esculenta*, and species of *Trillium*.[15]

ZOOLOGIST JOHN KEAST LORD

The other naturalist with the Boundary Commission, John Keast Lord, was born in Devon and in 1844 received a diploma from the Royal Veterinary College, London. After a few years wandering around North America, he served with a regiment of horse artillery during the Crimean War. The Zoological Society of London made him a Fellow. Soon afterward, he applied and was accepted by the Boundary Commission.

When not occupied with surveying the line on the mainland, Lord spent his time in Esquimalt, observing and collecting local natural history. He included many of his findings in a two-volume, lively, and entertaining account of his participation in the mission.[16] Crabs and other crustaceans caught his particular attention; he collected more than 40 species, several new to science. One of the experts back at London's Zoological Society who helped classify them noted:

> The extremely opposite and varied localities in which many of the species have hitherto been found, suggest the idea that Vancouver Island corresponds with the extreme limit between a

FIG. 11-3 A forest of bull kelp with stipes (stems) up to 90 metres long. The Linnean Society in London was pleased with the first specimens ever to be sent intact to Europe, by Dr. David Lyall. *Photo © Jackie Hildering, www.TheMarineDetective.com.*

northern and a tropical fauna. It is only in this way I can account for finding the representatives of tropical species with others that are found only (on the eastern coast of Asia) in the Arctic and perhaps, North Atlantic Oceans. Little, if indeed anything, is as yet known of the deep sea productions from the west side of the Island, which still offer a rich harvest to future explorers.[17]

Lord also investigated the local fish and was particularly interested in the migration cycles of the various species. He not only cast nets and lines for them, but also inspected fishmongers' stalls at the market. One species struck him as remarkable, the one he called the *Chirus*, noting the Lekwungen name as *Thatlegest*. He described it as

> [a] handsome, shapely fish, about eighteen inches in length. . . . Its sides rival in beauty many a tropical flower. . . . Quite as delicious to the palate as pleasant to the eye, the chirus is altogether a most estimable fish.[18] [From his description, it appears to be the rock, or kelp, greenling.]

In another, lyrical, passage, Lord recounts:

> Macaulay's Point [in Esquimalt], a long ridge of rocks running far out to sea, but bare at low water, was a favourite hunting-ground of mine, the snug little rock-basins left prisoner by the receding water. An unusually low tide disclosed a ridge of rocks I had never before seen, an opportunity for exploration not to be neglected. Clinging to the slippery wrack, and scrambling down a vertical ledge, I discovered a regular cave, its sides and floor literally covered with the strangest collection of marine wonders I have ever gazed upon. . . .
>
> *Actinia* [sea anemones] spread their treacherous petal-like arms, gorgeous in every variety of exquisite colouring; huge

holothuria, like brilliantly-painted cucumbers, clung to the dripping rock; starfish of all sizes and tints—chitons in black spiny mail—shells of *purpura* and *trochus* [sea snails], and hosts of kindred. Annelids [segmented worms] too were peeping from out their cases of stone and horn, their exquisite feathery tufts, fishing lines, and traps wondrously beautiful, but, like the embrace of a siren, fatal in its clasp; all these creatures, hungry and anxious, awaited the incoming tide.[19]

He also sought birds for his collection:

> The Pigmy Owl. This rare and beautiful little owl, the smallest of all North American species, I shot for the first time on Vancouver Island. The habits of this tiny bird appear little known. Its diminutive size, shy solitary habits—for it always hides amongst the thick foliage of the oak or pine, except when feeding—renders the task of observing it, or obtaining a specimen, at all times difficult. How the recluse lives, where it lives, or what it does, are secrets.
>
> Early in the spring, while collecting the migrant birds which arrive at Vancouver Island in great numbers and variety of species—some to remain the summer through, others only to rest awhile as they journey farther north to their breeding grounds—Dame Fortune, fickle though she generally be, deigned for once to smile, and afford me an opportunity to watch the habits of the Pigmy Owl.

He went on to describe how he observed a pair of the owls and their hunting strategy, until an unknown predator raided the nest, "devouring, perhaps, both parents and children." Later, he did find and collect another specimen, but discovered a problem:

> The Indians, without exception, hold this little owl in terrible dread. . . . To kill one is an unpardonable heresy. I nearly got

FIG. 11-4 The amazing variety of intertidal life forms J.K. Lord described as "the strangest collection of marine wonders I have ever gazed upon." *Photo © Jackie Hildering, www.TheMarineDetective.com.*

into very serious trouble for shooting a specimen of this little owl. An Indian deputation, headed by their chief waited on me, and protested against my risking theirs and my own inevitable destruction. All reasoning was futile, and there was nothing for it but to procure all the mystic birds and mammals by stealth.[20]

In 1860, Lord went to California to help buy a large quantity of pack horses and mules, and then drive them 1,000 miles (1,609 kilometres) to the Columbia River. During the journey, he also managed to collect zoological specimens for the society in London. Colonel Hawkins praised Lord's enthusiasm and abilities in his collecting activities, both in the field and at winter quarters, as well as his skills in caring for the pack animals.

On returning to London, Lord gave a series of lectures and wrote magazine articles and two books on his experiences. To volume 2 of his book on his time with the Boundary Commission, he appended an 84-page "List of the Mammals, Birds, Insects, Reptiles, Fishes, Shells, Annelids, and Diatomaceae, collected by myself in British Columbia and Vancouver Island, with notes on their habits." He acknowledged the help of several specialists from the British Museum in describing and classifying the various classes of his collection.[21]

Lord later participated in a scientific expedition to Egypt, the Red Sea, and Arabia, publishing books on the beetles and flies of the region, including many new species. His last position was as manager of the new Brighton Aquarium, but he died in 1872, soon after it opened.[22]

THE PRIZE ESSAY

In March 1860 the gunboat HMS *Topaze* arrived in Esquimalt with Dr. Charles Forbes, who had been the original surgeon to *Plumper*. On learning that Forbes was also a geologist, Governor Douglas requested his services for a survey of the route from

FIG. 11-5 Of the pygmy owl, J.K. Lord wrote, "How the recluse lives, where it lives, or what it does, are secrets." *Photo © courtesy of TJ Watt.*

the head of Harrison Lake, Port Douglas, to the Lillooet trail.[23] This was the favoured access for prospectors headed for the new gold diggings. The Royal Engineers Columbia Detachment were also blasting a wagon road through this same route. This work revealed the geological strata in greater detail, allowing Forbes to improve his final report to Douglas. At the Victoria Theatre, during the winter of 1861/62, he gave a four-part public lecture series on geology.

Apparently Forbes took a great interest in all matters related to Vancouver Island. Although their accounts do not record it, he certainly would have met with his fellow naval surgeon Wood during the winter respite at Esquimalt, and quite probably also with Dr. William Tolmie. From these men and, indirectly, from Wood's discussions with Lyall and Lord, Forbes would have acquired a far greater knowledge of the region's natural history than he could have gleaned in just a single year's personal observation. When, in late October 1861, the Colonial Secretary announced a public essay competition to extol the features of the colony, Forbes decided to enter.

To follow up on the huge success of London's 1851 Great Exhibition, the British government planned a second for 1862. Douglas needed booklets to distribute there to attract British settlers to both the island and the mainland colonies. So he launched twin competitions, each with a prize of £50. The stated objective was to "set forth in clearest and most comprehensive manner the capabilities, resources and advantages of Vancouver's Island as a Colony for settlement." The panel of three judges included Dr. Tolmie, and entries were required by the end of the year.

Forbes's essay won the prize for Vancouver Island and the colonial government published it in booklet form in June 1862. The booklet consisted of 63 pages of text, plus an appendix of data from various sources. Clearly structured, it fulfilled all the requirements, although the *Daily British Colonist* complained about

> the multitude of technical words. Some of them to the unscientific reader are perfect jaw-breakers. There are so many facts . . . that we might excuse the display of so extensive a knowledge of the natural history of the country.[24]

Conscious that his target readership included potential farmers and landowners, Forbes took care to mention the opportunities for traditional countryside leisure pursuits:

> The sportsman will find abundant use for both rod and gun, and as a hunter he may distinguish himself in the forest, the puma, the bear and the wolf, being worth of his prowess. . . . Great numbers of [deer] are shot annually, and the great red deer, or elk, as he is popularly called is indeed a prize any sportsman may be proud of. . . . Grouse shooting begins on the 12th of August, but the sport is very different from that enjoyed on the breezy moors of Yorkshire, or of Scotland, and more resembles pheasant shooting. . . . In the early winter snipe and wild duck afford good sport. . . . Excellent trout fishing may be had on every stream, and in the arms of the sea into which fresh water runs. . . . Trolling with minnow and spawn, are the only means by which salmon can be caught, these lordly gentlemen refusing to show a fin to any fly.[25]

He devotes eight pages to "The Natural Productions of Vancouver Island in the animal, vegetable and mineral kingdom." Forbes describes the fisheries as "inexhaustible," the timber as "unrivalled," and the coal as "the best on the whole North Pacific Coast." He provides details on the types of fish available for commercial activity, and similarly for the trees. He describes the coal found and already being exploited as "almost inexhaustible wealth." He mentions that traces of gold have been found in many places but not, so far, in worthwhile quantities.

The appendix provides a variety of official statistics and relevant proclamations, as well as three lists of the wildlife and three of the botany found on Vancouver Island, giving their popular and scientific names "in accordance with Vols 8 and 9 of the Pacific Railroad Reports."[26] With one exception, he did not provide sources for the information in the lists. The first cited 24 animals, some of which are questionable: he listed a red fox, which did not occur on the island, and a "Black Bear" and a "Brown Bear," both as *Ursus Americanus.*[27] He did not list any mammals smaller than the ermine, nor any cetaceans (although, in the text, he did mention that there were several found in local waters).

The second list of birds contained 97 species and included the pygmy owl, which could indicate the observation by Lord. The list is clearly a composite one. Several of the names Forbes gave are no longer in use, so identification is not always straightforward. For example, his "Suckley's Gull" is now Heermann's, and his "Oregon ground Robin" is now the rufous-sided towhee. There appears to have been little correlation in Mayne's book between Forbes's zoology list and that of Wood. Different species were mentioned, and the names, both common and scientific, were given differently. Wood's identification seems the more reliable.

Forbes's third list was of shells collected "from the rocks and dredges off Esquimalt and Victoria Harbours." Again, this seems to have been the work of zoologist J.K. Lord. Forbes cited 38 species from five orders, but for these he did not provide any common names. Nor did he list any crustaceans. The botanical lists included 22 species of "Trees and Shrubs of Economic Value," 23 species of "Shrubbery Under Growth," and 8 species of "Grasses, Leguminous Plants &c., &c." It was these botanical lists that Mayne later incorporated into his book.[28] In all, Dr. Forbes provided the most comprehensive record of wildlife and plants found on Vancouver Island up to the date of publication.

The tour of duty for *Topaze* at Esquimalt concluded in June 1863, and Forbes returned to Britain with the ship. He then seems to have retired from naval service, to take up private practice. On March 14, 1864, he read a paper to the Royal Geographical Society in London entitled "Notes on the Physical Geography of Vancouver Island." The society published it the following year in its journal, accompanied by a map. Coincidentally, one of the survey officers with the Columbia Detachment, Lieutenant H.S. Palmer, RE, also read a paper at the same meeting: "On the Geography and Natural Capabilities of British Columbia, and the Condition of its principal Gold-Fields," published with another map.

A.H. MARKHAM, ARCTIC EXPLORER AND COLLECTOR OF SEABIRDS

Two decades after *Topaze* had entered Esquimalt Harbour, another gunboat of the Royal Navy, the ironclad HMS *Triumph*, arrived with Captain Albert Hastings Markham, RN, in command. *Triumph* was the flagship of Rear Admiral Frederick Stirling, commander of the Pacific squadron. The vessel was to undergo a refit, so, they remained in Esquimalt for three months during the summer of 1880.

Triumph's captain was renowned as an Arctic explorer and a keen amateur naturalist. He was a cousin and close friend of Clements Markham, the long-serving secretary and, at the time, president of the Royal Geographical Society. As a young man he had served as second mate aboard a whaling voyage into Baffin Bay. The experience gained led to his appointment as second-in-command of the British Arctic Expedition of 1875/76, where he led a man-hauled sled party on an attempt to reach the North Pole. Poorly clothed, they managed to get as far as latitude 83°20'26", a record that lasted for the next 20 years. The RGS awarded him an inscribed gold watch in recognition of his achievement.

He had recently returned from Novaya Zemlya, the large Russian island in the Arctic Ocean. Markham acquired specimens of Arctic birds and the scarcely known eggs of the king eider, and also collected 15 botanical specimens, crustaceans, molluscs, insects, rocks, and fossils.[29]

When service duties aboard *Triumph* permitted, he had again collected birdskins and lepidoptera. As they steamed north from the Straits of Magellan, he acquired specimens at anchorages and at times at sea.[30] His collection included species taken in Chile, Juan Fernandez, Peru, Galapagos, Panama, Acapulco, and Esquimalt. He sent them to London for identification and description by the Royal Zoological Society.

The first part of the collection consisted of 13 species of Laridae, the large family of gulls and terns. His second group of birds consisted of another 149 species, many of them of the pelagic tube-nose family such as petrels, shearwaters, and albatrosses, several new to science.[31] Among the collection was a specimen of the giant petrel,[32] called by earlier maritime explorers "Quebrantahuessos." They confused this bird with the immature short-tailed albatross seen in numbers on the west coast of Vancouver Island, now very rare.

The 12 species listed as obtained from Esquimalt were, curiously, far fewer than might be expected, given the time and the number of species available and his earlier enthusiasm for collecting. They were ovenbird,[33] cedar waxwing, violet-green swallow, white-crowned sparrow, chipping sparrow, Steller's jay, pileated woodpecker, northern flicker, belted kingfisher, American kestrel, bufflehead, and least sandpiper.

He could have acquired such a list on any single morning during his three-month visit. He seems to have temporarily lost the fervour. Victoria did not impress Markham: "There was a depressing air of poverty about the town."[34]

Two specimens of a golden-winged warbler were of unlabelled origin but supposed by Osbert Salvin (editor of the British ornithological journal *The Ibis*) to have come (impossibly) from Esquimalt. Salvin, who described and published the second list,[35] noted:

> Captain Markham deserves the thanks of ornithologists for his
> industry in amassing so large a collection. . . . We only hope that
> his example may frequently be followed.

After his retirement, Admiral Sir Albert Markham served on the council of the Royal Geographical Society for many years, providing advice and encouragement to new generations of polar explorers. He helped select Commander Robert Falcon Scott, RN, to lead the south polar scientific and exploratory expedition of 1901–04.

FIG. 11-6 The diminutive bufflehead. One of the Victoria region's favourite autumn arrivals. *Painting by Allan Brooks, from W.L. Dawson's* Birds of Washington, *1909 [image edited].*

FIG. 12-0 A stand of old-growth Sitka spruce near the Nitinat River. Botanical collector Robert Brown, on finding a similar specimen in 1863, thought his sponsors in Edinburgh would be pleased to know about it. *Photo © courtesy of TJ Watt.*

CHAPTER TWELVE

COLONIAL NATURALISTS, PART I

"Strange things, wild men, new places . . ."
Robert Brown Botanizes and Explores

O N MAY 6, 1863, ROBERT Brown—yet another young Scottish botanist—arrived in Esquimalt on a mission to collect seeds, roots, and plants from the region. His sponsor, the Botanical Society of Edinburgh, had raised enough to cover his passage and a modest stipend for a three-year expedition. This was the same group of eminent landowners that had contracted with John Jeffrey in 1849, for a similar mission to what they termed the Oregon Territory.

The son of a Scottish farmer and a Danish mother, Brown was born in 1842 near the remote town of Wick at the northeastern tip of Scotland. Nineteen years later he enrolled in the University of Edinburgh Medical School, studying to qualify as a research scientist, and while there he won a silver medal for botany. Opting for adventure, Brown interrupted his studies to sail as ship's surgeon aboard the *Narwhal* for an eight-month whaling and sealing voyage to Spitsbergen, Iceland, and Greenland.

This experience reinforced his urge for perilous travel. He abandoned academic work and agreed to take up the mission offered by the Botanical Society of Edinburgh. He was 21 years old and considered himself overqualified to carry out the society's objectives. He knew that Jeffrey, his predecessor in the position, had been simply a gardener. Brown hoped, however, that the opportunities the mission would afford justified his decision. He envisaged making a far more ambitious, scientific investigation of parts of the island so far unexplored.

Brown's first journal entry after arriving in Victoria mentioned talking with some of the many Indigenous Peoples around, for he was intent on learning their language. He strolled over the James Bay Bridge into the grounds of the government buildings, where the carpet of fawn lilies and camas in full bloom caught his botanist's eye.

Calling in to see Governor James Douglas, Brown presented his letters of introduction and explained his purpose. Douglas, after admiring his "grit" in planning to venture into unexplored territory, cautioned that the local people were currently most unwelcoming to unescorted white men. Brown responded that he intended to proceed anyway, and Douglas asked to be kept informed of his progress.

FIG. 12-1 *Wild Easter Lilies and Camas.* On Robert Brown's first morning stroll in Victoria, he noted fawn lilies and camas in full bloom carpeting the grounds of Governor Douglas's residence. *Watercolour by Emily Sartain, date unknown, from author's collection.*

Brown also had a letter of introduction to Dr. William Fraser Tolmie, and had called upon him shortly after he had arrived. A few days later, Tolmie introduced him to Gilbert Sproat, an executive with the Anderson lumber company operating at Alberni. Over dinner, Sproat told Brown that so far, no naturalist had investigated the area, and offered him a berth in the company schooner about to go there. Brown accepted.

While in Victoria, Brown had told people, including the press, that he had come "for the purposes of exploring Vancouver Island and British Columbia in its scientific aspects" and that the California Academy of Sciences had appointed him a corresponding member. Respectable Victoria society took his story and apparent status at face value and admitted him to their circle.

BOTANIZING ON THE ISLAND'S WEST COAST

After a few days' delay awaiting favourable winds and tide, the schooner *Alberni* sailed for Barclay Sound, and up the inlet to anchor at the new sawmill. The mill manager politely provided the visitor with "a famous woodman" to guide him over a four-mile trail that led to a large lake. The guide was Quassom of the Opetchesaht (now the Hupačasath, a Nuu-chah-nulth community), whom Brown described as "a shaggy, thick-set, tremendously strong individual." At the lake's shore, they found an old canoe, which they patched up and paddled, until meeting a local with a better canoe who took them to the company's logging camp.

In the surrounding forest, Brown "collected everything most religiously,"[1] then reboarded the canoe to paddle to where the lake discharges into the Somass River. He named the lake after his benefactor and friend, Sproat, and called the upper reaches of the Somass River the Stamp, after the local director of the Anderson lumber company. A better canoe bore Brown downstream back to the settlement, "overshaded" all the way by flowering dogwood trees.

Another Anderson Company schooner, *Codfish*, was due to call in to the mill on a trading trip to villages all along the west coast of the island. Brown persuaded the captain to take him along. Leaving Alberni at the end of May with a crew of Tseshaht men, *Codfish* cruised the coast for three weeks, visiting villages in Barkley and in Clayoquot and Nootka Sounds to trade for dogfish oil and furs.

While Hugh Walt, the "trader," negotiated with chiefs, Brown was ashore collecting plant material. To enter Nootka was fraught with risk—the last trader to go there, six months earlier, had been murdered. Facing a fierce gale with torn sails and damaged yards on *Codfish*, the captain opted to bypass Friendly Cove. They ran for shelter in Esperanza Inlet, only to discover that they were in the midst of an intertribal conflict and coming under pressure to take sides.

Brown discovered collecting to be difficult—there was continuous torrential rain, and he was pestered by troops of children wherever he went. His bunk and blankets were soaked, as was the material for drying his specimens. Someone had stolen his waterproof coat. He recorded that "in this wooded country it requires infinitely more labour to get a few plants here than the roughest journey at home."

Some days later *Codfish* did enter Nootka, as Brown—having read accounts of the place by Cook, Vancouver, Menzies, and Meares—had hoped it would. After a nervous greeting, the Mowachaht welcomed the party and allowed Brown to go ashore at Yuquot, their summer village and what had been the old Spanish settlement. There he found potato, cabbage, turnip, and raspberry plants, all probably introduced by the Spanish militiaman Captain Pedro de Alberni in 1790.

Brown returned to the mill at Alberni to dry out his clothes and reflect that, despite continuous pouring rain and cramped conditions, he had "seen strange things, wild men, new places." He had also acquired a working knowledge of Chinook Jargon, the trading lingua franca understood by most of the west coast peoples.

After just one day's rest, Brown took a canoe, some provisions, and two local paddlers to ascend the Somass River. Quassom, the elderly but renowned Hupačasath hunter, again agreed to come along as their guide at the going rate of a dollar per day. They had to portage around several sets of rapids and falls, where he saw groups of men spearing salmon. At the logging camp across the lake, he found his previous companion, Charles Taylor, who wanted to join the party to explore the main section of the lake Brown had called Sproat.

Brown had not brought blankets or sufficient food for the trip, so they went to sleep hungry, lying on moss in the open, listening to the howling of wolves. He returned to the logging camp to better provision for a longer expedition, and immediately set out again for the western end of the lake, some 12 miles (19 kilometres) distant, botanizing as they went. At the head they found a river flowing into it, which Brown named after Taylor. The river was flanked by snow-capped hills that Brown estimated to be 4,000 to 4,500 feet (1,219–1,370 metres) high. One of these was Klitsa Mountain, at 5,387 feet (1,642 metres). Brown dedicated some of these peaks to prominent members of his sponsoring group, but unlike Sproat Lake, and Stamp and Taylor Rivers, these names were not generally accepted—and, of course, all of the features already had traditional names given by the Indigenous Peoples. Brown's presumption of the right to impose personally chosen names for geographic features in inhabited but poorly mapped territory was not unusual in that era, but some of them were overruled.

They camped and explored the woods for some distance upstream, "discovering" the aptly named *Oplopanax horridus* (devil's club), a dreaded, spiny, poisonous shrub found near streams.[2]

Hordes of insect pests tormented them. Brown noted several species of trees, including a fine specimen of Sitka spruce, which he thought would please his sponsors in Edinburgh. But once again, he realized rather late that they had left all their food back in camp. Further exploration was not possible.

In his report to his sponsors, Brown made excuses for the limited collecting he had managed:

> On such excursions a botanist can only collect one or, at most, two specimens of each plant he meets with; and frequently, so limited are his means of conveyance in an almost trackless country, he can only take such as he has not seen in other places.... So many mishaps come over one's precious load before it gets to a place of safety, that sometimes I have been mortified to find, after a laborious excursion, the tangible results, notwithstanding all my care, consist of only a few blackened, indifferently dried specimens.[3]

Brown had hoped to reach Qualicum and Nanaimo by the already established trails, but the weather turned to several days of continuous downpour, making such a traverse impossible at that time. Brown returned to Victoria by the steamer *Thames*, having been away five weeks.

The morning after his return, as agreed, he made his first call to the governor, who listened to his adventures and findings with interest and relief at his safe return. Douglas furnished him with letters of introduction to colonial officials in the Fraser Valley, where Brown planned to go next.

The local press had followed Brown's travels, particularly his visit to the infamous Nootka territory. They interviewed him and even suggested that he give lectures, which he declined, being too busy. He publicly thanked Gilbert Sproat and the

FIG. 12-2 Devil's club, a source of discomfort for unwary travellers on riverbanks, but of great medicinal value to Indigenous Peoples. *Chromolithograph of a 1925 painting by Mary Walcott, from author's collection.*

Anderson Company for making the venture possible. Brown re-established contact with a few friends and collected specimens of the local flora, then in full bloom.

He found that the wet conditions in the field and aboard *Codfish* had rotted his collections, rendering them all but value-less. He had very little material to send to his sponsors but did make a long report of his trip and his plans for the future. He was disappointed that the mail service between Victoria and Edinburgh was unreliable—several of his letters had gone astray. After three weeks in Victoria, he set off for Washington State, where he hoped his collecting would be more successful, since it was the season for seeds. Unfortunately, when crossing a river in spate near Seattle, he lost most of his collection and returned to Victoria empty-handed.

During his travels Brown discovered just how the requirements of a plant collector were incompatible with a more general scientific reconnaissance. He operated on a very tight budget, depending on the goodwill of contacts for his logistic needs. A plant collector needed to be there at the time of flowering and again when seeds were ready to be dispersed. His collecting equipment was bulky: plant presses, vascula (carrying containers made of tin, usually cylindrical), and tree-climbing gear.

He had to convey it to and from remote, hard-to-access places, frequently under wet conditions. This required employing porters, known locally as "packers." Those packers also needed provisions, adding to the loads to be carried. Brown's collecting efforts inevitably suffered.

After a month in Victoria, he collected in the Fraser Valley, reaching as far as Lillooet before returning to the island in late September, just in time to collect pine cones. After another three weeks, he dispatched a small collection of seeds and dried plant material to his sponsors.

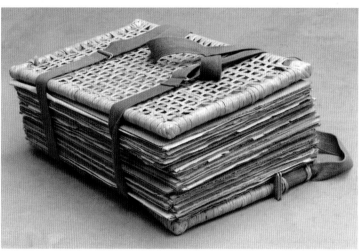

FIG. 12-3 (TOP) A botanist's vasculum, a metal case for carrying plant material from the field to base camp. *Photo courtesy of Jurgen de Vries, the Netherlands.*

FIG. 12-4 (BOTTOM) Cane plant press. Dr. Ching-Chang Chaung, curator of botany, Royal BC Museum, between 1973 and 1976, used this to dry specimens for later study and identification. *Courtesy of the Royal BC Museum and Archives, photo by author.*

Hoping that the weather would permit one more expedition to Great Central Lake to collect material from the magnificent trees he had seen earlier, Brown left for Alberni. He organized a canoe to take him the length of the lake and back, a journey of three days, during which he added several more species to his collection. Under continuous rain, he visited the Tseshaht islands in Barkley Sound, but by this time, late October, he found that all the seeds had been dispersed, so he returned to Victoria for the winter.

VICTORIA, WINTER OF 1863, AND A NEW OPPORTUNITY

Brown spent much of the next few months indoors, noting, "Raining every day, mostly all day, little frost." He spent the period researching and talking with knowledgeable locals on a variety of topics, including the history of previous explorations of the island's interior. He also found time for social activities like attending the theatre.

By this time his sponsors had let him know of their dissatisfaction with his performance. His finances must have been precarious. In that era, the cost of living in Victoria was high, and his first year's stipend of £80 would not have lasted long. He must have called upon his own, or borrowed, money to live and employ assistants—at a rate higher than he was earning. He despaired that lack of funding would prevent further forays, but he still nursed ambitions to make a general scientific study of the region.

Understandably, the relationship with his sponsor deteriorated over the winter and spring. Even by the middle of May 1864—after he had been on the project a full year—they had not received a single seed from him. The few that he had sent seem to have been lost. The tone of Brown's letters to them, emphasizing the importance of his scientific studies, struck them as arrogant and missing the point of their primary objective—supplies of seeds.

In December 1863 the Colonial Office in London announced that Douglas's term as governor of the two colonies would conclude. He was to be succeeded by two people: Arthur Edward Kennedy for Vancouver Island, and Frederick Seymour for British Columbia.

Kennedy arrived in Victoria on March 25, 1864, to find an urgent need to identify and exploit the natural resources of the island to provide funds for its administration. He challenged the local business community to fund an expedition of exploration. He would match two-for-one with government money any private funds raised. Brown immediately identified this as a heaven-sent opportunity to realize his goal of a properly funded, broad-spectrum mission of scientific enquiry, which he, of course, would lead.

He took immediate measures to enhance his profile: he quietly adopted the self-awarded title of "Dr." for his contacts with the press—presumably on the strength of his eight months as ship's surgeon aboard *Narwhal* while still an undergraduate. He sent the Scottish newspaper *Evening Express* a copy of his report to Edinburgh about the *Codfish* and the Sproat Lake trips. Then, on May 4, he submitted a 2,500-word article, under the pseudonym "GEOGRAPHICUS," to the Victoria newspaper *Daily Chronicle*. In it, he summarized what little was known of the interior of the island, and who had explored into it.[4]

In the article, Brown briefly referred to earlier explorations by various people from the HBC and Royal Navy. He did not mention the explorations made, and reported, by Eddy Banfield[5] in the very area into which he had recently ventured, the Somass Valley and lakes.

One-quarter of the article, however, was a "third person" account of how explorations by a certain Dr. Robert Brown "opened up a large portion of the island hitherto unexamined." He concluded the piece with a disavowal of having a "private object to serve," and an extravagant offer: "Should I be a member of the party, it will be as a volunteer and not as a salaried servant." Brown's motives for this are puzzling. Perhaps he hoped that the organizing committee would value the idea of saving one salary, particularly that of the leader, thereby improving his chances of inclusion. To make such an offer does seem reckless, given Brown's shaky financial state.

His application to lead the expedition, sent to the committee two days later, restated his offer to serve "free of expense to the Association." He also proposed to act as "Botanist, Zoologist & Geologist . . . [and] report on the topography, soil, timber & resources." He suggested that a professional surveyor should be appointed as "second officer."

On June 1, 1864, the committee announced the nine members for the Vancouver Island Exploring Expedition. They also appointed Robert Brown, Esquire, as its commander. Among the members was John Buttle. He was the sapper surveyor with the Boundary Commission, trained at Kew, who had assisted Dr. Lyall with his botanical collecting. Buttle, as did many from the ranks of the two military contingents, had opted to remain in the colonies when they returned to Britain, taking a land grant of 150 acres. Brown nominated him as assistant naturalist with the expedition, but neither of them managed much botanizing.

The expedition spent the rest of the summer exploring, usually in smaller groups, through the valleys of the Cowichan, Nitinat, Sooke, Leech, Nanaimo, Puntledge, and Stamp Rivers, as well as the streams entering Alberni Inlet. They frequently faced extreme difficulty and privation, but the team did manage to acquire a considerable amount of new geographic information.

As Brown was coasting in a canoe south from Port San Juan, he noticed a sandstone cliff at the mouth of Muir Creek. In it he found some bivalve fossils, and nearby, coal-bearing strata. Those fossil beds proved of interest to paleontologists in subsequent

FIG. 12-5   A slab of sandstone from the Sooke Formation at Muir Creek bearing 25-million-year-old marine fossils. *Photo by author.*

eras. The so-called Sooke Formation held not only many varieties of mussels, clams, barnacles, and snails, but also fossil teeth of two extinct species related to the manatee or sea cow, teeth and bones of other marine mammals, tarsus bones from two extinct species of cormorant, and many different plants.[6] Other members of the team found more coal seams along Brown's River, near today's Comox.

Most significantly, at the junction of the Sooke and Leech Rivers, they discovered deposits of placer gold, which triggered a minor gold rush. This entitled them to an earlier reward. The discovery also served to mollify members of the organizing committee who had grown unhappy with Brown's more general objectives about scientific knowledge. They viewed their investment, and therefore his purpose, as a simple search for gold. Brown declined the offer to lead the following season's expedition, recommending John Buttle for that role.

He sent a summary of his expedition to the Royal Geographical Society in London, which published it in its journal in 1865. He also had plans for his future; he would compile a popular version of his expedition, including illustrations by Frederick Whymper, an artist who had been with the team, and maps by Buttle.

Brown's other sponsors in Edinburgh remained unhappy with his performance. In early January 1865, he sent another consignment of seeds, dried plants, and samples of wood, all listed and described. He accompanied it with a letter tendering his resignation. Although disappointed with even this large batch, the association declined to accept his notice—to his relief, as he was running short of money. Fortunately, his share of the reward for finding gold, amounting to $400, came in the spring and enabled him to settle his debts.

Brown spent the summer of 1865 collecting plants in the western United States. He sent off another batch of seeds and specimens to the association. Unfortunately, when the consignment was opened, it was "a mass of corruption"—all rotten. This proved the final straw. His Scottish sponsors decided to not renew his contract. Brown remained based in Victoria for another year, making odd sorties that included a visit to Quatsino Sound from Fort Rupert, another to Haida Gwaii, and an unsuccessful attempt to climb Mount Baker. He returned to Scotland via California, across Nicaragua to the West Indies, and thence through the eastern United States and Canada's Atlantic provinces.

In 1867, Brown joined the mountaineer/artist Frederick Whymper[7] on an expedition out of Copenhagen to Greenland, collecting botanical and zoological specimens. He soon gained respect and a reputation as a "zealous naturalist." He became a prolific writer of articles on exploration and the natural sciences. The University of Rostock in Germany awarded him a doctorate for his report and book on the Vancouver Island exploration. For a while, he taught geography and science in high schools, and later became a professional journalist. The Linnean Society elected him a Fellow, and he served for several years on the council of the Royal Geographical Society.

BROWN PUBLISHES ON THE BIRDS OF VANCOUVER ISLAND

In 1868, the authoritative British ornithological journal *Ibis* published a paper by Robert Brown, FRGS (note: not "Dr."), entitled "Synopsis of the Birds of Vancouver Island." In it, he declared:

> During my various visits to and explorations of Vancouver Island I lost no opportunity of studying its ornithology; and though often unable to convey any specimens over the almost impenetrable wilds which it was my duty to traverse, I made full notes of the species, and resolved my doubts on return to civilization. I also examined every local collection of which I could hear.[8]

He started with a summary of "what little has been written on the birds of the country," mentioning Sclater's article about the birds collected by Prevost, and the lists provided in the books by Charles Forbes, John Keast Lord, and Charles Wood. His principal acknowledged resource was James Hepburn, "whose knowledge [of the birds of the North Pacific] is only equalled by his liberality in imparting it to his less fortunate brother naturalist." He referred to works of regional ornithology by Cooper and Suckley, Townsend, Nuttall, and Baird. He also mentioned meeting the HBC agent at Fort Rupert, Pym Nevins Compton, who was a keen observer and collector of birds.

In all, Brown listed 153 species of the island's known avifauna, arranged according to Baird's *Birds of North America* taxonomy. He appended another list of an additional 52 species "which ought to be looked for . . . as residents or visitants to the islands," which he had inferred from the regional literature. He gave, as the "local name" for the pileated woodpecker, the delightfully apt "logcock." He did not include the California quail, knowing it as introduced in Metchosin. The short-tailed albatross appeared listed among those species known to be present.

During his life, Robert Brown published more than 40 papers in many different learned journals, as well as hundreds of more popular articles. One of his last letters was in response to an enquiry by Dr. Charles F. Newcombe in 1894, requesting details of his years in this part of the world. In it, Brown noted:

> There was a time when everything about British Columbia interested me. I passed in that region some of the most instructive years of my early manhood at a time when I did not know six people in it who had any knowledge of or interest in Natural History.[9]

Who were the five that he did know? Possibilities include Dr. William F. Tolmie and his son, John W., James Hepburn, Pym Nevins Compton, and Alec Anderson.

FIG. 13-0   Blue-fronted jay, now known as Steller's jay. Seeing this bird convinced Georg Steller, a German botanist with the Vitus Bering expedition, that in 1741 they had reached the American continent. *Painting by Allan Brooks, from W.L. Dawson's* Birds of Washington, *1909.*

CHAPTER THIRTEEN

COLONIAL NATURALISTS, PART II

Two More Gentlemen-Naturalists of the Colonial Era

JAMES HEPBURN, ORNITHOLOGICAL AMATEUR

The naturalist James Hepburn, whom Brown effusively acknowledged in his "Synopsis," the list of birds, was a wealthy Scottish amateur, who was based in Victoria from 1860. Born in London in 1811, educated at Trinity College, Cambridge, and the Inner Temple, he had been called to the bar in 1842.[1] During his youth he became fascinated with natural history, a passion that stayed with him for life. In 1851, he arrived in California to manage a gold mining enterprise. The venture folded after three years, but Hepburn remained in San Francisco. He then devoted his time to collecting birds and other natural history specimens until 1860, when he decided to move to Vancouver Island, where he rented rooms on Pandora Street in Victoria.

From there he made collecting expeditions throughout the island, to the mainland, and to Washington State, frequently aboard ships of the Royal Navy. These included a voyage in 1862 to Sitka, then in Russian territory. For this he required a formal letter from Governor Douglas to his Russian counterpart, requesting both permission and protection. Douglas was

apparently quite taken with this personable member of his small community, a man of wealth who chose to devote his life to the study of natural history.

That same year, back in Victoria, Hepburn made an interesting acquisition:

> I once bought an adult male [short-tailed albatross] in its full white plumage from some Indians, who had caught it somewhere in the neighbourhood. I kept it upwards of a month. . . . it is now in my collection.[2]

Apparently, Indigenous Peoples occasionally sold these birds, usually immature, on the street in Victoria.

Hepburn established a good relationship with many of the naval officers and ships' surgeons stationed in Esquimalt, and several of them provided birds and eggs for his collections. Among them was Commander Daniel Pender, RN, who, after Captain G.H. Richards, RN, had returned to Britain with HMS *Hecate*, had continued the survey with HMS *Beaver*. Pender named two places Point Hepburn after his friend: one at the narrowest part of Grenville Channel, the other on the western side of Admiralty Island, in Southeast Alaska. Another such naval friend was Dr. David Lyall, then with the Boundary Commission, who, appreciating Hepburn's skills as a preparator, brought him several specimens that needed skinning, preserving, and stuffing, for his own collection.

Usually on his forays, Don, Hepburn's enormous black Newfoundland dog, served as both companion and assistant. Don was intelligent and a skilled retriever for even the most fragile specimens, even a hummingbird, or tiny eggs. Another frequent companion was Alec, another son of Alexander Caulfield Anderson. Anderson had noted that Hepburn was an accurate marksman, despite an injury to his right hand that required modifications to his gun and his aiming technique.

Hepburn died in Victoria from pneumonia in 1869, aged 58, and "was highly esteemed for his many good qualities"[3] and for being "a genial man and the type of a fine old English gentleman."[4] He left considerable property in San Francisco, together with most of his natural history collections. His family distributed a few specimens to friends and the Smithsonian Institution, but the bulk of them, including the short-tailed albatross bought in Victoria, went to Cambridge University Zoological Museum. Dr. J.W. Clarke, the curator, described the accession as

> one of unusual importance.... There are over 1500 skins, all in excellent condition, representing about 300 species, of most of which the series is extremely good.... They are accompanied by a large collection of eggs and nests carefully identified and authenticated.

There was also a small series of mammal specimens, including two complete skeletons of the northern fur seal, which Clarke noted were

of very great value, being so far as I know, the first ... acquired by any European Museum. Of Reptiles, Amphibia, and Fish, there is a considerable number preserved in spirit. Of Invertebrates, there is a very large collection, consisting of Mollusca in spirit, shells, crustacea, and insects.... It certainly consists of many hundreds of species. A small but important series of minerals, chiefly indicating gold.... There are also a few fossils. Mr. Hepburn's specimens have reached us in the most admirable condition and order.[5]

Earl Larrison, in his biographical article, calculated that, in all, Hepburn collected and catalogued 1,500 birds at various locations along the north Pacific coast between 1852 and 1868.[6] According to reports by Anderson, Hepburn continued collecting during the last 15 months of his life, but the results weren't included in his catalogue.

In the Newcombe family fonds in the BC Archives,[7] an anonymous and undated list analyzes Hepburn's specimens in various museums, and the associated catalogues and notebooks. Seemingly made in, or soon after, 1936, the list abstracts part of his ornithological collections (only the birdskins) made "1860–1869, on and near Vancouver Island." The analyst further subdivided the list into eight districts: Victoria (including Esquimalt), Saanich (including Prospect Lake), Salt Spring Island, Nanaimo, Fort Rupert (including Hardy Bay, McNeill's Harbour, Klickseewe, and Bentinck Arm),[8] Barclay Sound (including Somass and Alberni Canal), Neah Bay (including Strait of Juan de Fuca), and the Gulf Islands.

In all, the list's author[9] identified 352 specimens from 103 species. These included 13 skins of glaucous-winged gull, 18 of "Wrangel's or Marbled Auk" (now marbled murrelet), and 3 of short-tailed albatross. There seems to have been confusion between the listed 7 skins of "American Goshawk" (5 taken in Saanich), and the unlisted Cooper's hawk. In the accompanying

FIG. 13-1 A male Cooper's hawk, a fearsome predator of songbirds, well known in gardens throughout southern Vancouver Island. *Chromolithograph from a painting by Louis Agassiz Fuertes, 1902, from author's collection [image edited].*

notes, the goshawk is described as "not common on VI," "never seen the adult bird alive." Hepburn's specimens would seem to have been Cooper's hawk.[10]

Hepburn's name is acknowledged in one bird, the Hepburn rosy finch, an Alaskan subspecies, apparently taken near Fort Simpson (later Prince Rupert). Spencer F. Baird, taxonomist and curator of natural history at the Smithsonian Institution, with whom Hepburn had corresponded, named it so. Brown's list noted it, but Hepburn's own catalogue or notebooks did not.[11]

PYM NEVINS COMPTON, HBC TRADER, LINGUIST, NATURALIST, AND ARTIST

The other fellow bird enthusiast whom Robert Brown mentions having met and exchanged notes with was at the time chief trader for the HBC at Fort Rupert.[12] Pym Nevins Compton was born in 1838 into a respectable family of Quakers in Tottenham, just north of London, England. Details of his early life and education are uncertain, but by the time he was 20, Pym had travelled and had reportedly learned eight languages. He had also acquired business skills and an interest in natural history. In 1858 friends considered him fortunate to have secured a clerk's position with the HBC. His first job was as purser aboard the maiden voyage of the coal-fired sidewheeler *Labouchere*. The vessel was bound for Fort Victoria, destined to replace *Beaver* as the company's supply and trading vessel on the north Pacific coast.

As they were crossing the south Atlantic, nearing the Falkland Islands, they witnessed an extraordinary spectacle:

> A fight between the sperm whales & a very large kind of fish called "thrashers"; as far as I could judge they are from 10 to 20 feet long [3 to 6 metres] this & huge creatures jumping out of the water & coming down on the whales, they kill them, the whales spouting & lashing the water with their tails. The thrashers jumping entirely

out of the water is a very fine sight, very interesting for a landsman fond of natural history.[13]

From Compton's description of the hunting behaviour, it seems probable that the "thrashers" were a pod of transient killer whales.

On arriving at Fort Victoria, Compton continued aboard *Labouchere* to Fort Simpson. Near present-day Prince Rupert, it was the major coastal trading post of the HBC's New Caledonia region.[14] Compton remained there for two years, learning the fur-trading business and the Indigenous languages, Tsimshian and Chinook Jargon. He then rejoined *Labouchere* as trading clerk, and for the next few years he travelled the intricate coastline between Victoria and as far as Skagway at the north end of the Lynn Canal. It seems that James Hepburn sometimes travelled with them, using trading stops to collect specimens. Compton learned more local languages and their grammatical and linguistic subtleties. He began compiling a portfolio of watercolours of scenery, birds, and fish.

In July 1862, Compton married 14-year-old Kath McCauley at Fort Simpson in a service conducted by someone whose name is noted, but indecipherable, in Compton's bible.[15] The following year, the Reverend Edward Cridge revalidated the union in Victoria. Kath, his bride, travelled with him aboard *Labouchere*, as did the wives of the captain and the engineer.

Kath's first voyage after the marriage proved dramatic. While trading for a large collection of sea otter pelts with Tsimshian villagers at Point Couverdon, at the mouth of the Lynn Canal, a dispute arose over price. The situation suddenly turned into the seizure of the ship by a large party of armed men. The captain and Compton were both disarmed and held captive, while the rest of the crew, well armed but outnumbered 10 to 1, awaited orders from their skipper. After a few hours' standoff, the raiders

FIG. 13-2 Painting of a female big skate fish, by P.N. Compton, 1866. Known to commercial fishermen as "barn doors," mature specimens can reach 8 feet (2.4 metres) in length. *Image pdp05328-141 courtesy of the Royal BC Museum and Archives [image edited].*

released their hostages and left the ship, with the disputed furs still aboard. Steam was raised and *Labouchere* beat a strategic retreat, chased by canoes for 60 miles (96 kilometres). When they next called in to the village some months later, officers and crew kept watch for signs of hostility, but trading proceeded as if nothing had happened.

In a village at the northern end of Admiralty Island, near today's city of Juneau, Compton made a delicious discovery:

> Near the residence of [Aukequon] people are found some of the finest crabs I have ever seen & and do not know if they are found in any other place at least I have never seen them; The body is of a rounded form and about 8 inches [20 cm] in diameter the legs are about three feet [one metre] in length & and about an inch [2.5 cm] through filled with a firm fine flesh more resembling that of our lobster than of our English crabs, the claws are very small & altogether the animal looks like a huge crustaceous spider but far surpasses in flavour any of the crab tribe with which I am acquainted. [The animal was, of course, the now-much-sought-after Alaskan red king crab.][16]

In 1865, Compton took up a new responsibility, in command of Fort Rupert. During the next eventful year, Kath bore him a son, and Robert Brown and Hepburn separately visited, as did a party of gentlemen aboard another HBC steamer, *Otter*. They were on an excursion led by Dr. Tolmie, headed for Metlakatla and back. One of the party, writing under the initials "G.W.M.," posted a lengthy report in the *Daily British Colonist*,[17] recording:

> Arrived Fort Rupert at 3 o'clock where we were kindly received by Mr. Compton, HBC Agent, who is a fine fellow, good talker and quite hospitable; spent a pleasant evening.

In his later memoir, Compton noted differences in diet between various Indigenous groups:

> All these southern nations living on the coast subsist in great measure on dried & fresh clams & other shell fish, which are always procurable, whilst those living up inlets are obliged to depend more on dried salmon & roots of ferns & other herbs with the flesh of the mountain goat & of bears. The flesh of the seal also forms a staple article of food (& is by no means bad) as also that of the porpoise. Deer are very plentiful about the parts inhabited by this nation [Kwakwa̱ka'wakw] & the Elk (*Cerons Canadenses*) is found in abundance in Vancouvers Island. Berries of various species of *Rubus*; *Gaultheria* &c are also very plentiful & the Indians find good subsistence with comparatively very little trouble.[18]

Mr. and Mrs. Pym Compton, with their infant son, John, returned to Britain in early December 1866, aboard the company's ship *Prince of Wales*. According to the brief record in the HBC Archives, the following year Compton applied to rejoin the company, with unspecified result. He did return to Vancouver Island, however, for his bible records the birth of a daughter, Edith Mary, in December 1867, in Shirley (a tiny community west of Sooke). It seems that during the next few years, he began writing the manuscript of his memoir. He clearly intended it for publication, but it was never completed or published. The manuscript is in the BC Archives, together with a later transcript and his watercolour portfolio.

Much of the text covered ethnology and fine points of the linguistics of local languages, but it concluded with a section titled "Natural History." In this, he devoted most space to discussing the bears found in the region, including this intriguing paragraph:

The black bear is subject occasionally to albinoism like most of the other animals on this coast thus I have seen, White (black) bears, White otters, white racoons, white martens, and white minks, & this not from having changed colour in the severe winter as many of the skins had evidently been in the summer time and the fur was comparatively thin. The Indians set great value on the white bear skin & I was shown one which was supposed to be the skin of the paternal originator of the Tsimpseen race after the flood for their tradition of the deluge is that only a woman and a bear were saved on a mountain & that from this peculiar miscegenation the Tsimpseen race arose. I offered to purchase the skin in a moment of mercenary impiety but the price demanded was far beyond what it was worth so the Indian still ret[d] the hide of his ancestor.[19]

Had Compton's memoir been published, this reference to the spirit bear would have been highly significant. It would have been one of, if not the very first, to have drawn the attention of the scientific community to what was later identified as a geographically separate subspecies of black bear, the *Ursus americanus kermodei*. It was not described scientifically until 1905.[20] It is now British Columbia's official animal.

Compton's last completed paragraph of his memoir was also about bears. It included a culinary anecdote:

The flesh of the black bear when young and in the spring is very good, and I know a gentleman who not knowing what animal he was eating, made an enormous dinner off young roast bear & declared it was the best mutton he ever tasted. When properly cured the hams are excellent but the old bears meat is very strong.[21]

Little is known about the last few years of Compton's life. His bible recorded the birth of a second daughter, Katherine

FIG. 13-3 A mature male Roosevelt elk in velvet, photographed near Youbou on Cowichan Lake [image edited]. *Photo © courtesy of Malcolm Chalmers Photography.*

Chimo Koomah

HIII Chronoa Burnt...

FIG. 13-4 *Chimo Koomah* (spotted ratfish). Another painting from P.N. Compton's 1866 portfolio, of a very ancient species still common along the Pacific coast of North America. *Image pdp05325-141 courtesy of the Royal BC Museum and Archives [image edited].*

Milecent, in December 1867. He died in Victoria in August 1879, aged 41, to be survived by his daughter for less than a year. His naval friend, Daniel Pender, commemorated Compton's name by two geographical features on the regional chart: an island in Blackfish Sound, and a prominent point at the northern entrance to Wells Passage. Both are in the Broughton Archipelago, an area close to Fort Rupert that Compton would have known intimately.

Compton's artistic legacy, his portfolio,[22] contained many watercolours of natural history subjects. The birds he included were varied thrush, Harris's woodpecker, American robin, and bufflehead, each depicted as a specimen hanging from a nail, and the heads of a surf scoter and ring-necked duck. The fish were sockeye and chinook salmon, salmon trout (Dolly Varden char, in salt water and fresh, and as a brook trout), spotted ratfish, tube snout, grunt sculpin, snake prickleback, sand lance, and big skate. Compton also painted a squid that washed aboard *Prince of Wales* in the mid-Atlantic, during his return to England.

FIG. 14-0 *Mallards Heading South,* circa 1950. Shooting one of these reawakened botanist John Macoun's boyhood fascination with birds, an interest that remained for the rest of his long life. The American artist Louis Darling also illustrated books for Roderick Haig-Brown and for Rachel Carson's *Silent Spring. From a print in author's collection.*

CHAPTER FOURTEEN

JOHN MACOUN, PART I

"The Professor"

I N AUGUST 1866 THE TWIN colonies of Vancouver Island and British Columbia agreed to amalgamate under the name of the latter. On July 20, 1871, the united colony formally joined the Canadian Confederation as a province of Canada, with its capital in Victoria. One of the terms of that agreement was that Canada would construct a transcontinental railway to link the west coast with the rest of the Dominion. A year later the first reconnaissance survey for that route—the Canadian Pacific Railway (CPR)—commenced under the direction of their engineer-in-chief, Sandford Fleming. One of his team members was the botanist John Macoun, who arrived in Victoria in December 1872, having traversed the continent.

MACOUN'S START IN LIFE

Macoun was born in 1813 into an impoverished Protestant family in a village in County Down, in the north of Ireland. Fatherless from the age of six, he immigrated in 1850 with his mother and three siblings to Seymour in Upper Canada. They came for a new life and to be near his mother's brother, already farming

there. During his childhood and first few years in Canada, Macoun's only formal education was sporadic attendance at parochial schools. Nevertheless, before leaving for Canada he had managed to obtain a clerical job in Belfast, which opened up opportunities beyond manual labour.

He brought with him a stubborn self-confidence and devotion to the Protestant-Loyalist cause known as the Orange Order. He had also acquired a fascination, bordering on obsession, with the plant world, becoming an autodidact in botany. He also recalled that, as a boy,

> I loved to live outside and be going to out-of-the-way places and later it became a passion with me and I knew more birds' nests than any other boy in the country . . . being credited with the knowledge of one hundred and eight birds' nests in one spring.[1]

In Canada, Macoun expanded his general knowledge through reading, sufficient to teach in local, one-room schools, where qualified teachers were hard to find and retain. He began a wide and lifelong correspondence with such eminent botanists as Asa Gray, Sir William Jackson Hooker, and George Lawson, sending them plants he had collected. In Kingston, Ontario, he attended the inaugural meeting of the Botanical Society of Canada, instigated by Lawson, where Macoun's knowledge and enthusiasm were noted. He established many friendships with kindred spirits. In 1862 he married Ellen, and they began a family of five children, starting with the birth of a son, James. He continued reading avidly, including such new and disturbing works as Darwin's *Origin of Species*, Huxley, Lyall, and Humboldt. Much of this material conflicted with his profound religious beliefs.[2]

"THE PROFESSOR"

After successfully completing a semester at the Toronto Normal School (teacher training college), Macoun joined the staff at a larger school in the nearby Loyalist town of Belleville. Six years later he accepted an offer to teach natural history at Albert College in the same town. The college, which had recently been chartered as a university, arranged that an Episcopal college in New York grant him an honorary master of arts degree.[3] Macoun's reputation as an expert in the local flora and his network of distinguished fellow botanists in Canada and abroad smoothed this elevation to a professor's chair. For the rest of his long life, he was known as "the Professor." As an academic, the head of a young family, and a stalwart member of the Presbyterian Church, the Conservative Party, and the Orange Lodge, he now enjoyed respect and status in Belleville. Throughout his life, he abstained from liquor.

In his new position, Macoun learned, with envy, that a recent official exploring mission had included another botanist. Now he too was given an opportunity to collect farther afield. Lawson, teaching at Dalhousie University, invited and funded Macoun to join summer expeditions to the Muskokas and the north shore of Lake Superior. He revelled in such botanical fieldwork and wished his financial situation permitted him to devote all his time to it, but it did not. In the summer of 1872 his fortunes once more changed for the better. Setting out from Prince Arthur's Landing (now Thunder Bay) for a collecting foray on Lake Superior, and quite by chance, he encountered someone who would offer just such an opportunity: Sandford Fleming.[4]

As Macoun boarded the steamboat at Owen Sound, he "noticed a company of gentlemen in peculiar dress and thought they were English sportsmen."[5] One of them, "in semi-clerical costume," approached and chatted briefly. Then another of the group came up and did the same, asking questions, including about his current excursion. This person, "a fine looking man," introduced himself as Fleming, explaining that he and the group were just starting a survey for a new rail route across the prairies to the Yellowhead Pass and through the Rocky Mountains to the Pacific. He invited Macoun to join them as expedition botanist, which he accepted immediately.

The cleric had been the Reverend George Monro Grant, later principal of Queen's University in Kingston, and the team's secretary. He recorded how the enthusiasm of the new member of the group impressed him:

> At whatever point the steamer touched, the first man on shore was the Botanist, scrambling over the rocks or diving into the woods, vasculum in hand, stuffing it full of mosses, ferns, liverworts, sedges, grasses, and flowers, till recalled by the whistle that the Captain always fortunately sounded for him. . . . The sight of a perpendicular face of rock, either dry or dripping with moisture, drew him like a magnet, and with yells of triumph, he would summon the others to come and behold the trifle he had lit upon.[6]

FIG. 14-1 "The sight of a perpendicular face of rock, either dry or dripping with moisture, drew [the botanist Macoun] like a magnet." *Getty Images, #806380982.*

While fit and fearless, Macoun had had little preparation for the practical rigours of a long expedition: he was a poor horseman, had never used snowshoes or canoed, and seemingly could not swim. Nevertheless, as he had done with botany and other academic subjects, he set about acquiring all these skills, except the last. He got on well with most of his fellow team members, but almost came to blows with the photographer Horetzky during a later phase, as the two traversed the Rockies. Horetzky had been a clerk with the Hudson's Bay Company fur brigades and disparaged Macoun's abilities in wintertime travel through the forests. In the event, having separated at the Peace River to continue on different routes, and to the amazement of HBC's man in Victoria, the neophyte Macoun beat the seasoned Horetzky through to Victoria.[7]

The 3,000-mile (4,800-kilometre) journey from Winnipeg to Victoria had taken Macoun nearly five months. He had warned Albert College and his school that he might be late in returning from his summer's collecting. He was further delayed by having to debrief with Fleming in Ottawa. However, his standing with his employers and in the Belleville community had been enhanced by his entertaining accounts, published in the local paper. He was welcomed back to teaching while preparing his formal report. It was full of enthusiasm for the agricultural potential of the northern prairies and the Peace River district.

The luxuriant vegetation he had seen, and its variety of species, convinced him that these lands would grow excellent crops of grain, findings contrary to a previous report by John Palliser.[8] In this, Macoun erred somewhat by not considering the variability of seasonal rains. The region was subject to extended periods of drought, at times creating a disastrous dust-bowl effect. However, the report delighted the government, eager to promote settlement and a coast-to-coast confederation.

Macoun's report was distributed in early 1874. By then there had been a change of government, and the new one considered using an alternative route by the Peace River. The director of the Geological and Natural History Survey of Canada, Dr. A.R.C. Selwyn, planned to investigate the area in the summer of 1875. He admired Macoun's report to Fleming and felt that the writer would make a useful contribution to his own team. Selwyn asked Macoun if he would be interested in joining the upcoming expedition. Selwyn, in a reversal of his earlier view, now supported the creation of a new of position of staff botanist to the department, and funding was in place. Despite his immediate delight, Macoun took his time in responding. His own political views were known not to be in line with the new government, so he feared he might be denied the permanent position. Having been reassured by a well-connected friend, and with the full support of his employers for another extended absence from teaching, Macoun accepted. He asked Fleming and other influential contacts to lobby for his confirmation in the position. It proved just as delicate as he had imagined, but just one month before the Selwyn expedition was due to start, the new prime minister, Alexander Mackenzie, approved Macoun's appointment as the Survey's botanist.

THE DOMINION'S BOTANIST

At home, Macoun had to reassure his wife, Ellen, now mother to their five children, of his devotion despite his long absences. He made no-doubt-implausible promises that this would be the last time. He also took steps to bolster their financial situation and his standing as collector, by contracting with a popular London journal for regular instalments. Secretly, he also planned to acquire multiple specimens of the rarer plants he found, for sale to his wealthy collector contacts. He arranged with fellow botanist George Barnston, a retired HBC factor, for a letter of introduction to fur-trading establishments along their route. This would secure cooperative treatment in the remoteness of the Peace River.

Macoun set out for Victoria in mid-April 1875. Selwyn's plan was to retrace much of Macoun's 1872 route in reverse. In all, the expedition's route would cover about 8,000 miles (13,000 kilometres).

To get to Victoria, Macoun took trains via Laramie in Wyoming, across the Sierra Nevada to Sacramento, thence by sea, arriving in Victoria at the beginning of May. Even though his first few days there were rainy, the botany of the city and its surroundings impressed Macoun, particularly since his previous, brief visit had been in late December. He immediately started work:

> I carefully examined the flora in the vicinity of Victoria and collected on Cedar Hill and Mount Tolmie and many other localities. I noticed that, on these two mountains, there were many species that seemed peculiar to them but which plainly indicated that a part, at least, of the California flora had worked its way thus far to the north. . . . The climate is everything that can be desired and a large number of settlers with more advanced ideas of agriculture is alone required to make Vancouver Island what nature intended it to be—the Garden of Canada on the Pacific Coast.

He astutely observed

> what seems to me the cause of the mild climate of the Pacific Coast, and, in my opinion, it is precisely the same as that of Western Europe. A stream of warm water, a little to the south of Formosa . . . analogous to the Gulf Stream, is observed moving to the north east. [He was referring to the North Pacific Gyre that does bring water and associated weather systems to Vancouver Island's west coast.]

Macoun had only two weeks in Victoria to observe and collect, and during that time he noted that the plentiful apple blossom indicated that the season was three weeks ahead of Belleville. The locals also informed him that things were late this year. He continued:

> A careful examination of the map . . . will show the relationship existing between Europe and western America in the same parallels. . . . Both regions have their shores deeply indented by inlets. "Fiords," in the one case and "Canals" in the other. . . . There are four hundred miles [640 kilometres] of coastline in our western possessions north, with a forest growth superior to anything else in the world at present. Its shore is indented with multitudes of harbours, bays, and inlets teeming with myriads of fish. Its rocks and sands contain gold, iron, silver, coral and other minerals. And beside all this, a climate superior to England in every respect . . . and yet, men ask me what it is all worth? I answer: 'Worth more than Quebec, and all the Maritime Provinces thrown in', and skeptics may rest assured that the day is not far distant when my words will be found to be true.[9]

Macoun eventually arrived at Winnipeg in early November, after an arduous and nerve-racking journey. He returned to Belleville by the middle of that month, a total time away of eight months. Despite nearly starving, capsizing, and getting totally lost while on his own in the vast, featureless landscape, he had collected and brought back more than 20,000 botanical specimens during the expedition. What he had witnessed had reinforced his opinion of the immense agricultural potential of the northern prairies. He met Prime Minister Alexander Mackenzie in Ottawa but failed to convince him of its merits. To cap it all, after requesting and receiving an exhibition of specimens, Selwyn informed him that the department's budget

FIG. 14-2 John Macoun in 1895 showing a bird's nest with eggs to a young friend. *Photo from Library and Archives Canada, MIKAN 3193103.*

could not afford his services after the end of the year.

In his report to the director, Macoun listed 12 trees and 40 herbaceous plants in flower in and around Victoria. He particularly admired the camas, shooting stars, and fawn and chocolate lilies "for the brightness of their colour and beauty of their forms."[10]

He continued gathering energetically throughout the expedition; even during the rain he was busy collecting mosses. In the evenings he prepared the acquired specimens for preservation and examination. For this, he had brought a large quantity of sheets of absorbent paper on which to mount his specimens. He carefully cleaned and arranged each one to display its significant characteristics, noting the location in and date on which it was collected, and covering it with another sheet of the paper. Each such "sandwich" would be piled with others within a pair of boards strapped tightly to flatten and dry the included specimens, and the whole wrapped in waterproof material for transportation. He needed to change the papers frequently as they absorbed the plants' moisture. A botanist in the field was kept extremely busy even when not actively acquiring plant material.

Macoun wrote to Hooker at Kew, giving details of the 1875 expedition and his collection. He explained that one of the official sets would be sent to Kew, but he requested help in disposing of the additional specimens,

all of which I would like to sell or exchange for botanical works or botanical specimens of European plants. My great want is books or money to purchase them.... For many years I have been working to obtain a knowledge of the Flora of the Dominion, a new want stares me in the face—botanical literature. My only way to obtain it is by the above method and hence my appeal to you.[11]

For the next few years Macoun continued teaching at the college and making collecting expeditions during the summer. By 1877 his eldest son, James—by then 14 years old and a budding naturalist—was able to accompany him and became his companion in the field for some years after that. The political situation changed again with the election of 1878, with a new Macdonald government in power. Between 1879 and '89 the department's official title was the Geological and Natural History Survey of Canada.

The new minister for railways, Mackenzie Bowell, his old mentor from Belleville and later prime minister, called for more surveys to be mounted and invited Macoun to lead one of them as Explorer in the Northwest. He led exploring parties into the prairie country for each of three years, starting in 1879. In 1881 Sir John A. Macdonald declared Macoun's position official, with the title of Dominion Botanist.

During his 1880 season Macoun shot a mallard, which reawakened his boyhood interest in birds, and he began to study them in earnest. As he had done with plants when a boy, he made field notes on the species he encountered: "Because I had no books with the descriptions in, I wrote out descriptions and then hunted them up in books afterwards."[12]

On subsequent field trips, he added the collecting of birdskins to his work, donating them to the department's growing museum. The year 1882 proved a momentous one for Macoun: he published a book, *Manitoba and the Great Northwest*,[13] and assumed his duties in Ottawa. He moved his family, extensive herbarium, and growing collection of birdskins to the capital, where he gave well-attended public lectures. That same year, he was among the 20 esteemed men of arts, science, and learning invited to be founding members of the Royal Society of Canada. He began preparing his monumental *Catalogue of Canadian Plants*.[14]

Two years later, the British Association[15] decided to hold its annual event in Montreal, sponsored in part by the Canadian government. The CPR then invited the group, as their guests, to take the train as far west as construction of the line had then reached. W.C. Van Horne, the president of CPR, requested that Macoun attend as an authority on the prairies.

Accordingly, Macoun joined the party, nearly 100 strong, at Owen Sound, keeping a low profile at first. His wide range of scientific knowledge, however, soon gained the attention and respect of the eminent visitors, who included the president of the British Ornithological Union, and a senior botanist from Kew. The party managed to get as far west as Castle Mountain, near Lagan (now Lake Louise) before returning. Macoun wrote, "I had a wonderful time and made many friends who aided me in years to come."[16] The contacts he had made proved valuable much sooner than he imagined.

At the end of April 1885, continuing budget limitations obliged Selwyn to again lay off Macoun and several other staff members. Having seen the Rocky Mountains briefly the previous year, Macoun decided to devote that summer to returning privately and botanizing the region more thoroughly. With his younger son, William, he took the Grand Trunk Railway to Calgary by way of Chicago. From there they made their way to Canmore, Alberta, where they collected plants and butterflies among the mountains, and thence to Golden and the Columbia River Valley.

They met the CPR crews constructing "the Loop" of tunnels under the summit of the Selkirks, near Rogers Pass, and befriended the company's head of western operations. He, Mr. Marpole, was about to travel in his private railcar to the eastern limit of construction at Biscotasing in Ontario, to meet the governor general. Marpole invited the two Macouns to accompany him to Ottawa. Macoun later marvelled at having

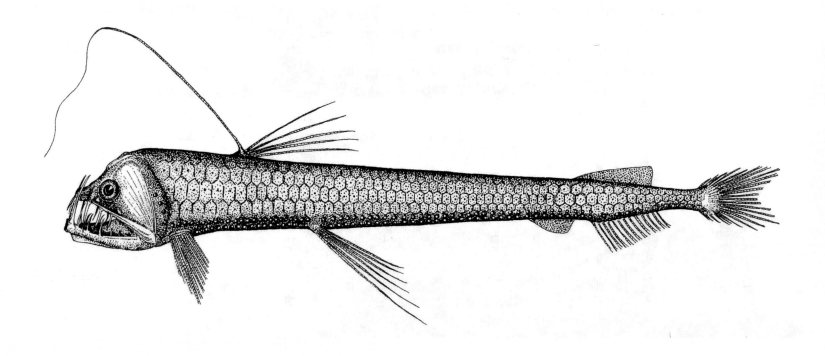

FIG. 14-3 The Pacific, or fanged, viperfish, *Chauliodus macouni*. Little is known about them, since they are oceanic, found at depths between 550 and 2,200 fathoms (about 1,000 and 4,000 metres). The longest found to date measured 11.4 inches (29 centimetres). *Drawing by S.L. Bourque from the* Encyclopedia of Canadian Fishes, *1995*.

seen forests of trees "so tall that birds could not be killed with an ordinary shotgun," trees that, within his remaining lifetime, were lost to logging and fire.

Macoun returned from his vacation to find the department preparing for the Colonial Exhibition in London the following year. He was to organize a display of timber and a selection from the herbarium as part of the Canadian pavilion. He had not been included in the initial delegation to accompany the exhibit, which displeased him. He contacted some of his friends in the British Association, indicating that they might exert some influence to have him sent. This they did. Sir Charles Tupper, the high commissioner in London, was "deluged with letters from eminent literary and scientific men of England[17] saying that Macoun's presence would be very acceptable." His ploy worked, and Macoun's name was added to the list.

In the event, his influential friends listed him as a "distinguished visitor," and as such he was invited to the most significant functions and aristocratic stately homes. He even lunched with the president of the Royal Society. This in turn led to his attending the grand dinner of the Inner Temple, where he met the Marquis of Lorne, and the brother of the then governor general, Lord Lansdowne. He was also given a private showing of the treasures of the library of Hatfield House by the Marchioness of Salisbury. During the royal visit to the Canadian pavilion, Macoun chatted about birds with the Duke of Argyle,[18] "a typical Scotsman with red hair and a red face." The young lad who had left rural County Down had ascended the social ladder quite considerably.

The Irish National Party invited the Canadian and Indian delegations to Dublin. Home rule for Ireland was the topic of the day and about to be debated in Westminster. Macoun, still a loyal monarchist, was opposed to the concept, but, alone among the delegation, accepted the invitation. He had already planned a trip to Ireland to visit his boyhood home. After sightseeing and formal events in Dublin, he went to Maralin, the home village he had not seen for 36 years. He stayed with a distant relative, also named John Macoun, with whom he kept in contact for many years afterward, and whose daughter would later marry William, Macoun's younger son.

When Macoun returned to Ottawa in 1876, he realized that his family had grown up, but they all remained close. That year he served as president of the Ottawa Field Naturalists' Club.[19] In December of the same year, the Linnean Society elected Macoun as a Fellow; this confirmed full acceptance by his international botanist peers.

FIG. 15-0 The scalyhead sculpin with prey. This species was initially named after Macoun, but renamed *Artedius harringtoni*. Image © Jackie Hildering, *www.TheMarineDetective.com.*

CHAPTER FIFTEEN

JOHN MACOUN, PART II

"The botany of Vancouver Island is the most interesting in the Dominion . . ."

—John Macoun's letter to C.F. Newcombe, March 18, 1890

I N 1886, HAVING BEEN AWAY from his desk for eight months, Professor John Macoun turned his attention back to his major project, compiling and shepherding to publication the *Catalogue of Canadian Plants*. The first volume, in three parts, would be more than 600 pages long, but the work was nowhere near completion. His botanical expeditions had already ranged over a vast area, from the Bay of Fundy to the Rockies, but he had not yet collected in the far west. He needed to devote time to Vancouver Island and the rest of British Columbia. He elected to spend the summers of 1887 and 1889 remedying those deficiencies.

He chose to visit the island first. In April he and his son William[1] boarded the CPR at Ottawa and travelled the length of the newly completed track to Port Moody, and from there went by steamer to Victoria. On his brief visit in 1875, Macoun had befriended the Reverend George Taylor, who had taken him to some key locations for botanizing. The friendship renewed, Rev. Taylor invited the visitors to stay with him.

Soon after his arrival, the professor gave a press interview, in which he explained the purpose of his visit and said that he would "pay particular attention to the character and extent of [the island's] timber and . . . make a collection of plants, birds and mammals." In this connection, he commended the wisdom of the government in establishing a provincial museum,[2]

> where people who come to the province can see what is in it instead of having to travel over the country to get the information. . . . The fruit growing industry should soon become one of the most extensive and profitable of the coast. The soil and climate are particularly adapted for it.[3]

The Macouns and their host again investigated the nearby places of good botanical potential: Gordon Head, Mount Tolmie, Cedar Hill (by this time, officially called Mount Douglas), and Lost (now Blenkinsop) Lake, finding many species that, with increased settlement and farming, became rarities, such as the endemic Macoun's meadowfoam.

Rev. Taylor and his archdeacon had planned to visit the Comox Valley by the newly opened Esquimalt and Nanaimo

The man who first guided Professor Macoun around the Victoria region in 1875 and '76 was the Reverend George Taylor, MA, FRSC, FZS.[4] In addition to his busy schedule ministering to the parishes of St. Luke and St. Michael, Taylor was an avid and knowledgeable amateur naturalist.

Born in Derby in the English Midlands into an educated, devout family, he succeeded at the local grammar school and planned to go on to study mathematics at Cambridge University. Instead his father, a mining engineer, persuaded him to follow him in that profession. Despite disliking the life underground, he persevered until qualified. Throughout his boyhood, natural history, particularly entomology, fascinated him, and, having fulfilled his father's directive, he took a job in the local museum. There he specialized in conchology, the study of mollusc shells, in which he became a recognized expert.

In 1881 he decided to visit his cousin in Victoria to explore new opportunities, and decided to stay there. While he had some private money, coal mining in Nanaimo seemed a good place for him to establish a viable living. The coalfields so appalled him that he soon returned to Victoria. He needed respectable employment that allowed time for natural history.

His solution was to take holy orders. In 1886 he was ordained as a priest, the first to do so in British Columbia. He then devoted much of his life and resources to building churches and associated congregations in Saanich, Ottawa, Nanaimo, and their surrounding communities.

In 1885 he married Bessie.[5] During his training and early years as a priest, he actively pursued his other great interest, entomology. He became a corresponding member of the Entomological Society of Ontario, submitting papers for its journal[6] and building a close friendship with the club's founder, James Fletcher, the Dominion Entomologist and Botanist. In

FIG. 15-1 Rev. George Taylor, distinguished entomologist and the first curator of the Marine Biological Station, Departure Bay, now part of the Science Division, Fisheries and Oceans Canada. *Portrait courtesy of Fisheries and Oceans Canada. Photo by author.*

1887, the lieutenant-governor of BC appointed Taylor as honorary provincial entomologist. After moving to Ottawa, he joined the very active Ottawa Field Naturalists' Club.

After less than two years, the Taylors returned to Victoria and another new parish. In 1890 he was a charter member of the Natural History Society of British Columbia. Four years later, the Royal Society of Canada (RSC) elected him as a Fellow. He then moved to Nanaimo to take on a "turbulent" parish, and subsequently lived on Gabriola Island, and then in Cedar and Wellington, establishing parish churches in the region while continuing his natural history avocation.

In 1901 he became the first president of the Entomological Society of British Columbia and four years later was elected to the BC Fisheries Commission. In 1907, he made the case to the RSC for a biological research station on the Pacific coast,[7] reinforcing this concept with a paper to the BC Fisheries Commission.[8] The federal government responded by voting funds to build a research facility at Departure Bay in Nanaimo. Upon its completion in 1908, Taylor was appointed curator,[9] responsible for supervising scientific work by visiting specialists. Early on, he hosted Macoun's team.

The following year he welcomed a large group from the British Association for the Advancement of Science, accompanied by the Canadian prime minister[10] for a two-day visit. Macoun, who had been working at Ucluelet, came to join the company.

That same year, Taylor suffered his first heart attack, which obliged him to give up his parish work in order to devote himself to science. He founded the British Columbia Academy of Science in 1910, declaring:

> We are all helping to increase the round total of human knowledge; and that I believe is one of the highest and noblest objects which mortal man can strive to attain.

Two years later, he died from a massive heart attack, and was buried in Nanaimo.

During his career as a natural historian, George Taylor reported to the RSC 250 species of land and freshwater shells, and 492 species of Pacific marine molluscs. His personal collection of limpets was the largest in the world, and his was one of the largest general collections of land and water shells (7,000 species) in Canada. An editor of the RSC's *Transactions* for 1895 noted:

> Any attempt to summarize Mr. Taylor's labours in various fields is impossible.

FIG. 15-2 Macoun's meadowfoam, now listed as a species at risk, is endemic in seasonally wet microhabitats within Garry oak ecosystems. Recovery efforts are underway at sites on southeastern Vancouver Island. *Photo © courtesy of Matt Fairbarns, Aruncus Consulting.*

Railway, and Macoun felt he should go with them. As they paused at Nanaimo, while awaiting the steamer to carry them north, he noted the prominent nearby peak, Mount Benson. He decided that he and William should explore it at some later opportunity.

Macoun collected plants from different altitudes as he climbed, noting the correlation of species and elevation.[11] He also spotted, with pleasure, the snow-covered Mount Arrowsmith, adding it to their list for future climbs. The steamer's captain informed him that a local innkeeper, "Qualicum Tom," would be able to guide them across the island to Alberni and the neighbouring mountain.

The Comox settlement was then surrounded by impressive, old-growth forest giants. The Macouns made several botanical forays in the vicinity before returning to Victoria. They explored and collected on Salt Spring Island, climbing Mount Erskine. They also climbed Mount Finlayson near Goldstream, and Mount Prevost at Somenos near Duncan.[12]

After a few weeks, they returned to Nanaimo for the attempt on Mount Benson. At the time, a "pathless forest extended nearly all the way to the summit." A farmer near Wellington, who was also a hunter and had been up to the top, agreed to guide them. Leaving the farm at first light, they

> climbed through a forest of beautiful pine and fir in which the underbrush was Salal and it was with great difficulty we could force our way through it.... [On the top, they had] a most glorious view. What I had never seen before nor since was a thunder-storm below us along the slope of the mountain. In other words, we were in bright sunshine on the summit and, 1,000 feet below us, the thunder was rolling.[13]

They went to Qualicum and met "Tom," who agreed to take them to Mount Arrowsmith. Four of them set out in his canoe:

Tom, his son, and the two Macouns, up the Little Qualicum River as far as the falls. A trail through the forest led to where a new road was being cut to link Nanaimo and Alberni that made the going easier. A fire in the canopy gave Macoun some concern, but Tom reassured them that it would pose no threat once they had reached Cameron Lake. They carried provisions for four days, but minimal camp gear. After passing an uncomfortable night plagued by mosquitoes, they reached the foot of Arrowsmith.

It became clear to Macoun that Tom was inexperienced in planning the ascent of a mountain, so he took the lead. Despite his age, 74, he was the fittest of the party and had to wait for the rest to join him on an open plateau near the top with clear access to the summit. Leaving them to make camp and their meal, he went to the top, "a mile, above the sea,"[14] to watch the sun setting over the cloudless Pacific.

> As I stood there, each summit was bathed in sunlight, the mountains on the mainland also shone out, and the mountains to the northward of the Island stood out boldly also. Gradually darkness seemed to walk in the light and put out the light and, as the darkness increased and rose on the mountain slopes, we were in twilight.[15]

Returning to Qualicum, they immediately made a second excursion to climb Mount Mark overlooking Horne Lake. It was covered in fog, but some collecting was possible. A third foray took them by an old trail across the same lake to Alberni. It proved easier going than the previous two outings. Once there, Tom secured a canoe for them to paddle upstream to Stamp Lake, which provided fruitful botanizing, as did the meadows around the old sawmill at the head of the inlet. Tom rented a larger canoe to carry them down Alberni Canal to Barkley Sound. On seeing the huge swells rolling in from the ocean, the usually fearless professor acknowledged his limits and chose to remain on an island, collecting, while the others braved the seas to visit Cape Beale.

Once more back in Qualicum, Macoun thanked Tom "for his great care and kindness," and returned to Victoria. At the end of August, he became one of the first to travel from Vancouver to Ottawa without changing trains. He came away from the trip justifiably well pleased with his summer's achievement. During their 1887 season on Vancouver Island, a little over four months long, Macoun and his younger son William had assembled several different collections. The annual report of the Geological Society of Canada, 1887–88, recorded

> 56 bird species in 90 skins, also a large number of marine shells and other *invertebrata*, and of land and fresh water shells, two mammals [including an adult female puma], and fifteen hundred species of plants.

Macoun had also started keeping notes on bird distribution and migration patterns as well as other aspects of natural history. He wrote:

> I may say that the botany of Vancouver Island is the most interesting in the Dominion.... There is no better field in Canada than [the] island for collecting interesting things.... I discovered a new species of fish at Oak Bay.[16]

To round off a highly satisfactory year for the professor, the federal minister of the interior Thomas White—without consulting the Geological Survey's director, Selwyn—appointed Macoun as assistant director and naturalist. This effectively gave him responsibility for enumerating the flora, and now also the fauna, of the northern half of North America.

Unfortunately, budgetary restrictions continued, exacerbated by political turmoil. In the field, Macoun could call upon only the resources of a part-time assistant. Back at the Geological Survey's museum, the herbarium was in good hands, those of his elder son, Jim. The zoology collections, particularly birds, however, neglected because of tight budgets, suffered from damage by mould and insects. Storage and display space were nowhere near sufficient. Internal rivalry and resentment about Macoun's promotion did not help matters.

He resolved problems of difficult identification and taxonomy by sending material to specialists in the United States and Europe, who were helpful and grateful but used the findings for their own purposes and credit. Nonetheless, a great many species new to science were identified from his collections, and *macounii* frequently appeared as the species taxonym. He also maintained correspondence with a wide circle of advisers. One of his most reliable contacts was his American counterpart, C. Hart Merriam, who was very knowledgeable about the care of zoological specimens. Merriam, in turn, valued Macoun's field data from north of the border for his study on continental faunal distribution.

The following summer, 1888, Macoun's eldest daughter, Clara, married a prominent land surveyor, Arthur O. Wheeler, an Irishman who specialized in working among the highest mountains. They would soon move to New Westminster, BC, so he could survey the BC mountains using a new photographic technique. Macoun felt he owed his wife, Ellen, and their two other daughters a long-overdue holiday together, and they all went to Prince Edward Island. He could pass the days happily botanizing and birding, returning each night for family and social time.[17] William did not join them, as he had taken a job at the federal government's Central Experimental Farm as assistant to the director. He did well in this career, going on to become Dominion Horticulturalist and an expert in cultivating apples.

Jim Macoun also missed the family vacation. He was working as the naturalist in a field party. It happened that during their work, he discovered a man who would become an invaluable aide to the Macouns for the next 30 years: Bill Spreadborough.

On the basis of Jim Macoun's recommendation, his father employed Spreadborough for the 1889 season. Starting from Vancouver, the three—father, son, and field assistant—followed the CPR line eastward for 400 miles (644 kilometres) to Eagle Pass, with a side trip down Okanagan Lake. Macoun noted, "This being the first season of my duties of naturalist, we devoted much more time to general natural history than to botany." Nevertheless, the prodigious trio collected over 1,400 species of plants (in 15,000 specimens), 141 species of birds and mammals (431 skins), nearly 100 reptiles, and several hundred insects. The professor concluded his report with a warning that his room was so overcrowded with flammable material, it constituted a grave fire hazard. At the end of the year, John Macoun suffered his first attack of angina. He was soon up and working again, but the warning signs were there.

The following year, the three returned to the BC interior. In 1891, James was needed on a special mission connected with the fur seal industry, but the other two returned to the west of Canada, exploring the mountains around Banff. For the 1893 season the professor chose to return to Vancouver Island, sending Spreadborough on ahead. As he explained in his 1892 report:

Our knowledge of the birds of the Pacific coast and islands is very scanty, and before publishing any catalogue of these, it would be desirable to devote at least another summer to collecting and observing in that region.

BILL SPREADBOROUGH

A faithful, long-term field assistant to John and James Macoun, William (Bill) Spreadborough[18] was born in Surrey in southern England in 1856 and brought as a child to the remote woodlands of eastern Ontario. As the elder son of a pioneer farming family, he attended log schoolhouses and the local church. He also learned practical outdoor skills, and about the local vegetation and wildlife at first hand. He later worked in logging gangs and with seasonal survey parties. He married in 1883, but two years later his wife died in childbirth, soon followed by his infant daughter, to his profound grief.

In 1888 he took a job as camp cook with a government survey party mapping rivers and lakes in northern Manitoba. Another member of that party was the naturalist James Macoun, who recognized that the cook had an aptitude for natural history, knew the woods, and was an excellent shot. He took Spreadborough under his wing and taught him to prepare the skins of birds and small mammals. James recommended Bill to his father, John, who employed him the following year in his own party. Thus was formed a closely bonded and highly effective team of field naturalists. While the two Macouns botanized, Bill focused on collecting, skinning, and preserving birds and animals, while also managing their camp and sustenance.

He travelled from his home in Ontario each year to work with summer field parties, although not always with the Macouns. The professor tried, unsuccessfully, to get the department to give Bill a permanent position. In the off-season, necessity obliged him to take odd jobs. Sometimes Macoun employed him to come early to the work area, as the advance man establishing camp. This put him in a position to begin collecting the spring migrants. At the close of the 1901 field season, he decided to remain in Victoria for the winter, and thereafter made his home in Esquimalt.

His skills in operating in Canada's remote forests were exceptional. These included selecting sheltered spots for a camp and deftly using an axe to furnish it with tent poles, seats, a table, fir boughs for bedding, and firewood. His camp meals were legendary, often using meat from the day's collected specimens. Over an evening fire, he proved an enthralling teller of yarns from his wealth of experience.[19]

From the Macouns Bill learned, and retained, the scientific names of mammals, birds, fish, amphibians, crustaceans, insects, and other invertebrates sought by the scientists, and understood how they needed to be preserved. He had a remarkable memory for where and when the specimens had been collected. At times, he would lose the feeling in his fingers from handling the arsenic used for preserving specimens. In 1892, the accidental discharge of Bill's shotgun killed Nathan White, a wagon driver. Although exonerated, he felt responsible and supported the widow and family.

The *Daily Colonist* of August 12, 1897, carried[20] a minor but intriguing news snippet about a W.T. Spreadborough. Apparently, eight years earlier he had deposited $2,000 with the Bank of British North America in Victoria, and he had "never drawn a dollar of it or asked any questions about it." It poses a curious mystery about a man renowned for his good memory, and for whom a sum that size would have been a fortune. One must hope that he remembered it a few years later when he moved to Esquimalt. In 1914 he married for the second time, to Janet Dumbreck, a Scottish immigrant.

After the deaths of James Macoun and his father in 1919 and '20, Bill declined to work with other field parties, and found employment with Esquimalt Township until he was obliged to retire in 1931. Fearing that his savings were insufficient for two, he took his own life. Taverner wrote to a friend, "Too bad, poor old Spreadborough."[21]

Macoun's daughter Sara was now living in New Westminster. He brought his wife and their youngest daughter, Nellie, out by train to visit Sara, while he, with friend Frank Wallbridge of Belleville, joined Spreadborough on the island. They had a perilous passage over the Rockies, being locked in by avalanches across the track, behind and ahead. They had to be rescued and make the final descent in a special train.

Macoun met up with Spreadborough in Victoria, to find he had been successful in collecting birds and mammals. The initial plan, exploring the mountains around Comox, was not possible because of the heavy snowpack, so the two men turned their attention to the sea. They dredged and collected invertebrates and seaweeds over the extensive tidal flats around Cape Lazo. They did similar work around Nanaimo, Victoria, and Sooke, before Macoun took a month's respite stop in Victoria, where his wife joined him, seeing "our friends, the Tolmies and others."[22]

Charles F. Newcombe, MD,[23] took Spreadborough to Clayoquot Sound and Stubbs Island, where they collected 134 species of shells, "many of which were of great interest and some peculiarly so." On their return journey, they paused to make similar collections at Burrard Inlet and New Westminster. In all, during the 1893 season they gathered 1,400 species of land plants and seaweeds. They noted about 150 species of birds and collected nearly 400 skins of birds and small mammals, plus a "very large and valuable collection of marine invertebrate shells, and many species of crabs and other articulates." In addition, Newcombe presented the Geological Survey of Canada with 21 Cretaceous fossils from the Comox River, 20 post-Tertiary fossils, and some rare recent shells from Vancouver Island and the coast of BC.

The Macouns did not return to Vancouver Island until 1908, but Spreadborough came to collect in 1907. He returned with 94 skins of mammals, 172 of birds from the west coast, and a few

FIG. 15-3 Macoun (centre) with Bill Spreadborough (right) and "Bugs" Young, at Ucluelet in 1909, inspecting part of their haul of 50 sea urchins. *Geological Survey of Canada 2021772 [image edited].*

eggs from the Victoria region. The professor and his son Jim had been occupied in preparing exhibits for the new Victoria Memorial Museum in Ottawa. They were also completing various catalogues of Canadian flora and fauna for publication. Because of increasing interest in Canada's forest resources, much of their time was devoted to a new project to assemble a collection of photographs and examples of trees for inclusion in the museum.

At the beginning of April 1908, Spreadborough again arrived in Victoria to collect the spring-flowering plants, list the incoming migrant birds, and collect the nests and eggs of 24 species. He also obtained 19 specimens of rare birds and 146 eggs. Macoun arrived at the end of May and they began work on two additional projects. They sought specimens of forest trees for the new museum, and they collected fauna and flora of the sea for the newly established biological research station at Nanaimo. This was the concept initiated by Macoun's long-time friend, the Reverend George Taylor, who was now the station's first curator.

The professor and Spreadborough travelled to Nanaimo to work on both projects. Joining them was an expert on the preservation of sea stars and similar organisms, Charles "Bugs" Young. Taylor placed the resources of the station at Macoun's service. These included accommodation, a boat and dredging equipment, and an extensive library, as well as the guidance of some resident specialists.

Spreadborough collected five-foot sections from 17 species of tree. He assisted Young in collecting "156 starfishes [sea stars], 195 crabs of various kinds, over 100 sponges of various kinds, a fine collection of barnacles, over 50 bottles filled with specimens in spirits and a very large collection of marine shells." At night, Young went out with lamp and net, eventually gathering 600 specimens of moths and beetles. Macoun and Spreadborough

also collected 1,100 species of flowering plants, about 400 species of cryptogams,[24] and nearly 150 species of seaweeds. Macoun noted in his summary:

> It will be seen by the above that we have made an excellent beginning, and another season's work will enable me to write an exhaustive report on the whole fauna and flora . . . [of Vancouver Island], provided I have the assistance of Messrs. Spreadborough and Young.

Selwyn had earlier approved the concept of such a report and agreed that a team of three should return to the island the following year.

It proved a wise decision. The summer of 1909 generated numerous additions to a range of lists of Vancouver Island and Canadian species, including many that were new to science. Toward the end of April, they came to Ucluelet, working from a house with a wharf,[25] intending to study the marine fauna of Barclay Sound and vicinity. They all collected, first at low tide and then by progressively deeper dredging to 35 fathoms (64 metres). They realized their collections would reveal much about the food of the large fish abounding in these waters. The professor took some time out to visit the biological station at Nanaimo and meet with the visiting scientists from the British Association.

During their four months' activity on the west coast, the three collectors amassed the astounding totals of

> 400 starfishes, 400 crabs and shrimps, 100 fish, 500 isopods, 90 tunicates and ascidians [sea squirts and their allies], 250 sponges, 150 hydrozoa, 4 jellyfish, 37,927 shells, 850 insects, 9 birds, 2 mammals, 15 toads etc., 150 seaworms, 50 sea urchins, 75 seaslugs, 35 barnacles, 45 polyzoa [Bryozoa or moss animals], 25 actinozoa [stony coral], 10 sea-spiders, and 15 anemones . . . [and

FIG. 15-4 Macoun with ornithologist Percy Taverner in 1911. Note that the latter is equipped with old-style, Galilean field glasses. Although prismatic binoculars had been invented, they did not become readily available until after the First World War. *National Museums of Canada J5535 [image edited].*

thousands of plant specimens from] 361 [species of] flowering plants, 226 mosses, 123 lichens, 134 liverworts, and 164 seaweeds.

Macoun sent some of these lesser-known life forms to American taxonomists for identification, but the bulk of the work fell on himself and his very few assistants. Seventeen of the shells were new species. One of the fishes was so obscure that a new genus had to be created. It was named *Pterygiocottus macouni* to commemorate the professor. The molluscs sent to the Smithsonian Institution's Dr. Dall yielded another surprising discovery—that the waters of Clayoquot were warmer than those of the Gulf of Georgia, a fact confirmed by the specialist on seaweeds.

That year, the 761-page revised edition of the *Catalogue of Canadian Birds* was published, with John and James M. Macoun credited as authors.

Late in 1909, Spreadborough was re-engaged and deployed to collect seabirds from Vancouver Island. From the station at Departure Bay, he collected "20 mammals, 289 birds, 340 shells, 19 crabs and shrimps, 4 sponges, 90 starfishes, and 80 breastbones of seabirds." The following summer, he received instructions to do similar work in the Queen Charlottes.[26] From Skidegate he made a much more substantial collection, including 2,000 shells, 200 fish, and 225 sea worms.

The wealth of new biological knowledge brought back from Vancouver Island drew attention to the scarcity of comparable data from the east coast. Consequently, Macoun and Young spent the summer of 1910 in Yarmouth and other locations in Nova Scotia.

In 1911, the new Victoria Memorial Museum[27] was opened in Ottawa. This meant that the professor was kept busy organizing the collections and completing various catalogues for publication, while Young needed to arrange and label the huge volume of invertebrate material collected in the previous few years. Both men did some collecting in and around Ottawa. An experienced ornithologist, Percy Taverner, took charge of the department's vertebrates section. Meanwhile, on Vancouver Island, Spreadborough went to Cowichan Lake where he collected 5 birdskins and 13 small mammal skins, and the skin and skeleton of a black bear.

The professor had planned to return to Vancouver Island for the 1912 collecting season, but in early March he suffered a paralytic stroke to his right side and was unable to travel until late April. He and his son Jim went to Sidney, where his daughter Clara and her husband, the surveyor/mountaineer Arthur O. Wheeler, now lived. Slowly recovering, the family patriarch was able to make short forays on the Saanich Peninsula. He needed a cane for walking and had to learn to write with his left hand. His son Jim, who could roam farther afield, visited many of the Gulf Islands and as far as Nanaimo, but mostly he stayed close to home to support his parents.

That year the provincial premier, Richard McBride, had announced the creation of a huge new park called Strathcona, in the island's mountainous interior. He intended it as a tourist attraction to rival Switzerland.[28] The premier challenged the Alpine Club of Canada to make a first ascent of Elkhorn, a dramatic, major peak within the park. Wheeler, a leading figure in the club, took charge of the expedition, which included his son Oliver, also a skilled alpinist, who would lead the ascent.[29] The Macouns followed the planning with interest.[30]

Jim Macoun decided that the new park required biological exploration as well. He spent six weeks there, generously hosted by the park's development team. Disappointed with what he found, he reported to the department:

There is very little animal life in Strathcona Park. No elk or deer were seen either by [me] or anyone else in the park during the

FIG. 15-5 *Polystichum andersoni.* In 1912 Jim Macoun discovered Canada's first new fern in 50 years in the new Strathcona Park. It was named for R.M. Anderson, who had taken over as head of the biological section at the Geological Survey in Ottawa. *Photo © courtesy of Steve Ansell.*

summer and even small mammals and birds were rarely noted. . . . Only 350 species of flowering plants—twenty-four species new to Vancouver Island were found, and six new to science, among the latter, a fern *Polystichium andersoni*, the first new species of fern found in Canada in over fifty years.

Close to a cougar trap set near Buttle Lake, he discovered the skinned carcass of a wolverine and was able to collect the skeleton for the museum. He also reported to the Alpine Club for its 1913 journal on the flora and birds he had seen. He endorsed the campaign to encourage tourism:

> A week spent in Strathcona Park will give the botanist or plant-lover a better idea of the flora of British Columbia than can be obtained elsewhere in the same time. . . . Cedar, Douglas Fir, Pine and Hemlock form as fine an example of Pacific coast primeval forest as can be found in British Columbia. . . . It is worth a visit to see the trees alone.

He also listed and praised the shrubs, berries, and ferns, adding:

> Only a few mountains were climbed in 1912, and on each of these plants grew that were not found elsewhere. Until all have been botanized, and botanized carefully, any visitor to Strathcona Park may expect to find not only species that have not before been recorded from Vancouver Island, but which are new to science.[31]

In his list of 29 common birds seen, he pointed out that he had visited after the breeding season, so had heard little birdsong. Respecting the park, he did not shoot any, so described his list as "incomplete . . . and will serve for a basis for future work."[32]

At the close of the 1912 season, Professor Macoun and his wife, also ailing, agreed to make their home with their daughter and son-in-law, Mr. and Mrs. Wheeler, in Sidney, north of Victoria. The Wheelers built an addition to their house for them. But the venerable botanist was certainly not finished with his work. He took a nearby cottage as his office and herbarium. The department kept him on staff as chief of the biological division until James took over in 1917.

The professor began building a collection, in duplicate, of the flora of Vancouver Island. One set would be used for his own reference before going to the museum in Ottawa; the other was destined for the provincial museum. He remained fascinated with the cryptogams. Within two years, he amassed 247 species (937 specimens) of fungi, 128 species (605 specimens) of lichen, 31 species (118 specimens) of liverworts, and 195 of the known 264 species of island seaweed, as well as 700 species (3,000 specimens) of flowering plants. He had found 20 species of flowers new to the island's list, 8 species of fungi new to science, and an extremely large number of mosses, not yet arranged.[33]

Using his left hand, Macoun wrote a series of popular articles on botanical subjects for the local paper, under the pseudonym "Rambler." He also corresponded on botanical technicalities with Newcombe at the newly established provincial museum. The community of enthusiasts in natural history in and around Victoria felt honoured to have such a venerable expert nearby to whom they could bring their findings for help in identification.

In 1914, Jim Macoun (by then aged 51, too old for military service), planned to complete fieldwork for the flora of Vancouver Island project by spending a few weeks on the Gulf Islands, and then do the same at the northern end of Vancouver Island, "which has never been studied botanically." He met with his father to go over the previous season's collections. Then they went to Mayne Island, where they botanized for a short time, before Ottawa directed a change of plan. Jim was to leave immediately for the Pribilof Islands in connection with his duties with the international fur-seal commission.

Taverner, with the help of Young, was compiling a new, more detailed catalogue of birds that would form the basis for his books *Birds of Western Canada* (1926) and *Birds of Canada* (1934).

In the summer of 1915, the two Macouns and Spreadborough were reunited for the first time in a quarter-century for a field excursion. They visited locations on the east coast of Vancouver Island and adjacent islands from a base at Comox. The professor "collected flowering plants and large numbers of cryptogams of all families." He now had a microscope from the department, essential for identifying moss and lichen species.

Jim Macoun and Spreadborough spent three weeks on Texada Island, where they did some dredging for marine species.

> The flora of Texada island is of special interest as this island and those adjoining it form the northern limit of the plants of the Arid Transition zone on the coast, many species being found there that are characteristic of the flora of the dry interior of British Columbia. The flora of Whidby [Whidbey] Island[34]... is very similar.

CLYDE PATCH'S EXPEDITION TO BARCLAY SOUND

In the winter of 1915/16, Percy Taverner sent newly recruited preparator/collector Clyde L. Patch to Victoria, in response to an invitation by the provincial government. Barclay Sound now had a salmon cannery, whose owners had complained of fish depredation by sea lions. C.F. Newcombe, MD, was sent to investigate. "Nootka Indians" (presumably from Nuu-chah-nulth communities in Barclay Sound) would hunt the animals on contract, for examination purposes. Of those that were killed, he offered the hides and skeletons to the Dominion's museum, provided they send a representative to prepare them for shipment.

Patch obtained permission from Francis Kermode, director of the BC Provincial Museum, to collect some ornithological specimens while he was there. Newcombe would be supervising the hunt from a motorboat, giving Patch excellent opportunities to collect seabirds. Accompanied by three locals, he visited Nahmint, Uchucklesit Inlet, Effingham, and the Broken Group Islands. He acquired specimens of 37 species of birds—all those seen, with the exception of the coot—plus two raccoons, a harbour seal, and two black-tailed deer.

He saw flocks of surfbirds "numbering two or three hundred individuals. One charge from a twelve-gauge shotgun brought down twelve Surf-birds and two Purple sandpipers." The numbers were significant because

> [surfbirds'] breeding grounds have never been discovered[35]... heretofore they have been known to winter only on the South American coast.... The occurrence of this species in this latitude as late as January 4 was something of a surprise.[36]

Patch skinned, cleaned, and prepared 14 sea lions for the museum's collection. To help with the modelling of an exhibition group for display, he made plaster casts of the heads and limbs of an adult bull, a juvenile male, and a cow.

Jim Macoun correctly surmised that the reason for the difference in species from nearby regions was that they lay in the rainshadow of mountains. Spreadborough reported collecting "8 mammal skins (squirrels, deer mice, and bat), 48 birdskins, 58 lots starfish, crabs and marine specimens, and 100 marine shells."

In 1916 Jim Macoun, "Bugs" Young, and Bill Spreadborough collected along the new Pacific Great Eastern Railway line between Lillooet and Squamish. The professor joined them for a few weeks at Brackendale, a short way upstream from Howe Sound. It must have been wonderful for the four naturalists and close friends to work together in the field. It was to be the last time they did so. The professor noted that the location "being near the coast was an excellent place for cryptogams and many fine species were collected there which do not occur on Vancouver Island." Bugs, too, noted that "it proved an excellent locality for bird collecting." The two Macouns then spent some time working in the provincial herbarium, which had been transferred to the provincial museum.

In 1917, the professor gave the provincial museum his collection of flora, mounted and named by him since he had lived in Sidney. The samples included 640 flowering plants and 117 Musci (mosses and lichens).[37] Francis Kermode, the museum's director, went in person to collect the precious contribution.

In 1919, Jim Macoun was collecting along the Grand Trunk Pacific Railway line when he fell ill. In Ottawa, surgery revealed advanced cancer, and in the new year he died, aged 57. This loss devastated many of his colleagues, including Taverner. Spreadborough, with whom the deceased had formed a close bond, was particularly hard hit. The blow of losing his "brother" was followed less than a year later by another, equally severe: the death of the elder Macoun. Spreadborough felt unable to continue such work, even with Taverner.

The professor had passed peacefully away in his 90th year. He was buried in Patricia Bay Cemetery, but his remains, along with those of his wife, whose death followed his a few months later, were taken to Belleville to be reunited with those of their son James.

The professor's other son, William, completed his father's autobiography and published it in 1922. In it he listed the species named *macounii*: there were 20 flowering plants, 14 mosses, 2 lichens, 6 liverworts, 1 starfish, 2 molluscs, 1 butterfly, and 2 fishes. In his editorial notes to the second (1979) edition of the work, W.A. Waiser added to that list 12 flowering plants, 10 mosses, and 5 lichens. But he also pointed out that any from these two lists might have referred to John or to his son James. Waiser added that most of the names have gone into synonymy— superseded by later taxonomists. The professor's vast collections of Vancouver Island flora were bequeathed to the provincial museum, now the Royal bc Museum.

Not long after the professor's death, the museum published *A Preliminary Catalogue of the Flora of Vancouver and Queen Charlotte Islands*.[38] Staff member William Carter, who "had done considerable collecting on Vancouver Island," compiled lists from both Macouns with those of Dr. Newcombe and his son, William, and of W.B. and J.R. Anderson, and Professor Joseph K. Henry.[39] The nomenclature was adjusted to conform with the new manual of the Gray Herbarium, Harvard University.

The lists, in an 80-page report, included scientific and common names, with brief notes on frequency and distribution. Kermode acknowledged that this list was incomplete, but he hoped "that it may prove to be useful as a basis for future workers to build on." That was surely Professor John Macoun's sincere intention.

FIG. 15-6 (ABOVE) The sea star, previously called *Leptasterias macounii*, was renamed *Evasterias troschelii* by taxonomists. The popular name is the mottled star. *Image © courtesy of Neil McDaniel.*

FIG. 15-7 (RIGHT) Macoun's Arctic butterfly, on Canada Post's 1988 stamp. Its close relative, the great Arctic, is found on Vancouver Island (see Chapter 19). *Photo by author.*

Macoun's Arctic · Nordique de Macoun

37 CANADA

FIG. 16-0 *Wild Lilies*, painted by the young Emily Carr in the early 1890s. She gave the work to the Sisters of Saint Ann in gratitude for care provided to her ailing sister, Lizzie. It is now on permanent exhibition at the Art Gallery of Greater Victoria. *Image © courtesy of the Sisters of Saint Ann.*

CHAPTER SIXTEEN
WOMEN AND BOTANY

I N THE LATE 17TH CENTURY and through most of the 18th and 19th centuries, gentlemen in British society were permitted, and admired for, active participation as serious amateurs in science and most of the fields of natural history. The same courtesy, however, was not extended to women. Members of the learned societies were almost exclusively male.

Only botany was an exception to this societal discouragement of women in science. It was considered quite acceptable for respectable ladies to take an active interest in their gardens and conservatories, in wildflowers, and even in seeking out new species away from their homes. Painting floral subjects was viewed as a most becoming accomplishment for a well-educated young lady. Botany also resonated with society's perception of women as being knowledgeable about edible and medicinal plants. And most botanical learning could be carried out close to home or under suitably modest and chaperoned field excursions. It was, thereby, compatible with the social requirements for decorum by women of that era.

Following the example set by Queen Charlotte, wife of George III, many English women responded enthusiastically to such licence, acquiring in the process considerable knowledge. They studied botanical science and horticulture, corresponded with experts, and sought out rarities. A few with the financial ability assembled and cared for collections of exotic flora, even commissioning expeditions to acquire even rarer specimens. "Herbals" or books on botanical topics were largely written by, and for, women. Some became highly regarded botanical illustrators. They were able to combine aesthetic awareness and artistic dexterity with technical fidelity.

Men continued to exert control of what they considered to be the more serious aspects of botany, such as taxonomy and morphology. Should a collecting expedition be dispatched to an unstudied region, such as the Himalayas or British Columbia, only men would be considered for the team. The rationale for this was not just men's physical strength and endurance, but what was perceived as their superior mental capability.

WHAT IS BOTANICAL ART?

In order to describe the ways that flora are depicted on paper, some discernment is required. Is the artwork botanical illustration, botanical art, floral painting, or none of the above? The most practical way to tell is by the artist's emphasis.

Where that emphasis is on the scientific aspects of the subject, to enable accurate identification, the depiction is considered **botanical illustration**. It depicts all the important aspects of the plant, including its form and life cycle, often with parts dissected, and including the key features that distinguish this plant from another.

Where the artist's emphasis includes aesthetic value as well as scientific accuracy, botanically correct but without all the specific information required by botanists, the depiction is termed **botanical art**. It is seen as "art in the service of science."[1] Such works are usually in colour against either a plain background or against the plant's natural background, and carefully arranged. Examples are found in the works of Emily Woods, Emily Sartain, and Sophie Pemberton.

Where the artist's intent is to make an aesthetically pleasing work of art of a botanical subject, usually flowers, and often in a still-life context, the result is called a **floral painting**. It can be in a natural setting or cut and arranged in a vase. Artistic licence is often applied to colours, size, and setting, and can be impressionistic, such as in Emily Carr's *Wild Lilies*.

Artists' depictions of landscapes, including trees and forest scenes, are not generally considered to be within the genre of botanical art.

In 1979 the Botanical Garden at the University of British Columbia mounted an exhibition, *Plantae Occidentalis: 200 Years of Botanical Art in British Columbia*, accompanied by a descriptive catalogue by Maria Newberry House and Susan Munro.[2] It included examples of all three forms mentioned above.

JOHN LINDLEY AND HIS DAUGHTER SARAH

A change was happening in the natural sciences, including botany, away from the amateur toward the professional, academically trained scientist. In this process, the Linnaean system of classification came under question, in particular by John Lindley.[3] He had devised his own "natural system" of botany, and held that the subject should be studied by trained scientists, under a microscope in the laboratory, and from a modern, non-Linnaean perspective. The approach by collectors and traditional taxonomists (such as Archibald Menzies, David Douglas, and John Macoun, whose activities he termed "polite accomplishment") was, he felt, for amateurs. In his inaugural lecture at the university he declared:

It has been very much the fashion of late years in this country, to undervalue the importance of this science, and to consider it an amusement for ladies rather than an occupation for the serious thoughts of man.[4]

In 1834 he wrote *Ladies' Botany*, an attempt to simplify his own system of plant classification. The book was still too abstruse for all but an educated specialist. His aide, Sarah Ann Drake, provided illustrations for the book. A close family friend of the Lindleys, and known affectionately as "Ducky," she lived in their house for 17 years. Under Ducky's tutelage, Lindley's daughter Sarah became adept and worked on her father's copious publications, including the renowned *Gardener's Chronicle*.[5]

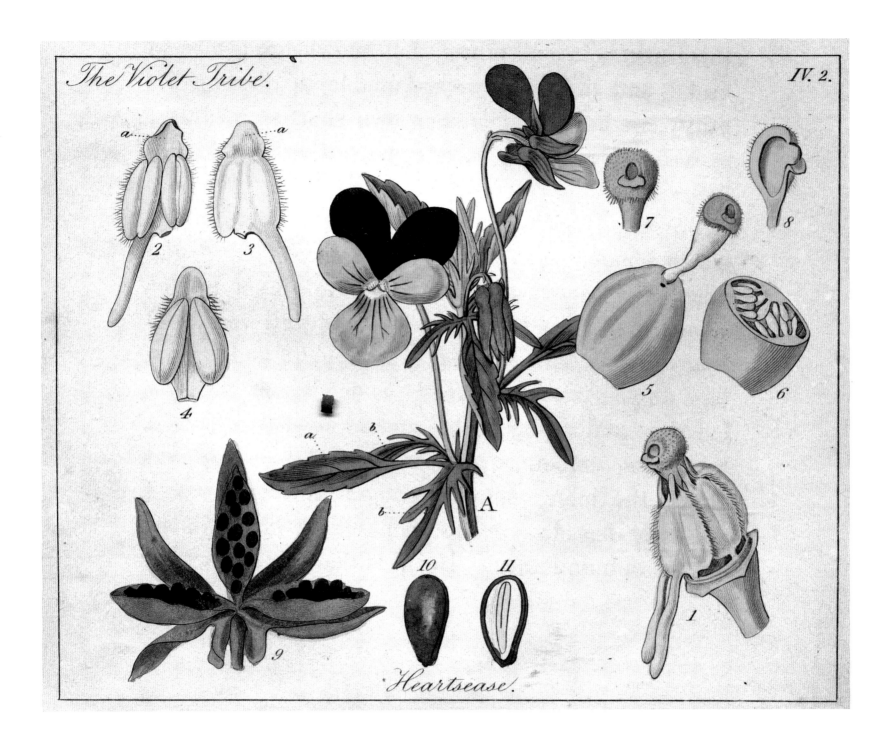

The Violet Tribe.

IV. 2.

Heartsease.

FIG. 16-1 Heartsease violet, a plate from John Lindley's *Ladies' Botany* probably painted by Sarah Lindley guided by "Ducky" Drake. *Plate IV2 from Lindley's* Ladies' Botany, *1834, from author's collection.*

FIG. 16-2 An English oxlip. Sarah Crease, née Lindley, painted this watercolour before coming to Vancouver Island, and kept it for the rest of her life. *Image pdp04851 courtesy of the Royal BC Museum and Archives [image edited].*

From early childhood Sarah had been immersed in the sciences of botany, horticulture, and the taxonomy of all manner of plant life. She had also studied with another family friend, Charles Fox, a distinguished portraitist.

These two mentors taught Sarah pencil and watercolour techniques and also how to convert drawings into woodblocks and engraved copper plates for printing. These were important commercial skills, as photography and lithography had not yet come into practical use. By helping her father, Sarah not only acquired technical ability and an intimate knowledge of botany, but also was able to earn some money of her own.[6]

At 22, Sarah met one of her brother's fellow law students, Henry Pellew Crease, whose family was from Devon. They fell in love and married five years later in 1853. After qualifying, instead of practising law, Henry managed a tin mine in Devon, but this did not turn out well. To recoup his losses, he sailed for Victoria, leaving Sarah with their children in England. In one of her letters to him she wrote:

> I have been eagerly searching for what information I can find respecting the country. I have as yet found nothing about the island itself[7] but in [David] Douglas's journal in the years 1825 & 6 of his botanical wanderings along the river Columbia from Fort Vancouver, he mentions many beautiful shrubs, trees and flowers which we cultivate in our gardens and are so familiar with that to see them again in so distant a country, would be something like meeting the face of an old friend. He gives also a good account of the kind & inoffensive ways of the native tribes. Frost, he also notes, did not commence until the 15th of December.[8]

In Victoria, Henry was soon granted the first licence to practise as a barrister and was able to call for his wife and family to join him. A fellow Devonian, the assistant surveyor general Benjamin

Pearse was a bachelor who had done well in the property market and had built "Fernwood," a fine stone mansion. He offered to share it with the Crease family. Sarah was happy there, spending time sketching and painting a series of landscapes and scenes in and around their new home. By this time, her artistic inclinations had drifted away from botanical illustration.

Thereafter, Sarah's life revolved around their growing family and Henry's ascending career, the pinnacle of which was to serve as a justice of the Supreme Court. They built their own handsome villa, "Pentrelew," which had a large, lush garden, and took their place as pillars of the community. As well as actively participating in her church, Sarah worked with several charitable causes. She continued painting until glaucoma diminished her eyesight. In 1862, 12 of her watercolours of the fort and city of Victoria were displayed at the International Exhibition in London.

Four years later, with Henry's knighthood, she became Lady Crease, and in 1910 was founding patron of the Island Arts and Crafts Society. She died in 1922, leaving an immense collection of archival material chronicling life in colonial and early provincial British Columbia, and including many botanical illustrations from her early years.

EMILY HENRIETTA WOODS

One of three women artists who lived in Victoria (and were coincidentally named Emily), Emily Woods was born in Parsonstown,[9] Ireland, in 1852. When she was just 13, her family came as settlers to Vancouver Island. Her father, Richard, soon obtained a senior administrative position at the Supreme Court, and the family set up a comfortable home, "Garbally,"[10] on the Victoria Arm waterway, just outside Victoria's city limits. Emily's parents could afford to send her to the exclusive Angela College, where she took lessons in drawing and watercolour that revealed her considerable artistic talent.

FIG. 16-3 A scene on the Comox River in 1877. A pencil-and-wash sketch by Sarah Crease of an angler casting from a canoe while a figure, perhaps the artist, seeks somewhere to set up a drawing board. *Image pp04195 courtesy of the Royal BC Museum and Archives [image edited].*

Her particular love was for the wildflowers that surrounded the Garbally property, and she devoted her life to finding and painting plants, travelling throughout the province to do so. The accuracy of her work shows her keen interest in botany. She usually provided both common and scientific names for the plants, and in some cases she also noted how the Indigenous Peoples made use of them. In 1884, one of her pen-and-ink sketches won a first prize at the annual provincial exhibition.[11]

During her time at the college she met two sisters, Edith and Clara Carr, who also shared her art lessons.[12] Later, Emily gave drawing and painting instruction at some small elementary schools. At one of these, a younger sister of her friends from Angela College took her first art lessons. This was Emily Carr, who later wrote:

> I was allowed to take drawing lessons at a little private school which I attended.[13] Miss Emily Woods came every Monday with a portfolio of copies under her arm. I got a prize for copying a boy with a rabbit. Bessie Nutthall nearly won because her drawing was neat and clean, but my rabbit and boy were better drawn.[14]

Emily Woods never married. For a while, she taught at St. John's church and participated in various patriotic and charitable associations. In later years, she shared a home on Bourchier Street with her unmarried sister, Elizabeth Ann. Emily died from cancer in 1916. During her life she produced more than 200 watercolours of flowers, or flowering shrubs and trees, and some 50 landscapes or scenes. The BC Archives holds four albums of her work. In 2005, the Royal BC Museum published Kathryn Bridge's compilation of charming vignettes written late in life by Emily Carr, each devoted to one plant, and exquisitely illustrated with an Emily Woods watercolour.[15]

FIG. 16-4 *Mentha Canadensis var Glabrata.* Watercolour of field mint by Emily Woods, who was Emily Carr's first art teacher. *Image pdp04001 courtesy of the Royal BC Museum and Archives.*

EMILY CARR

One cannot think of Vancouver Island landscapes and art without calling to mind the genius of Emily Carr. She is, of course, renowned for her powerful, dramatic depictions of forest trees. These were executed primarily from an artistic and spiritual perspective rather than for botanical accuracy, but clearly show her deep love of nature. A quote from her journal reinforces this sensibility:

> There is a cold, mysterious wonder amid the trees. They are not so densely packed but that you can pass in imagination among them, wonder what mysteries lie in their quiet fastness, what creeping, living things, what God-filled spaces totally untrod, what voices in an unknown tongue.[16]

The wildflower vignettes and passing comments within her written body of work, such as those included in the book with Emily Woods's watercolours, reveal that she was deeply interested in the individuals of the floral kingdom that surrounded her, and could illustrate them beautifully in words.

One of Emily Carr's youthful floral paintings is particularly memorable. In the early 1890s while studying at art school in San Francisco, she painted in oils an exuberant display of *Erythronium*—fawn, or Easter, lilies—in two vases on a table. She called it *Wild Lilies*, and it was a personal favourite of the artist and one of the few of her works that her sisters admired.[17] Decades later, her sister Elizabeth fell sick with cancer and was cared for by the Sisters of Saint Ann at St. Joseph's Hospital in Victoria. On Elizabeth's death, Emily gave the painting to the order in gratitude for the nuns' care of her sister. The Sisters of Saint Ann treasured it in their holdings for many years. They recently transferred it, and other paintings in their collection, to the Art Galley of Greater Victoria, where it hangs in the permanent display.[18]

EMILY SARTAIN

While another artist named Emily arrived in Victoria much later than the others, she was very much of the same tradition, so should be included with them.

Emily Sartain was born in Berkshire, southern England, in 1903, into a family of Huguenot descent. Her father was a master baker in Reading. Emily's artistic talent was apparent from the age of six, so her education was steered into training in embroidery and needlework. She did well, becoming the supervisor of 26 milliners in an exclusive salon, until suffering a nervous breakdown. Her return to health was helped by rediscovering her love for floral painting. Soon, she found contract work with the Royal Horticultural Society, producing botanical illustrations for it for several years.

Her work with the society gave her access to the botanical library established by and named in honour of Professor John Lindley, father of Sarah Crease. The collection included works by such masters of floral painting as Sandro Botticelli, Pierre Joseph Redouté, Albrecht Dürer, John James Audubon, and Sydney Parkinson, the artist taken by Sir Joseph Banks on James Cook's first great voyage. Inspired by such artistry, Emily decided to focus her own work on floral portraiture and found a ready market for her paintings. She supported herself as a professional artist for the next 60 years.

In 1931, Sartain joined the Society of Women Artists, submitted one of her early works for its annual exhibition, and was delighted when it was accepted. Queen Mary, patron of the society, bought the painting, and with such royal recognition came immediate fame. A year later, Emily was granted fellowship in the Royal Horticultural Society, a credential bringing privileged visibility by the highest levels of English society. Members of the nobility and many of the most influential families acquired her paintings. The Peninsular and Oriental

Steam Navigation Company (P&O, as it became known) commissioned works from her to adorn the first-class sectors of its vessels. Over the years, the Royal Horticultural Society awarded her its Grenfell medals for "outstanding contribution to the advancement of the science and practice of horticulture." She received one gold, one silver-gilt, five silver, and three bronze Grenfell medals.

In early 1939, Emily travelled to visit her sister Winifred, who lived in Vancouver, marvelling at the bounty of new wildflowers she found here. When war broke out, she was unable to return to Britain. After remaining for the duration, she decided to take Canadian citizenship, and participated in many art shows in BC and beyond. In 1947 she spent three months in Victoria, while exhibiting at the BC Provincial Museum. The following year, noted Toronto art critic Paul Duval pronounced her the "Audubon of Flowers."

In England, she had a pre-war commission to fulfill, so in 1951 she went back there to find that she was still remembered and appreciated. Soon after her arrival, Lord Beaverbrook invited her to dinner at the Dorchester Hotel. The following year, a display of 100 paintings from her collection of BC wildflowers won the Grenfell gold medal at the Royal Horticultural Society show. There was appreciative demand for her works at many shows throughout England, including at BC House, Canada House, and the Canadian Club in London.

Since the reign of George III, the Royal Horticultural Society has kept a treasured Royal Autograph Album.[19] During their reign, each royal patron is invited to sign a page, which is decorated by a suitably qualified Fellow. In the 150-year history of the album up to 1953, only 35 such pages had been incorporated. That year, Emily was invited to submit five designs for King George VI and Queen Elizabeth to select from, for the pages they were to sign. In 1971 she illustrated pages signed by King Gustav VI and Queen Louise[20] of Sweden, and in 1953, that of Her Majesty, Queen Elizabeth II. Emily Sartain became the only living artist to have contributed more than one page to the album.[21]

In 1956 she returned to the west coast, soon setting up home in Victoria, where she exhibited at the Victoria Art Gallery's spring show. Clifford Carl, the curator of the provincial museum, asked her to help preserve Thetis Park as a nature sanctuary. Devoted to the cause of conservation of native flora, she agreed. As membership secretary, she single-handedly increased the roll from 15 to 750 members.

In 1958, BC's centennial year, the Legislature displayed Sartain's "RHS [Royal Horticultural Society] Grenfell gold medal collection" in the rotunda. The royal visitor for the celebration was Her Royal Highness, Princess Margaret, who recognized Emily's work, since her mother and grandmother both owned her paintings. She also knew of Emily's efforts to conserve local wildflowers and asked to see the locations where some of those shown in the paintings grew.

The last time Emily exhibited her paintings was in 1979, when she participated in *Plantae Occidentalis: 200 Years of Botanical Art in British Columbia* at the Museum of Anthropology of the University of British Columbia. The catalogue's historical overview noted that

[Emily Sartain's] skill and control in the difficult medium of watercolor are superb and her dedication to accuracy, delicacy and beauty in flower painting had remained constant throughout her long career.[22]

She was no longer able to prepare and attend exhibitions—normally held during the painting seasons—as well as meet orders for her work. The provincial government often commissioned

her to paint gifts for royalty and other important visitors. For the 1968 National Centennial Celebration, Hallmark Cards commissioned her to paint the official flower of each province. The company presented the original artwork to each premier and the combined set to the Government of Canada, describing it as the very best of Canadian art.

Emily Sartain died in Victoria in 1990, aged 87. During her life she painted 5,000 watercolours and only six (experimental) oil paintings, the vast majority being of flowers. Many of her works have been donated to the BC Archives.

SOPHIA THERESA "SOPHIE" PEMBERTON

Known as Sophie, this artist is on record as "British Columbia's first native-borne painter to achieve professional distinction." During the brief flowering of her career, natural history subjects did not feature prominently. She did, however, leave at least two portfolios of botanical watercolours. These clearly demonstrate that this was an art form close to her heart. The 1979 *Plantae Occidentalis* exhibition[23] included one of her floral studies.

Sophie was born in 1869 into a well-established founding dynasty of the new colony. Her father, Dubliner Joseph Despard Pemberton, had arrived in June 1851, aged 29, to take up the urgently needed role of surveyor for the Hudson's Bay Company. He was well qualified for the daunting tasks ahead, and proved competent, energetic, and proactive, and to have an excellent head for business. He did very well financially, and at one time, his estate, "Gonzales," occupied much of today's Oak Bay and Rockland.

Her father's favourite,[24] Sophie was first educated and trained in art in Mrs. Cridge's Reformed Episcopal School. During this time she would have known Emily Carr and, probably, Emily Woods. At age 13, she received an honourable mention for her painting in a school competition. In the late 1880s she briefly attended the San Francisco School of Art.

By 1890, Sophie had demonstrated sufficient proficiency and determination to have her parents send her to art schools in London. Six years later, she went to Paris to study at the Académie Julian. A year later her painting *Girl with Daffodils* was accepted for exhibition by London's Royal Academy. This was the first of many such acceptances, and Sophie was acknowledged as a professional artist. She was the first woman in history to win the Prix Julian for the best student painting in portraiture created in Paris in 1899. Her work was also shown at the St. Louis World's Fair.

She returned to Victoria in 1900 and taught life drawing classes at Christ Church Cathedral School, earning "a handsome income" from portraits commissioned by Victoria's elite. She painted, and became close friends with, Lady Sarah Crease. In 1902 a mysterious ailment affecting her walking necessitated treatment in San Francisco and hampered her work. Her mother took Sophie, with her sister, to Europe to recuperate. Despite her debility and the presence of her querulous parent, she loved Italy and while there did some of her finest work.

After a year away, she arrived back in Victoria, and the Natural History Society of BC commissioned a painting from her—a portrait in oils of John Fannin, the recently deceased first curator of the provincial museum—intended for presentation to the government. Sophie's likeness of the well-known character received universal acclaim.[25] Today it graces the executive offices of the museum.

At age 36, she married the cathedral's canon, Arthur Beanlands,[26] a widower with four children. Initially it was a happy union, but Sophie's frail health continued and now she faced the added pressure of caring for her new family. All this, coupled with her husband's ingrained view of the "proper" place for a cleric's wife, effectively meant the end of her professional career, but she continued to paint for her own pleasure.[27] She still managed, on occasion, to get outdoors to paint scenery and some floral studies, particularly her beloved lilies. In 1909 Arthur

retired, and they went to live in Kent, in southeastern England, close to his parents. Eight years later, he died, and she was badly injured in a fall from a horse.

Sophie married for a second time, to a dashing and wealthy plantation owner, considerably older than herself, Horace Deane-Drummond, and for the next 15 years they led a happy and glamorous social life. Sophie's artistic outlets during this time seem to have been mainly on exuberant interior decor and a few oil paintings, including one of her husband,[28] until Horace left her, again, a widow. She moved from the depths of rural Gloucestershire back to the London she had known as an art student, and where she remained for the duration of the war. In 1947, she returned to live in Victoria until her death at age 90 in 1959. During those later years, her love of botanical watercolours resurfaced. An album of such works, dedicated to her brother and sister, is held in the BC Archives.[29]

BOTANICAL COLLECTORS

In addition to these, and many other, Victorian women who painted floral subjects, others were active in support of the acquisition and recording of botanical collections.

> Colonial botany drew on the enthusiasms of women who botanized, often with lists of requested specimens in hand. . . . Many women contributed to nineteenth-century floras by supplying information about specimens and localities to those cataloging projects. . . . The field station was dependent upon good relations between collectors in the field and individuals who needed to receive specific plants from local areas and willingly handed out assignments to enthusiastic botanizers. . . . [Hooker] corresponded with many collectors about sending him specimens. Women were part of his circle. Correspondence networks like these were important sources of botanical information and actual specimens.[30]

BC women who were botanical collectors include a Miss Alice Williams from Victoria, who, in 1888, donated a collection of seeds of local wildflowers to James Fletcher, the Dominion Entomologist and Botanist. She was a 14-year-old girl who had recently arrived from New Brunswick, having come from England in 1872. The family had met Fletcher in Fredericton. Alice and her elder sister, Mary, would both go on to make major contributions to the Victoria community. She would take up nursing and, apart from a four-year hiatus on active wartime service, was a senior member of the nursing staff at Royal Jubilee Hospital for over 50 years. Mary was principal at the Girls' Central School for a similar duration.[31]

In 2013 a researcher from the University of British Columbia, Brittany Blachford,[32] investigated seven women who, during the late 1800s until 1919, collected specimens for the UBC Herbarium under the direction of John Davidson.[33] The women corresponded with him from different cities in British Columbia, including one from Victoria, a mysterious Miss (or Mrs.) J.T. Higgins. Blachford was unable to trace her, which she felt supported her argument about the paucity of acknowledgement of women's contribution to botany.

Such a person, however, did exist. There was a small florist's shop, J.T. Higgins, on the southeast corner of Fort and Cook Streets in Victoria in 1904,[34] and a professional nurseryman of that name had won several awards for plants at the Provincial Agricultural Exhibition of 1893.[35] In 1882 John Thomas Higgins married Mary Ann Wilby in Victoria. She, under her married name, Mrs. J.T. Higgins, must surely have been Davidson's Victoria collector-correspondent. Whether Davidson paid her (or his other six correspondents) is not clear. Despite not finding records of Mary Ann Higgins, Blachford's case is certainly valid. There were a great many women who contributed to building the body of knowledge in botany and other natural sciences but whose labours went inadequately recognized.

FIG. 16-6 *Lilium parvifolium.* Sophie Pemberton (in later life Mrs. Deane-Drummond) returned to Victoria in 1947. She then created an album of floral watercolours, *Book of Wild Flowers,* including this one of tiger lilies. *Image pdp00981, ms. 3330, courtesy of the Royal BC Museum and Archives.*

FIG. 17-0 On April 12, 1890, members of the Natural History Society of BC, plus three boys and one girl, made the first of their Sunday field excursions to Cadboro Bay. Note that none carry field glasses or even notebooks. John Fannin is seen at far left. *Image B-09586 courtesy of the Royal BC Museum and Archives.*

CHAPTER SEVENTEEN

THE FIRST INSTITUTIONS FOR NATURAL HISTORY IN BRITISH COLUMBIA

JOHN FANNIN: FROM COBBLER TO COMMUNITY LEADER

The man who would one day lead British Columbia's provincial museum came from humble beginnings. Known to his contemporaries as "Jack," John Fannin was born in 1837 to Irish immigrant parents who had settled in Kemptville, Upper Canada. Little is certain of his early years except that he was one of eight children and his father was a tailor. The local census of 1861 described John as a shoemaker, but it is evident from his later abilities and exploits that he was more than that. He had developed excellent backwoods skills such as using an axe, hunting, trapping, and fishing. He had also acquired a deep knowledge of wildlife behaviour, forest fauna, and useful plants.

Unusually for a "mountain man" with hard-won competence for survival in the wilderness, Fannin did not prefer solitude. He was personable, gregarious, and musical. He was rumoured to have taught school in early adulthood. This is not improbable, for he later wrote articles for magazines and was granted the status of land surveyor. As such, the provincial government awarded him contracts for reconnaissance surveys. Clearly, he could turn his hand, talents, and keen brain to any task for which there was a call. He was also a man of exceptional endurance, courage, and resilience.

In the early 1860s, news of the discoveries of gold in BC reached Upper Canada, and Fannin, like many of his fellows, decided to seek his fortune out west. He chose to join a large group of "overlanders" led by Thomas McMicking, who would be taking the "all-English" route across the continent. After six gruelling months, during which many died and Fannin lost all his possessions, the overlanders made it down the Thompson River to Kamloops. It was then late 1862.[1] For the next eight years he attempted to prospect and mine for gold in the Cariboo region, and tried his hand at ranching, all without success. Deciding to start anew, he abandoned the frontier and returned to his previous trade as a cobbler, setting up shop first in New Westminster and later in Hastings, on Burrard Inlet.

This change in strategy proved effective. His shoemaking provided a living while he explored other outlets for his multiple talents. He learned taxidermy, the art of preserving and presenting the skins of mammals, birds, and fish in lifelike positions. Initially his subjects were animals he had shot or trapped himself, but as his skills improved, other hunters commissioned him to prepare and mount their trophies. His workshop—for both cobbling and taxidermy—was small and open, and he welcomed spectators, especially children. He had acquired a small "parlour organ" on which he would play and compose songs for his delighted audience. He also played the cornet with a local orchestra.[2]

During this period he made reconnaissance surveys for the Department of Lands and Works. It sent him to investigate the lower Fraser Valley, the upper Stikine region, the coast of Vancouver Island between Menzies Bay and Alert Bay, and the Cassiar district. Such work made full use of his capacity as an all-round observer of natural resources, as well as of his wilderness skills and physical endurance, and his ability to prepare maps and lucid written accounts of his findings.

Further scope for his pen came from articles he wrote for such outdoors magazines as *Forest & Stream* and *Canada West*. The readers of his articles included wealthy sportsmen-hunters and fishermen, many of whom employed his services both as a guide into the mountains and headwaters of Howe Sound and Knight Inlet, and as preparator for their quarries and catches. He was among the first international big-game guides in Canada and became recognized as an expert on the birds and mammals of British Columbia. His personal collection of mounted specimens grew until it filled 12 large glass cases. No longer surveying, he was given appointments as a postmaster and a justice of the peace. By this time, 1884, Jack Fannin was a respected member of the BC community.

PROVINCIAL WORTHIES CALL FOR A MUSEUM

The first indication of public interest in establishing a provincial museum appeared in a news item in the *Daily British Colonist* of May 20, 1885. It mentioned a proposed

> British Columbia Museum Association, for the collection, preservation and exhibition of all the natural productions—mineral, vegetable and animal—and also Indian and other specimens of local interest. . . . No doubt large contributions will be provided by private liberality.

The proposal was for individual membership annual subscriptions of one dollar and governance by a council composed of city and provincial nominees and elected members. Later that year, two other ideas were floated in the same newspaper. One was for a city library and museum, the other for a museum of "Old World Arts," distinct from the proposed provincial museum.

Early in 1886 a group of 30 "of the most prominent persons, scholars or otherwise, in [the province]"[3] signed a petition to Lieutenant-Governor Clement Cornwall that a provincial museum be established. The list included provincial and city politicians, surveyors, clerics, lawyers, bankers, businessmen, and landowners. Among the names were W.F. Tolmie, Henry Crease, and Benjamin Pearse. (Surprisingly few of their number would participate in the soon-to-be-formed Natural History Society.) Most seemed to be motivated more by provincial prestige and economic considerations than by scientific curiosity. Exceptions to this, apart from Tolmie, were Sir Matthew Baillie Begbie, chief justice and also president of the Union Club; the engineer and surveyor Ashdown Henry Green; and another surveyor, Alcide LeMay Poudrier.

The stated rationale for their petition included concern that ethnographic objects were being removed from the province,

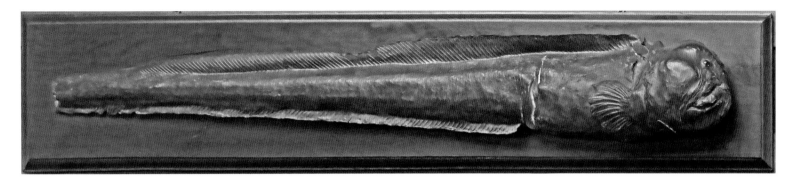

FIG. 17-1 A mounted wolf eel monitors the members' dining room of The Union Club. *Photo by author, with the kind permission of The Union Club of BC.*

that valuable mineral resources needed to be collected and classified, and that

> the Natural History of the country is by no means as yet perfectly understood, and it is trusted that if a centre for investigation be afforded, the interests of that science will be advanced, and that the attention and cooperation of naturalists of other countries will be gained. . . . [A museum was needed to] classify and exhibit . . . for the information of the public.[4]

From the composition of the list of petitioners, one might suppose the concept was hatched in the new premises of the Union Club. If so, any record of it was lost with all other club documentation in 1913.[5] Many of the members were keen shooters, and in Victoria at the time at least four professional taxidermists offered their services to "Sportsmen, Naturalists and Others": Joseph Dobinson, S. Whittaker, W. Lindley, and E. Langley.

The walls of the clubhouse were festooned with mounted heads of "doleful black, grizzly and polar bears, caribou, elk, moose, bison, and deer of every known species."[6] There would also have been bighorn sheep, giant chinook salmon, and trophy rainbow trout.

Many other members, of course, pursued less-conspicuous prey in the acceptable gentlemanly avocations of collecting butterflies, moths, birds' eggs, seashells, and fossils, as well as Indigenous cultural objects.[7]

The petition was approved in a remarkably short period from the time of its submission. A single room of 240 square feet (22 square metres) was dedicated to the "constant exhibition of natural products—mineral, vegetable, and animal—of the Province." The room adjoined the colonial secretary's office in the "Birdcages," the original legislative buildings. The legislature also voted a sum of $2,000 for the first year's expenses. (It was to be a further 27 years before the government passed the Provincial Museum Act in 1913, giving statutory authority for the Provincial Museum of Natural History, which had published its first annual report the year before.)

The Executive Council (of the BC government) appointed John Fannin as the first curator, effective August 1, 1886. He had a prior commitment to guide a party of American hunters into the Similkameen district after bighorn sheep. He also anticipated acquiring specimens for the museum, so he was not able to take up his appointment until mid-October.

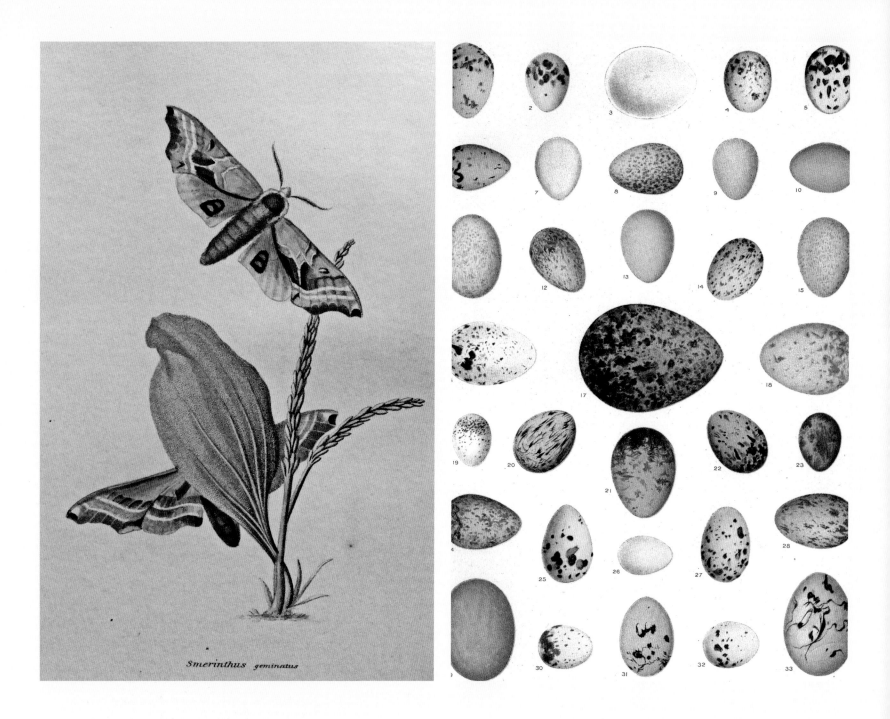

Smerinthus geminatus

FIG. 17-2 (LEFT)   Collecting spectacular nocturnal lepidoptera, such as this sphinx moth, was a popular avocation for English gentlemen in the Victorian era. *From a chromolithograph in author's collection [image edited].*

FIG. 17-3 (RIGHT)   Collecting birds' eggs, too, was socially acceptable. *From a chromolithograph in author's collection.*

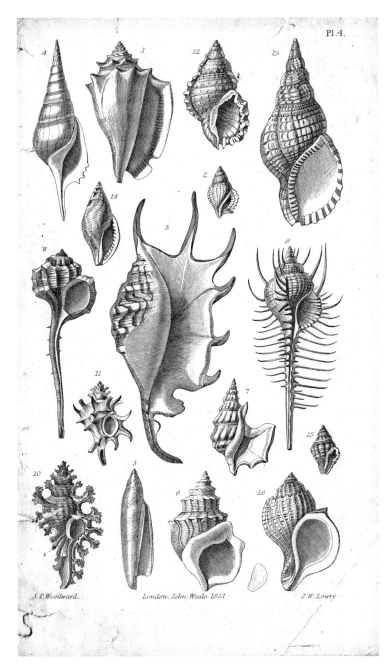

FIG. 17-4 Exotic seashells were another favourite subject for collection. *Plate 4 from S.P. Woodward's 1851 Manual of the Mollusca.*

The government had chosen well. By this time, Fannin had an unrivalled knowledge of BC's hinterland and its wildlife. He had an influential circle of clients, and was a popular writer on outdoors topics and an excellent raconteur with empathy toward all sectors of the community. As an early demonstration of Fannin's personal commitment to the museum, he donated his own collection of preserved and mounted specimens of birds and mammals in 12 glass cases, plus mounted racks of antlers. Some of these cases are still in the Royal BC Museum's collection, attesting to Fannin's superb skills in taxidermy.

THE MUSEUM OPENS, 1886

Fannin's appointment was officially confirmed October 23, 1886, and on October 25, the Provincial Museum of Natural History and Anthropology was founded in Victoria.[8] On December 2, it opened its doors. A long article in the next day's *Daily British Colonist* applauded both the exhibit and Fannin's appointment. The article relayed the museum's request to the public to donate specimens of local animals, birds, fossils, and minerals to build the provincial collection.[9] In the meantime, Professor John Macoun, on a visit to Victoria, had praised the concept of a new museum for natural history.

Frequent reports in the *Daily Colonist* reinforced the request for additions to the collection by listing donors and donations. For the next few years, the public responded generously to the call. In the first of such reports, dated two days after the long article, George Vernon had presented the "skin of a female caribou with the hoofs and horns attached," and Alex Anderson donated "a fine collection of British Columbia moths." "Articles of interest" had been received from four people in Victoria and other donors from New Westminster, Kamloops, and Revelstoke. In June, Ashdown Green donated "24 specimens of fish in glass jars, one shark's head, piece of lava, collection

FIG. 17-5 "John Fannin first curator of the Museum presented by the members of The Natural History Society of BC May 24 1905." Painted in oils by Sophie Deane-Drummond, née Pemberton. *Photo by author with the kind permission of the Royal BC Museum.*

of ancient coins, one hippocampus [seahorse], and a piece of pavement from Rome." Because shotguns were widespread in the community at the time, many birds, large and small, were donated to the cause.

HASELL, NEWCOMBE, AND FANNIN FORM A CLUB
EDWARD HASELL

In the late 1880s Victoria was well provided with physicians. New arrivals, even the most highly qualified, did not find it easy to establish a practice that could sustain them. One of those immigrant doctors was Edward S. Hasell, who arrived in Victoria in 1888 and hung his shingle at 81 Fort Street. He had been born in India to missionary parents 29 years earlier and was raised in England, attending Harrow School and Kings College, London. He studied medicine and qualified for membership in the Royal College of Surgeons in 1885. A cultured man, he enjoyed a wide range of interests including art, literature, and natural history.

CHARLES NEWCOMBE

Not long after Dr. Hasell's arrival, another physician came to Victoria: Charles Frederick Newcombe, MD. Born and raised in Newcastle, in northeast England, he studied medicine at Aberdeen, graduating with distinction. He interned as an alienist (a specialist in mental diseases) at an asylum in Yorkshire, under the tutelage of an enlightened, compassionate pioneer of the discipline. After serving as medical officer in another asylum, he qualified as an MD in 1878. By this time, he was 27.

He married and joined a general medical partnership in the county of Cumberland for a few years, then decided to immigrate to the west coast of North America. He came to Victoria in 1883, but soon realized that the chances of building a viable practice there were slim. Instead, he took his family to Hood River in Oregon. Newcombe practised his profession, revelling in attending settler-patients across a wide territory by horseback, boat, sled, and handcar. He helped build his house, a barn, and a fruit farm. He was also able to pursue his interests in natural history and archaeology, and began collecting local botany specimens and arrowheads. He built a small sailboat, *Cygnet*, learned to sail, and was able to explore and collect farther afield. His wife, Marian, found the winters too harsh for her delicate constitution, so after five years they returned to Victoria.[10]

After obtaining his licence to practise in BC, Newcombe found that he could not compete with already established, British-trained physicians in town. Having some inherited capital, Newcombe could manage despite the challenges of establishing a viable practice in Victoria, and besides, it allowed him time for his non-medical avocations. He joined in the collecting of specimens for the new museum, which brought him in touch with Jack Fannin. Fannin also struck up a warm friendship with another new doctor in town, Edward Hasell, who shared the two men's interest in natural history.

By 1890, Fannin's workspace had become overcrowded with specimens. Fortunately, a larger space became available in another part of the legislative precinct when the Supreme Court transferred to another building. In May of that year, the museum moved into the new location, and Fannin was able to take on an office-boy-cum-apprentice-taxidermist, 16-year-old Francis Kermode. While those developments were unfolding, the three newcomer friends—Fannin, Hasell, and Newcombe—discussed an idea. Why not form a club from those people known to be interested in natural history, to work with and for the provincial museum?

NATURAL HISTORY SOCIETY FORMED, 1890

They called an exploratory meeting on March 6, 1890, in Fannin's room, where it was agreed that the three should draw up a proposed constitution for such an organization, to be discussed and formally adopted at a second meeting on March 26. Notices would be sent out to all those who might be interested in membership, inviting them to attend. In the event, "more than forty gentlemen signified their wish to join the society."[11] The original constitution and bylaws of the Natural History Society of British Columbia, formally accepted at its first meeting, stated that the society's objectives were "to acquire and promote a more extended knowledge of the Natural History of the Province, and to act as an independent auxiliary to the Provincial Museum." The annual subscription for ordinary members would be five dollars.

The first appointed officers were President Ashdown H. Green; Vice-Presidents M. Lopatecki and Dr. Hasell; Secretary Dr. C.F. Newcombe; Treasurer J.K. Worsfold; Curator and Librarian J. Fannin; and committee—J. Deans, J. Fielding, Captain Deveraux, and H. Wooton.[12]

The society immediately began a series of fortnightly lectures in a room adjoining the legislative library, provided by the provincial secretary. The new president, Ashdown Green, an ardent fly fisherman, inaugurated the series with a two-part talk on the Salmonidae of BC. Throughout the ensuing year, talks by members followed. Poudrier spoke on entomology and on minerals in the Chilcotin, and Hasell on the origin of birds, on his recent visits to provincial museums in Britain, and on primitive forms of animal and vegetable life. Fannin lectured on the distribution of birds in BC and on provincial deer, Newcombe on the crabs of BC, C.P. Woolley on bears, P. Jenns on leaves, and W.H. Danby also on entomology.

Talks on topics other than natural history were presented as well. It had become clear that the members' interests included anthropology, which also matched the stated objectives of the museum. Deans spoke on the preservation of Indigenous remains,

FIG. 17-6 Plate of moths collected by Natural History Society member W.H. Danby. *Plate from the Natural History Society of British Columbia's Annual Report for 1890–91.*

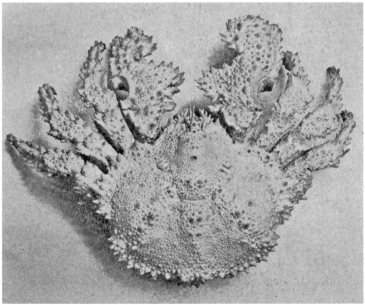

FIG. 17-7A (TOP), FIG. 17-7B (BOTTOM) Local species of crabs reported to the Natural History Society: (A) hairy lithodid crab and (B) Puget Sound king crab. *Plates from of the Natural History Society of British Columbia's* Annual Report for 1890–91.

and the myths, legends, and topography of the Queen Charlotte Islands; the Reverend Arthur Beanlands[13] made a presentation on jade implements. Distinguished visiting anthropologist Dr. Franz Boas discussed "The Skulls of the Indian Tribes of BC."

In addition to the lectures, during spring and summer the society organized field excursions. They went to Cadboro Bay, Macaulay Point, Goldstream, Aldermere (a member's estate in the Highlands), Shawnigan Lake, Beaver Lake, and Esquimalt Lagoon. They also made boat expeditions to dredge for shells, sea stars, and other inshore marine life off Victoria and Esquimalt Harbours and Trial Island, and off Sidney and James Islands in Saanich. Any specimens collected on such forays were destined for the museum's collections. Their excursions became popular social events as well as providing opportunity for more serious fieldwork.

Many of the participants on the field trips showed more interest in evidence of local Indigenous presence than in natural history. They looked for and investigated structures such as burial cairns, shell middens, petroglyphs, pictographs, and village sites. This aspect grew to form a significant part of the activity on such outings. Ethnology, the study of Indigenous Peoples, seems to have been treated as an extension of natural history. It was a curiosity to be examined, catalogued, and collected, rather than considered as a respectful examination of a society as valid as their own.

At the time of the annual report for 1890/91, the society's membership included 54 residents in Victoria, 4 near Shawnigan Lake, 2 each in New Westminster and Comox, and members in Massett, Enderby, and Vancouver. One of the previous vice-presidents, Maurice Lopatecki, had moved to California,[14] but continued his membership, for a total of 66 members.

For the upcoming year, Ashdown Green continued as president,[15] Deans replaced Lopatecki, and Hasell continued as vice-president. Worsfold, Newcombe, and Fannin remained as treasurer, secretary and curator, respectively, but Hasell took over as librarian from Fannin.[16] O.C. Hastings, C.P. Woolley, and Canon Beanlands joined the committee, and Fielding, Deveraux, and Wooton stepped down.

The first annual report[17] included transcripts of some of the presentations. These were the ones on salmon and other economically important fish by Ashdown Green, Beanlands on jade, Deans's paper on "Legend of Cowichan Indians," and some unattributed notes on entomology listing 29 species of diurnal lepidoptera (butterflies) taken in Victoria during 1890. The writer noted:

> Although Vancouver Island is an excellent field for Entomology, very little collecting was done here in 1890. It is hoped that more will be done this year.

The report also included Fannin's record of BC birds, a list comprising 313 species. Fannin explained: "It is more than probable that future observations will add to its numbers, as the extreme northern and northeastern portions of the Province still remain unexplored." The following year, BC's Queen's Printer separately published Fannin's list of birds annotated with distributions.[18] For reasons unstated, wealthy amateur ornithologist John Eliot Thayer, an American, shared author credit with Fannin for the list.

Early in 1891, Dr. Newcombe's wife, Marian, died, soon after giving birth to their third son. At age 39, he was now a widower with six young children. Leaving the three youngest with a housekeeper, he took the three oldest back to London, where he had extended family. He spent the next year there, taking courses in geology and natural sciences at the British Museum. Leaving the three oldest with family members, he then returned

FIG. 17-8 Henry Moody and Dr. C.F. Newcombe on a 1923 collecting mission to Tanu in the Queen Charlotte Islands (now Haida Gwaii). *Photo from* The Beaver, *Spring 1982, p. 38 [image edited].*

alone to Victoria to rejoin his two younger offspring. (While he had been away, the infant had died.)

Newcombe rented a home on Dallas Road, and from there he devoted more time to his avocations—dredging for molluscs, investigating local geology, and becoming progressively more interested in the Indigenous Peoples, and their cultures and artifacts. He used his sailboat *Cygnet* to explore for a while, then built a larger one, *Pelican*, that enabled him to venture as far as Haida Gwaii and beyond. In addition to collecting natural history specimens, he built a strong network of contacts among the Indigenous Peoples throughout the coastal communities.

He established a respectful relationship with Elders of many groups and began to purchase totem poles, decorated panels, dance masks, and other cultural objects from them for the provincial and foreign museums and for his personal collection. He kept meticulous notes on everything he acquired. His son Willie accompanied him and eventually took over his collecting and note-taking. Together, they assembled an enormous and unique collection of coastal First Nations artifacts, all carefully annotated, which in time was acquired by the Royal BC Museum.[19]

While Newcombe had been absent, the society had continued its series of lectures and field excursions, and adding to the growing collections in Fannin's charge. His good friend Hasell had been appointed "coroner for the city and county of Victoria" and was immediately kept busy with a smallpox epidemic, but remained active in the society. Newcombe compiled a checklist of the province's marine shells, which the society published in its 1893 *Bulletin*.[20] The same issue contained another of his papers, on some crustacea in the museum's collection. Fannin provided a preliminary list of the mammals of BC, Ashdown Green on some new and rare fish, and Danby and Charles de Blois Green[21] on provincial entomology.

In the introduction to his paper, Fannin pointed out that the list did not include the smaller mammals, because

we know that the number of small mammals in British Columbia is far from insignificant, but just what species we have, and as to their distribution and relative abundance we are with respect to many of them, entirely ignorant. It is therefore desirable that collecting in this direction be prosecuted more earnestly by members of the society and others interested in the natural history of the Province.

In 1896, the colonial secretary authorized Fannin to make a tour of museums in the eastern United States and England. He was to study their methods prior to moving the provincial collection into more spacious quarters in the new legislature building, then nearing completion. Newcombe was appointed his temporary replacement as curator. (Newcombe would make a similar tour of eastern Canada and the United States in 1901, where he sought opportunities to exhibit totems and other Indigenous cultural objects to wider audiences.)

The following year, 1897, as part of his official report to the premier, Fannin produced a classified list of the 577 objects held in the society's collection. He added a recommendation that the minerals they held should be placed under the care of the provincial mineralogist in the Department of Mines. The rest of the collection was transferred to the east wing of the new building. Starting in December 1897, the Natural History Society enjoyed the use of the splendid new reading room adjoining the new legislative library for their meetings.

The spectrum of topics addressed at the society's regular meetings and field excursions continued to expand. There was a growing interest in local history, both Indigenous and colonial. The membership had grown and now included several professional scientists, such as C.C. Pemberton and James R. Anderson, the first deputy minister for agriculture. These two, together with Professor Macoun, established and built the museum's botanical collection. Another active member was John Walbran.[22]

While some long-standing members wanted the society to remain focused on traditional "natural history," in 1903 a revised purpose was defined. In its incorporation document as a charitable association, the society retained its original name. Its objectives, however, became "to promote the study of the natural sciences and historical research" and the "collection of all available data." The society would continue to act as an independent auxiliary to the museum. Now, it would do the same for the Department of Agriculture and Department of Mines, and for the legislative library. The annual dues for ordinary members were set at two dollars. Ladies could now be elected as members but would form a separate branch and could not serve as officers or on committees. Dr. Hasell served as president at the time of the new constitution.[23]

WHO WOULD SUCCEED FANNIN?

Toward the end of that same year, Fannin's health deteriorated. His long exposure to arsenic—used by taxidermists to preserve skins—may have played a part. By the following spring, no longer able to work, he resigned. Newcombe was his expected successor and applied for the position. The executive committee of the Natural History Society had sent a formal letter to the premier, Richard McBride, strongly recommending that Newcombe be appointed to succeed Fannin as curator. Notwithstanding such endorsement, and to everyone's astonishment, on Fannin's formal resignation the government chose to promote his assistant curator, Francis Kermode.[24] In June 1904, Jack Fannin, universally admired and respected, died, aged 67,

from a "Cerebral Embolism—five weeks" as the death certificate recorded. The Natural History Society turned out in force for his funeral service at Christ Church Cathedral.

In marked contrast to his predecessor, Kermode proved to be more of an administrator than a naturalist or historian, but he managed the museum competently.[25] Despite a shortage of staff, he disdained the support given by members of the society, deliberately distancing them from the museum. He remained as curator and, from 1913, as director of the museum for a total service of 36 years. As such, he worked at acquiring a working familiarity in the areas of interest to the museum. The deputy curator, Ernest Anderson, continued actively as a member of the society. As one of his early acts as curator, Kermode published, under his own name, Fannin's revised list of BC birds,[26] to which 24 species were added.

Dr. Newcombe, although understandably crestfallen at not being appointed to lead the museum, did not hold a grudge. For many years he continued to explore by boat, gathering natural history specimens for the collection, sometimes accompanied by Kermode. He also produced many technical reports and lists related to local natural history, including one that published Menzies's journal of his voyage with George Vancouver.[27]

Through the press, the society raised a matter of concern with the mayor of Victoria and the public.[28] That favourite spring flower of Victoria citizens, the native white fawn lily, was being decimated by wanton picking of the blooms, particularly by children. E.A. Wallace[29] had pointed this out to the society. He explained how such wholesale gathering was damaging traditionally dense stands of the plant. Society members shared his concern and asked him to write a letter to the newspaper, requesting public restraint.[30]

In 1908 the society was obliged to find a new venue for its meetings and library. It secured the use of a room in the Carnegie

Library building, declaring it to be "very pleasant quarters." In March 1914, an editorial in the *Daily Colonist* highlighted and praised the work of the society:

> Its greatest benefit will be in creating here an atmosphere of culture, by which we do not mean mere superficial refinement of manner, but an attitude of mind towards the various aspects of Nature, an intelligent interest in every phase of animate and inanimate things.[31]

Initially neither the society nor the museum had been active in building a herbarium. Instead the Department of Agriculture did so. In 1911 the department's botanical collection was formally established as the Provincial Herbarium of the Native Flora. Four years later responsibility for the herbarium was transferred to the museum. At about the same time, the botanical garden and herbarium at the University of British Columbia were also instigated under the direction of John Davidson.

Over the decades following the First World War, activity by the Natural History Society of British Columbia dwindled. The society became inactive by 1930 and finally dissolved three years later.[32]

FIG. 18-0 The skylark proved the most successfully transplanted British songbird imported by the Natural History Society of BC in 1903 and 1909. A few survive in and around Victoria Airport. *From D.A. Bannerman's* Birds of the British Isles, *1953.*

CHAPTER EIGHTEEN

IMPORTING SONGBIRDS:
A SADLY FAILED PROJECT

I N 1897, THE NATURAL HISTORY Society of British Columbia instigated a plan to import British songbirds, but without adequate forethought, funding, and management the project failed, with tragic results for most of the birds. The scheme seems to have been initiated by some British "exiles," nostalgic for the birdsongs of their childhood. They yearned to hear the birds in their new neighbourhood of "silent woods." Recognizing that such an enterprise would be expensive, and reluctant to fund it themselves, they sought support. For this, they needed a stronger justification than their personal auditory pleasure, and they decided to portray the desired birds as "insectivorous," thus beneficial to farmers.

Before the society became involved, there had been private importations of birds from Europe. These included several attempts at bringing in game birds—California quail, pheasants, partridges, even black grouse and capercaillie from Scotland[1]— by "sporting" farmers, including Dr. Tolmie. In about 1874 a Mr. Roscoe set free a number of "English larks" at Ross Bay. In 1882 William Moock advertised in the *Daily Colonist* that he had for sale "150 German canary birds, goldfinches and robins."[2] Presumably, these were intended as cage birds.

In 1884 William Clarke offered at auction "Choice Birds, canaries, English goldfinches, linnets, thrushes," and later, the same species plus "black birds, larks, love birds, magpies, cardinals, parrots and other varieties of singing birds."[3] In 1886 a J.D. Campbell brought from Scotland 22 English skylarks,[4] for M.W. Tyrwhitt-Drake to release locally.[5]

A decade later, the society voted "to import several hundred specimens of each European songbird, care being taken to obtain only those suitable to the country and without destructive habits." They nominated a committee of three to draw up a list of suitable species.

J.R. Anderson, the deputy minister for agriculture, chaired the bird subcommittee. It anticipated needing $1,000 and having to set up a breeding aviary.[6] In it the birds would gather strength after their journey and hopefully raise offspring. Some would be released when their food was plentiful, until they had successfully established viable colonies.[7] While the public's reception to the

FIG. 18-1A (LEFT), FIG. 18-1B (BOTTOM LEFT), FIG. 18-1C (BELOW) Some of the other British songbirds selected with skylarks for importation into the Victoria region: (A) blackbird, (B) song thrush, and (C) nightingale. *Illustrations A and C from Thomas Bewick's* History of British Birds, *1809, B from C.A. Johns's* British Birds in Their Haunts, *1862 [images edited].*

plan was described as apathetic, the committee remained keen.

Fruit growers expressed the view that "English blackbirds, thrushes and linnets were liable to injure the fruit trees."[8]

A year later, the society countered this concern with a report from the fruit commissioner of Oregon. Having run just such a project for a few years, he strongly endorsed it as beneficial.[9] In 1900, farms throughout the province suffered a plague of cutworms, the larvae of certain moths that devour ground crops. This pointed to a need for more birds that feast on such pests, changing farmers' views of the project.

THE FIRST CONSIGNMENT OF IMPORTED BIRDS, 1903

In 1902 the government accepted the society's plan and offered $500 in support, provided the society raised a similar sum. The Central Farmers' Institute endorsed the importation of a large number of skylarks, goldfinches, English robin redbreasts, siskins, nightingales, and blue tits.

They were to be liberated on the mainland and the island. The committee had difficulty raising its portion of the funding and called urgently for donations.[10] In the event, with a budget of $504, it could afford to order only 100 pairs of goldfinches, 100 pairs of skylarks, and 50 robin redbreasts. The cost of the birds from an importer in New York was $1.50 per pair of goldfinches and skylarks, $2.25 per pair of robins. Freight would cost a further $50.

The consignment of birds arrived in Victoria via New York in November 1903. The news was disappointing. "All the robins are dead, and a number of the goldfinches have succumbed."[11] The survivors were temporarily housed in an aviary in Beacon Hill Park under the care of John McGraw, who was "well versed in the rearing of songbirds." According to a letter from his daughter, only the previous year McGraw had brought out from England

40 skylarks, 2 linnets, and 2 thrushes. The linnets and thrushes did not survive, but the skylarks did very well. After keeping the birds, & feeding them a special diet for some time, he released them in the Gordon Head district.[12]

After a month, the society's skylarks were liberated, some near the Jubilee Hospital and Beacon Hill, others in North Saanich, Cedar Hill, Colwood, and Duncan. The 16 surviving goldfinches also gained their freedom in the park.[13]

The committee investigated and reported that a Professor Hornaday, the New York dealer, had inspected the birds. It concluded that "it transpires that proper care had not been taken of the birds in transhipment, during which time [15 days] they had not been fed."[14]

In his presidential address to the society, Dr. Hasell downplayed the affair as "not as completely successful as anticipated at the outset." He hinted at future efforts in the same direction.[15] In March 1905, Keith Wilson of Salt Spring Island received his own delivery of "a large cage of . . . English robins, a few larks and thrushes. . . . The consignment arrived in excellent condition."[16] In June 1907 H.F. Pullen, a realtor and retired rear admiral, reported seeing at least three skylarks, maybe more, near the Royal Jubilee Hospital, for the first time in 12 years.[17] Two years later, news arrived about a retired doctor in Tacoma, who had been born in England and for the past five years had been importing, rearing, and releasing skylarks, linnets, goldfinches, throstles (song thrushes), and English blackbirds, which "are seen and heard all over the country."[18]

THE SECOND CONSIGNMENT OF IMPORTED BIRDS, 1913

In 1911 the Natural History Society of British Columbia again elected to attempt importing a large consignment of four species. J.R. Anderson, now retired, was in London and could place the

FIGS. 18-2A, 18-2B, 18-2C, 18-2D (CLOCKWISE FROM TOP LEFT) More British songbird species selected for importation by the Victoria Natural History Society: (A) goldfinch, (B) robin redbreast, (C) siskins, and (D) blue tit. *Illustrations A, B, and D from Thomas Bewick's* History of British Birds, *1809, C from C.A. Johns's* British Birds in Their Haunts, *1862 [images edited].*

order while he was there, if the money were available and sent to him. Dr. Hasell gave an illustrated talk to the society on the birds under consideration for importing. The society called urgently for donations toward a budget of only $100. This was a pitiful sum considering that the province was enjoying boom times. The previous total cost had been five times that amount. They eventually raised $125 and sent it to Anderson, with orders for

> six dozen male and female goldfinches; 6 dozen m&f brown linnets, 6 dozen m&f green linnets [siskins], 6 dozen m&f skylarks; the balance to be expended on the purchase of as many robins as can be acquired, also if possible, a few blue tits and chaffinches.[19]

The money arrived too late for Anderson to place the order. Britain's Wild Bird Protection Act prohibited the capture or confinement of songbirds during the breeding season. Another member of the bird committee, A.S. Barton, was to visit London in August and would be able to make the arrangement then. The consignment would arrive in Victoria in February or early March 1912.[20]

Just before that was to happen, Francis Kermode, the museum's curator, presented a well-reasoned and convincing case for the protection of birds throughout the province. He pointed out their value to the farming community as predators on the most-feared pests: cutworms and similar insect pests. The newspaper published his presentation in full and endorsed the view that songbirds were beneficial, and that the new "immigrants should be warmly welcomed."[21]

In May 1912, the schedule having slipped another year, the society requested the government's permission to import songbirds from Britain. Previously, this had been opposed by orchardists and fruit growers, but they now supported the scheme. The minister of agriculture promised to give the idea due consideration when he discussed it further.

The *Daily Colonist* reported that the shipment consisting of 500 English songbirds, carefully fed and tended, were on their way, in a specially constructed aviary built in the ship.[22] In fact, the government agent purchased the birds from a London "fancier," Shackleton of Leadenhall Market, in mid-October. The birds would be kept in an aviary until spring, when they would be shipped. This time, Shackleton's attendant, "well-known to the agent-general," would accompany them. The consignment had cost "in the neighbourhood of $425."[23] Just prior to shipment, the agent reported that "the song birds were looking well in London."[24]

At a meeting in December 1912, reports emerged of people recently seeing, or hearing the song of, English robins on Dallas Road and in James Bay, Rockland, and Fairfield. This was an odd series of sightings, since the entire 1902 batch of robins was reported to have died en route.

The bird committee reported to the society on March 25, 1913, that it appeared there would be a deficit of $150. They suggested that the birds, when they arrived, be exhibited at a suitable place, with a charge for viewing to raise more funds. The committee accepted an offer by member E.A. Wallace to use his greenhouses on Rupert Street.

The society's second batch of birds eventually arrived in late March 1913. A brief announcement noted that "their ranks [have been] greatly decimated by the rigours of the trip from England." Of the 450 birds shipped at Liverpool, 150 died during the voyage and a further 50 on the train to the west coast. Forty-four skylarks ordered by the government and 12 birds ordered by a private buyer were left in Vancouver; the remaining 150 were brought to Victoria. After being exhibited at the greenhouses for two days, raising an additional $273 in fees and contributions, they were distributed for release.[25]

Arthur S. Barton, president of the society, had met the birds and their attendant, Richard Miller, at Vancouver and

FIG. 18-3 Richard Miller, the attendant sent by the "fancier" or bird merchant in London, feeding his charges upon their arrival at Liverpool prior to embarkation. *Press photograph from the* Liverpool Echo *reproduced in the* Daily Colonist, *Victoria, March 23, 1913 [image edited].*

accompanied them to Victoria. Miller explained to the executive committee what had transpired. He had worked with Shackleton for two years, and had cared for the birds since October. During the various stages of the journey, he had lost 6 on the train to Liverpool and 11 more before they were loaded aboard the steamship. The specially built cages were put in the seamen's fo'c'sle, in the bow of the CPR vessel *Montcalm*, the place of maximum movement at sea. On the skipper's instruction, Miller was helped by the deck boy. Even so, it was impossible to keep the birds' food and water dishes filled during a passage across the north Atlantic against March gales. Fifteen more birds died at sea.

On arriving at St. John, the birds waited for 12 hours before being loaded into the baggage car of a train bound for Montreal. Miller travelled with them, but even so, 12 more died. On the next stage, he was not allowed into the baggage car except at junctions, which also provided his only opportunities to get food for himself. A kindly conductor, disobeying company orders, allowed him to travel in the baggage car to feed the birds, but he was not permitted to clean the cages for fear of causing damage to other parcels. From Fort William to the end of the line, he was not allowed into the baggage car. Five more of his charges perished. He had orders to keep the left wings of any birds that died during the journey. He produced 247 of them at Victoria.

Miller recommended that, for any future consignments, smaller cages be provided, and with cloth covers to keep the birds in the dark except for two hours after feeding. This would inhibit fighting. Also, drawers below the cages would facilitate mucking out, especially at sea. It would be important to minimize disturbance of the birds by visitors or by noisy porters moving baggage. For his three-week trip, he was paid just three pounds, with no provision made for his return journey. The executive planned to express their great dissatisfaction to the Dominion Express Company over the facilities provided, with the warning that their claim for compensation was to follow.[26] In the end, the express company made a $20 "donation." The unfortunate scapegoat, Miller, later asked for the society's help in finding work.[27]

Shackleton, when he learned of the society's unhappy view of the result, was sympathetic and helpful. He noted that "the robins are such fighters, and blue tits are hard to keep alive." He told of another customer who had had more success, "but they were put on the cattle deck. They had a canvas tent for them to travel in, and no other luggage near them so that my man could feed, water and clean them out. . . . They travelled overland [to Detroit] by American Express, there was a special car for the birds alone [the attendant insisted that he travel in the same car]." He further recommended that if there was to be another batch ordered, it would be better to ship them in September than in the spring. He added, "My boy Miller was one of the cleanest lads with animals and birds."[28]

The birds committee reported to the society that "rather more than half the birds had died on passage, that the survivors had been distributed from Cadboro Bay to Esquimalt, and that two pairs of blue tits were already nesting on Beach Drive. The cost of the exercise had worked out to $3.50 per surviving bird,"[29] nearly six times the original price in London. The following spring, the society announced that "several [sighting] reports were made of the English songbirds, larks, robins, and linnets which have all been seen in the environs of Oak Bay and the city recently."[30]

There were 43 robins, 32 linnets (more probably siskins), 20 goldfinches, 49 skylarks, and 6 blue tits released at 14 locations between Esquimalt and Christmas Hill.[31] Two weeks later, reports had come in that some blue tits, linnets, and robins appeared to be nesting. There were calls for bounties to be given on crows, jays, and raptors to protect the new arrivals. These calls went unheeded.

In his address as retiring president of the society in March 1914, Arthur Barton mentioned the project to import songbirds. He reported:

> We have every reason to believe that a sufficient number have survived the first winter of their life out here. . . . We have every hope that we have added to the pleasures of the people of Victoria and the surrounding districts, by introducing into their homes and gardens, some of the most beautiful Song birds in the world.[32]

SUBSEQUENT SURVIVAL

The song of skylarks continued to be heard over the fields of Gordon Head until the construction of new buildings and sports fields at the University of Victoria. They still appear in the August 2017 edition of the *Victoria and Southeastern Vancouver Island Checklist of Birds*. It notes them as year-round "uncommon—usually in low numbers or irregular, often local." With the exception of the siskin, which is listed in the checklist as common year-round and is known as the pine siskin,[33] the other species imported by the society failed to gain a local foothold.

The whole scheme, viewed from a modern perspective, seems to have been based on the self-indulgence of a few, was poorly executed, and had tragic results. Because of public indifference to the concept, as demonstrated by the lack of response to repeated calls for funding, there was inadequate budget to justify persisting. Nonetheless the small group of enthusiasts pressed ahead. They allocated too much of the budget to acquiring a large number of species and individuals, leaving too little to ensure the appropriate welfare of the subjects during their traumatic journey and recovery period.

Crowding 500 birds, trapped in the wild, into a confined space for a rough sea voyage followed by two weeks inside a railway freight car, kept short of food and water all the while, was inhumane. It seems incredible that any of the birds survived the ordeal. Those that did were not granted a period of recuperation on arrival, as originally planned. Instead, they were immediately released to fend for themselves in a foreign ecosystem.

It is further distressing to realize that so soon after the birds' release into the skies of Vancouver Island, so many island sons would hear the birds' song again. This time, in fields far distant:

> and in the sky
> The larks, still bravely singing, fly
> Scarce heard amid the guns below.[34]

GEORGE SPROT'S SKYLARK SURVEY, 1937

Two decades after the second introduction, an ornithologist from Cobble Hill, George D. Sprot, made a survey of the winter skylark population in and around Victoria.[35] He found 219 birds in groups resident in the area bounded by Gordon Head, Christmas Hill, and the Lansdowne slopes. Most of these groups occupied habitat still being farmed at that time, and six groups frequented what was already Cedar Hill Golf Course. He had earlier found 8 birds as far north as Sidney, and many more in the central Saanich Peninsula.

The major concentrations in the Victoria district were around today's Lansdowne Middle School (at the time an airport), the fields later used for the university's sports, and where Tyndall Avenue meets Ash Road.[36]

Sprot attributed the skylarks' comparative success in adapting to the ecosystem of southeastern Vancouver Island to a fortunate combination of several factors. First, they are evidently a hardy species. Only 2 out of 200 succumbed to the traumas of the first shipment, and most of the second batch survived to be released on the mainland and the island. They found the climate of their new situation comparable to that of England. The vegetation pattern of cleared fir forest and oak woodland, now cultivated, provided a year-round source of their preferred foods.

In the winter, skylarks especially thrived on cereal fields in stubble. Most significantly, this situation had not yet been "identified" and populated by competing native species. The skylarks' only competition for food in these fields came from other imported species such as domestic pigeon, pheasant, partridge, house sparrow, and semi-domesticated mallard. There was also a lack of natural predators.

Sprot anticipated that skylarks would continue to "hold their own." They did so for the next quarter-century, reaching an estimated peak of 1,000 birds in the 1960s. However, the inexorable increase in density of human occupation of the agricultural lands, combined with changes to farming patterns, crops, and pest-control measures, have led to their steady decline since his study.

There is some debate about the skylark's current status on Vancouver Island. One authority holds that the true subspecies of the Eurasian skylark is now extirpated on Vancouver Island. The occasional sightings of individuals are thought to be of storm-blown vagrants of another subspecies from Kamchatka or the Far East.[37] But this opinion is disputed by other people knowledgeable on the topic. They hold that all the birds recorded locally are descended from the deliberate importations.[38]

A more recent historical review of the story of the imported skylarks[39] reports that "populations totalling up to 65 birds have been heard, seen, and even photographed in the Saanich Peninsula. They were still to be found in the vicinities of the Victoria airport, Martindale Flats, and Vantreight's daffodil farm." But this report agrees that "the Edwardian-era skylark colony is now in dire straits."

FIG. 18-4 A painting by an unknown Japanese artist of the Asiatic race of the skylark. Evidently they are more vividly coloured than the European race. *From author's collection.*

FIG. 19-0 *Zacotus matthewsii*, a ground beetle first reported to science by brothers Henry and Joseph Matthews. They had found it during a brief visit to Vancouver Island in 1869. *Photo © courtesy of Andrew McKorney.*

CHAPTER NINETEEN
A STOOP OF ENTOMOLOGISTS [1]

NTOMOLOGY PROVIDES ONE OF THE clearest examples of the divide between approaches to the broad field of natural history. The rift lies between the methods of the amateur and those of the professional scientist, in this case, the entomologist. The former, from a wide range of backgrounds, generally focused on building a collection, often starting with butterflies and moths and then branching into other orders. The latter, the scientific entomologist, following formal training, was more engaged with the detailed biology of the animal, and particularly its economic effect on human society. As the late 18th century ended, the study of entomology on Vancouver Island traversed that divide.

JOHN KEAST LORD

A military veterinarian, John Keast Lord,[2] was the first significant contributor to the study of Vancouver Island's insects. Between 1858 and '62, he served as naturalist with the British contingent of the 49th parallel Boundary Commission. From the BC mainland and Vancouver Island, he collected a vast array of wildlife specimens. These included 148 species of insects, although a later analyst of this collection, John L. LeConte of Philadelphia, was dismissive of the collection's significance.

THE MATTHEWS BROTHERS: JOSEPH AND HENRY

The same expert was more impressed with the next collection he received from the island. It came from two English brothers, the Reverend Henry Matthews and Joseph Matthews. During a brief visit in 1869, they collected 186 species of beetles from the island, and gave them to their other brother, Andrew, also a vicar and gentleman-entomologist.[3] He, in turn, sent the collection to his friend LeConte, who was delighted. He described one of the specimens as "a magnificent copper-coloured *Brocade* . . . stands preeminent as one of the most remarkable additions made recently to the North American insect-fauna." To acknowledge its discoverers, LeConte gave it the name *Zacotus matthewsii*.[4]

GEORGE CROTCH

Four years later, a distinguished English coleopterist (collector of beetles), George Robert Crotch, followed the Matthews brothers

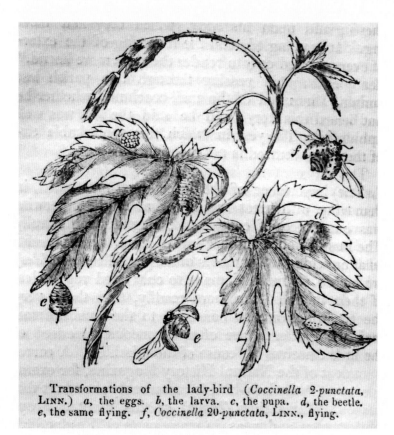

Transformations of the lady-bird (*Coccinella 2-punctata,* LINN.) *a,* the eggs. *b,* the larva. *c,* the pupa. *d,* the beetle. *e,* the same flying. *f, Coccinella* 20-*punctata,* LINN., flying.

FIG. 19-1 The life stages of the *Coccinella* beetle, or ladybug (known as ladybird in England). *Plate 122 from* Insect Transformations, *a volume in the series* The Library of Entertaining Knowledge *(London: Society for the Diffusion of Useful Knowledge, 1830).*

to Vancouver Island. He was born in Cambridge, England, and studied at the university there, where he became fascinated with entomology, specializing in beetles, and earning a master's degree. Crotch also published, and later revised, the *Catalogue of British Coleoptera*. He was an authority on the world's ladybirds.

In 1872, aged just 30, he embarked on an entomological tour of the world, arriving in San Francisco early in 1873. He spent the summer collecting in California, Oregon, the Fraser Valley, and, briefly, in the vicinity of Victoria. While there, in addition to beetles he captured more than 40 species of geometrid moths (a large family whose common name derives from their larvae, "inchworms," because of their locomotion that seemed to be measuring the ground).[5] In Cambridge, Massachusetts, he accepted a position as entomologist with Louis Agassiz's Museum of Comparative Zoology, but shortly afterward he died from tuberculosis.

GEORGE TAYLOR AND JAMES FLETCHER

In 1887, the BC provincial government appointed the Reverend George Taylor as its official, but honorary, botanist.[6] During his time in Ottawa, he had joined the Ottawa Field Naturalists' Club where he had met the founder, James Fletcher. They became friends and would remain in contact after Taylor returned to Vancouver Island.

Fletcher was by this time an expert taxonomist of Lepidoptera, of which 17 species of butterfly were named after him. He was born and educated in England and had started his working life as a bank clerk, but on coming to Canada he became an assistant in the parliamentary library. There, with ample spare time, he devoted all his energy to the study of science and natural history. He acquired sufficient expertise and reputation by 1884 to be appointed honorary Dominion Entomologist and Botanist. Three years later, his position was

made permanent and attached to the new Central Experimental Farm in Ottawa. He had crossed the divide from being a keen amateur to attaining the status of a professional scientist in the field of economic entomology.

In this role, Fletcher became central to the struggles against insects injurious to the nation's farms, nurseries, orchards, and forests. He battled with such scourges as cutworm, scale, locusts, and plant diseases, and made frequent visits to British Columbia. In Ottawa, Taylor had befriended John Macoun and his son, both active botanists, but who were also keen on many other aspects of natural history. The Macouns, too, worked in collaboration with Fletcher and respected him.

Taylor wrote several papers for the *Canadian Entomologist*, the journal of the Entomological Society of Ontario. In 1884, having recently arrived in Victoria, he submitted one on his first impressions. In "Notes on the Entomology of Vancouver Island" he reported that

> all kinds of vegetation are very luxuriant. . . . All our climatic conditions, except perhaps the wet winter, are favourable to abundant insect life. . . . In the first place the extreme abundance of Diurnal Lepidoptera must attract attention. Nearly 40 species may be marked as abundant. A patch of blossom in May, covered with Blues and Fritillaries, with an occasional *Colias* and two or three magnificent species of *Papilio*, is a sight such as an English entomologist, at least, never sees at home, and later in the year hundreds of *Vanessa, Chrysophanus, pamphila,* and *Limenitis*[7] make a very different but not less beautiful picture.[8]

A year after this paper, Taylor submitted another, this time relating how, in May 1885, he went in search of a butterfly with a group of fellow enthusiasts. Among the party were Fletcher, father and son Macoun, John Work Tolmie (son of the venerable

FIG. 19-2   A page of British Geometridae moths, whose larvae are popularly called "inchworms." *Chromolithograph plate 29 from* British Butterflies and Moths *by Kappel and Kirby (London, 1896), in author's collection.*

FIG. 19-3 Taylor's checkerspot, once common on Vancouver Island, then extirpated, but now a tiny, protected population survives on Denman Island. See Yip and Miskelly, p 94. *Photo © courtesy of James Miskelly.*

doctor and an enthusiastic entomologist), and several others, including women. They were after the *Chionobas gigas*—the great Arctic butterfly that had long been sought by Fletcher. Over a few excursions from Goldstream they climbed to the 1,300-foot (400-metre) summit of Mount Finlayson. They were rewarded with several specimens of this species, and some other butterflies new to their collections. Taylor noted that

> the locality is not very easy of access, but it is most interesting one both entomologically and botanically. Here are found no less than 15 out of our 20 native species of ferns, and many other rare plants.[9]

DANBY AND GREEN

In 1893 two enthusiasts prepared a "Report on the Entomology of British Columbia" for the first *Bulletin of the Natural History Society of British Columbia*. They were a land surveyor in the Okanagan, Charles de Blois Green,[10] and an American land broker, W.H. Danby, from New York but living in Victoria. Their combined lists featured 90 species of butterflies, which they had collected on the island and in the interior, 71 species of moths, plus some flies, beetles, and spiders collected in the vicinity of Victoria. The former list included "the beautiful *Satyrid, Chionobas gigas.*" Danby captured it on Mount Finlayson, reporting that it is "generally common in the Highlands of South Vancouver Island. As far as known, [it] is confined to this island."

Their list of moths did not include any geometrids (inchworms), since the specimens collected had been sent to specialists for identification. But the authors did note one species new to science, *Eumelia danbyi*.[11] They presented their specimens as an early contribution to the provincial museum's collection. Paul Riegert later wrote that "the [Danby-Green] report, though

FIG. 19-4 *Chionobas gigas*, the great Arctic butterfly, keenly sought by early lepidopterists on Vancouver Island. *Photo © courtesy of Mike Yip.*

brief, indicated that the state of entomology in British Columbia at that time was rather primitive, both in taxonomic and economic aspects."[12] Danby also wrote a paper for the *Journal of the New York Entomological Society*, "Notes on Lepidoptera Found on Vancouver Island." He based it on his and others' captures during 1892 and '93. He noted the *E. danbyi* moth as "Nov. gen. n. sp.," indicating a genus, as well as a species, new to science.

In the report of the Entomological Society of Ontario for 1901, an unknown correspondent from BC described a strange phenomenon. It related to *Neophasia menapia*, the pine white butterfly:

> The mode of occurrence of this species in British Columbia is very remarkable. In certain years it swarms in countless myriads, the caterpillars feeding on the coast upon the foliage of the Douglas Spruce, but in the interior on the Bull Pine, *Pinus ponderosa*. Towards the end of the season, in August, the dead butterflies may be seen in vast numbers floating on the sea around Vancouver Island, or thrown up along the beach in windrows, sometimes an inch or two in depth.

Also in 1901, Taylor, Fletcher, and J.R. Anderson made the first of their two climbing expeditions to Mount Arrowsmith, summitting then and in 1903. They identified many interesting plants, collecting some, but mainly focused on getting to the top and back.[13] During the 1903 expedition, Fletcher collected some insects, but his butterfly net was mislaid for much of the climb, and besides, the conditions were not conducive to this activity.[14]

ROBERT HARVEY

Robert V. Harvey, MA, founded and was headmaster of a private academy for boys, the Queen's School, in Vancouver in 1900. He was born in Londonderry, Ireland, and educated in Liverpool

FIG. 19-5 Lepidopterists coming to Vancouver Island after a childhood in Britain readily recognized many of the local butterflies. In particular the tortoiseshell (1 and 2), Camberwell beauty, called mourning cloak in North America (4), red admiral (5), and painted lady (6). *Chromolithograph plate 8 from* British Butterflies and Moths *by Kappel and Kirby (London, 1896), in author's collection.*

and at Magdalene College, Cambridge. From boyhood, entomology, particularly Lepidoptera, held a fascination for him. He compiled an extensive collection, which he brought with him to Canada and extended with local species, many of them new to the BC list. As did other enthusiasts who arrived from England, he found he was familiar with many of the butterfly species here.

He taught entomology as part of his biology syllabus, and other high schools in the province soon followed suit.

After moving his school from Vancouver to Victoria, Harvey redirected his interests from natural history to military-type pursuits. With the publication in 1908 of Baden-Powell's *Scouting for Boys*, Harvey organized a local troop. He also established an officer cadet training corps within his school. In September 1912, with expectation of a war in Europe mounting, the Victoria Fusiliers was formed. Called the 88th, it was the first militia regiment in Victoria. Harvey joined immediately and was commissioned as a captain. When war was declared two years later, Harvey volunteered. In command of a company, he was among the first Canadian forces to go to France. Shortly afterward, he was wounded and captured, and he died a few weeks later in a prisoner-of-war camp.

AMATEUR ENTOMOLOGISTS OF BRITISH COLUMBIA FORM A SOCIETY

Late in 1902 Fletcher, by then Dominion Entomologist and a Fellow of the Royal Society of Canada, visited a colleague in Vancouver, Tom Wilson. A Scot who had studied horticulture and forestry, Wilson had worked as a foreman at the Royal Botanic Garden, Edinburgh. He had spent five years supervising a tea plantation in India before coming to Canada in 1886, where he worked in agricultural positions with the provincial and federal governments.

Wilson introduced Fletcher to Harvey, still head of the Queen's School and a keen amateur lepidopterist, and the three discussed subjects of mutual interest. From this meeting came the idea of establishing a formal network of local collectors and enthusiasts. In the first week of 1903, "a small but ardent group of entomologists living in the environs of Vancouver and Victoria" founded the Entomological Society of British Columbia, whose work was to "include all branches of the Science of Entomology."[15] Most of the members, however, were amateurs, mainly interested in collecting.

FOUNDING MEMBERS OF THE ENTOMOLOGICAL SOCIETY OF BRITISH COLUMBIA

Founding members from Vancouver Island included Ernest Anderson, at the time assistant curator at the provincial museum; Abdiel W. Hanham, a bank manager in Duncan; and the Reverend George Taylor, then resident at Wellington. Four members were from Vancouver, including Robert Harvey, Miss O. De Wolf, and Louis D. Taylor, an American owner of a local newspaper, who would later become mayor of Vancouver. Two others were residents of Fairview, a short-lived mining community near Oliver.

Hanham was born in England and had immigrated to the United States at age 24. He joined the Bank of British North America, and during his career he had many postings, including Victoria in 1901, and finally Duncan until he retired. He was another lifelong collector and student of natural history. His main early interest was in Lepidoptera, but he also collected Coleoptera, and he donated his extensive collections to the provincial museum. Hanham was an active member of the Victoria Natural History Society and later of BC's natural history and entomological societies. He published 14 scientific papers for the *Canadian Entomologist* and also became an expert in conchology. He died in 1944.

For president, members unanimously elected the Reverend George Taylor, who would serve until his death in 1912. The key office of secretary-treasurer was undertaken by Harvey, and it was to his dedication and untiring efforts that the society owed its initial success. The first bulletins, mainly concerning interesting finds, were handwritten or typed and circulated among the members. At the time the only funding came from subscriptions. Because of the physical separation of the members, meetings of the society were few; they were held in private homes in rotation. Harvey wrote one of the first publications: "A Preliminary List of the Macro-Lepidoptera of BC." In 1905, the society formally affiliated with that of Fletcher in Ontario, to become the Entomological Society of Canada.

The following year, 1904, Harvey decided to relocate his school to Victoria, with a new name: the University School.[16] The workload associated with the new endeavour obliged Harvey to relinquish his activities with the society. This led to its dormancy for a number of years.

REGINALD TREHERNE

In 1911, a new champion for the entomological society emerged. Reginald Charles Treherne would bring radical changes to its focus, thereby reinvigorating it. He turned "a small but keen coterie of lepidopterists mostly, [into] one of the most important scientific bodies in the Province."[17]

Born in southern England, Treherne came to Canada in 1905 as a young man. After a year working as a labourer, he enrolled in the Ontario Agricultural College, earning a degree in agricultural science, while developing a special interest in entomology. He joined the Dominion Entomological Service and came to Agassiz in 1911, focusing on combatting the insect pests of orchards, field crops, and market gardens. He spent his working life in these campaigns.

Treherne demonstrated his energy, drive, and charming personality as he set out to revive and transform the local entomological group, then numbering 24 paid-up members. The society's new emphasis was on scientific research to aid agriculture. As a result, it received official support and funding for such activities as educational programs and the publication of proceedings. Within a year, membership in the society increased to 101, with a new majority of applied economic entomologists.

GEORGE DAY

In this transformation Treherne was supported—first by Wilson, who had replaced Rev. Taylor as president of the society, then from 1913 by George Day. An English gentleman, Day was given a private education, which included instruction in botany by the Reverend Charles Kingsley.[18] He became a bank manager and was honoured for public service. A lifelong avid lepidopterist, he collected almost all the British species and was elected Fellow of the Royal Entomological Society. On his retirement in 1905, Day came to Canada, residing in Duncan and joining the Entomological Society of British Columbia. He continued to collect and study the Vancouver Island species, publishing more than a dozen papers in the society's *Proceedings*, including a history of the society.[19] On his death in 1942, Day bequeathed his expertly mounted and displayed collection of British and local butterflies to Shawnigan Lake School.

EDMUND REED

In 1890, a very experienced entomology amateur came to Vancouver Island and participated in the society's activities. Born and educated in England, Edmund Reed was qualified as a lawyer but spent most of his working life as secretary-treasurer of a church diocese in Canada. He also had a lifelong interest in natural history and was a charter member of the Entomological Society of Canada, serving on the board in various capacities and contributing many articles to the annual reports. He was interested in the economic as well as the systematic aspects of the science and concerning many orders of insects. Because of his expertise in keeping meteorological records, he was given charge of the new observatory, a post he held until his death in 1916, aged 78.

ERNEST BLACKMORE

Yet another highly knowledgeable amateur lepidopterist, Ernest Blackmore added considerably to the local collections. He arrived in Victoria in 1908 as an employee of the federal postal service. Born in Shropshire, he had collected butterflies and moths since boyhood, with a particular focus on inchworm moths. In Canada, he switched his attention to the local micro-lepidoptera.[20] In 1917 the provincial museum published his list of BC lepidoptera. He served as president of the reinvigorated society in 1916/17. On his death in 1929, he bequeathed parts of his collection to the provincial museum and to the entomology museum at the University of British Columbia. He had amassed a collection of 8,000 specimens from 1,500 provincial species.

The Entomological Society of British Columbia continued in strength through to modern times. In 1991 the academic entomologist and author Paul Riegert compiled, on behalf of the society, a list of profiles of the *Entomologists of British Columbia*. He included short biographies of 27 "Collectors and Naturalists" and 122 "British Columbia Entomologists." He also listed graduate students in entomology from the University of British Columba and Simon Fraser University through to the date of publication.[21]

FIG. 20-0 Intertidal life near Ucluelet. At centre are leopard dorid and spiral white nudibranchs guarding eggs; at right, a purple or ochre sea star. *Photo © courtesy of James Holkko.*

CHAPTER TWENTY
AMERICAN INTEREST IN VANCOUVER ISLAND

I N THE LATTER HALF OF the 19th century, some American natural history institutions became interested in British Columbia, including Vancouver Island, and sent collectors and scientists to investigate its flora and fauna.

CLARK STREATOR

One of the first to arrive was Clark Streator, sponsored by the American Museum of Natural History of New York to collect skins of mammals and birds for its collections. During the summer of 1889 he visited the Fraser Valley, the Okanagan, and the Cowichan Valley. He returned to California, making two stopovers on the Columbia River on his way. The sponsoring museum's ornithologist, Frank Chapman, who analyzed Streator's collection, remarked: "So far as published records go Mr. Streator collected in an almost new field. . . . His efforts were remarkably successful."[1]

In all, Streator had collected about 1,000 bird specimens and 114 mammals,[2] among which were 87 bird specimens from 26 species from the Duncan area. He had spent just three weeks there in late September and October, noting:

[Duncan's station on the E&N Railway] is on the edge of one of the most improved and fertile valleys on the island. On all sides are numerous and extensive lakes. The land which has been cleared was [formerly] covered with heavy forests, which were largely coniferous.[3]

HENRY WICKHAM

The entomologist Henry F. Wickham,[4] of the University of Iowa, briefly visited Vancouver Island during the summer of 1890. His specialty was Coleoptera (beetles.) He spent much of June "in the vicinity of Victoria" busily collecting in a variety of habitats: the seashore, woods, ponds, and in the lanes between houses. He particularly noted the large quantity, both in species and individuals, of Elateridae (click beetles). Wickham reported his findings to the *Canadian Entomologist* journal,[5] beginning with "but little seems to have been written on the fauna of this interesting island." He appears to have been unaware of previous publications, such as those of LeConte, the Matthews brothers, George Crotch, or the Reverend George Taylor. Nor does Wickham mention contacting any local naturalists, such as W.H. Danby or J.R. Anderson.

Wickham reported that he had found beetles and that "insects from many orders seemed to be plentiful, with the exception of Lepidoptera. There may be more of these however at other seasons of the year." This comment also seems strange, given that he had earlier advised:

> I would recommend the island as a fine field for investigation by any Entomologist who wishes to spend his summer in a spot charming in itself and rich in insect life. There are enough [species] to keep one always happy by finding something new or of interest.

JOSEPHINE TILDEN

In 1898, another natural scientist from a US midwestern university arrived in Victoria. Josephine Tilden was a phycologist—a specialist in algae—and a member of faculty in the department of botany at the University of Minnesota. Seaweed was an unusual field of study for someone born in Iowa and educated in Minnesota, both landlocked states in the middle of the continental land mass, a thousand miles from the nearest ocean. Tilden was also a groundbreaker by her choice of career. Misogyny was rife in the scientific and academic culture of the era, and she became a role model for many women. She had come to the west coast to find the ideal site for a study centre in the natural sciences of her chosen ecosystem.[6]

The 29-year-old, accompanied, as societal norms dictated, by her mother, had travelled by train and ferry to Victoria. She learned from knowledgeable locals that there was a potentially suitable location on the coast of the Strait of Juan de Fuca, some 70 miles (110 kilometres) west of Victoria near Port Renfrew. There, she should contact a certain Tom Baird, a settler who had acquired the surrounding property. The only access to Renfrew at the time was by sea, but there was a regular run by the steamer *Queen City* to convey the two ladies there and back.

After a rough passage, they arrived to find Baird supportive of the concept, and he agreed to row them the 7 miles (11 kilometres) to his property at the mouth of the broad inlet called Port San Juan, the traditional territory of the Pacheedaht Peoples.[7] In pouring rain, he brought them around the eastern point of the entrance to their landing place.

They found massive waves from the open Pacific breaking upon a wide, rocky shelf. It was protected on the landward side by an unbroken, primeval coniferous forest with an impenetrable understorey of salal. This notoriously stormy coastline, the "Graveyard of Ships," had proved fatal to seafarers from vessels wrecked on the many subsurface hazards. Even people who had managed to struggle ashore were trapped there, only to perish of exposure and starvation.

Josephine Tilden, however, could only marvel at the wealth of intertidal life in the numerous pools, and the botanical riches onshore—from giant spruces and cedars to mosses, lichens, ferns, and fungi galore. There were two forest ecosystems here: that of the conifers and, more importantly for her, that of the giant kelp. She spent four days on site with only a makeshift shelter rigged by Baird and whatever they could forage from the bounty of seafood and edible plants. She was enthralled by the unlimited scope for research the place offered her and her students in Minnesota.

Responding to her enthusiasm, Baird agreed to subdivide his property and grant her a deed for her field laboratory without cost. It covered 4 acres (1.6 hectares) surrounding what would become known as Botanical Beach. Back once more on

FIG. 20-1 Botanical Beach near Port Renfrew became a favoured place for intertidal field research. *Photo © courtesy of James Holkko.*

campus, Tilden told her departmental head, Professor Conroy MacMillan, of her discovery and acquisition. Most supportive, he made the case to have this declared an official outstation of the university, to be called the Minnesota Seaside Station. Its purpose was to support advanced studies in the plants and animals of the west coast. The university agreed to provide instructors and appropriate scientific equipment but no funds for buildings or operational costs.

The Canadian Pacific Railway provided some financial support, but the start-up costs were mostly funded from her own and MacMillan's personal resources. They hoped the university would take on the financial burden and repay their costs to date, but they were disappointed. With the help of Baird and other locals, a patch of the land was cleared, and the first two log buildings erected for a small laboratory and for a kitchen and living area with dormitories above.

They were completed in time for the first season's courses in the summer of 1901. Students, almost half of them women, had to pay for their stay and instruction and were expected to participate fully in all the activities. Thirty people, including Tilden, her mother, MacMillan and his wife and daughter, departmental colleagues, and researchers—even a Professor Yendo from Japan—enjoyed that first summer at the station.

For the next six seasons the station provided month-long courses to more than 200 students and researchers, from the university and from across the United States and Canada. Students often managed to cram a year's coursework into their month at "the seaside." Additional laboratories were added to the station. Courses were offered in marine and terrestrial botany, zoology, geology, and the new field of photography, with a darkroom on site.

This idyllic arrangement lasted only until 1907, when academic politics struck a fatal blow. The board of regents of the

FIG. 20-2 Class working on the rocks near the Minnesota Seaside Station (Botanical Beach) at low tide. *Lantern slide #una508701, Ned L. Huff Collection, University of Minnesota Botany Records [image edited].*

university withdrew its association with the project. MacMillan resigned, leaving Tilden with the impossible task of running the station on her own. In 1948 Tilden sold her property, and for a few years the beach continued to be used for academic fieldwork by some local colleges and the provincial museum. The processes of the forest consumed the buildings. The beach was declared a provincial park in 1989 and is now accessible by a road and footpath. It remains a favourite place for tide-pooling among both youngsters and marine biologists.

A digital archive of the collection of photographs from the active years of the station is accessible though the University of Minnesota.[8]

ANNIE ALEXANDER'S VANCOUVER ISLAND EXPEDITION

In 1910 a 43-year-old American heiress named Annie Alexander funded and led a zoological collecting expedition to Vancouver Island. With her was her friend Louise Kellogg, who would be Annie's partner for the rest of her long life.

By then, Alexander had lived an adventurous life. Born into a wealthy family of sugar plantation owners in the Kingdom of Hawaii, she had studied in California, Massachusetts, and Paris, where she studied painting. He father, leaving his business for others to run, took her cycling through Europe, sailing on the Pacific, camping in Oregon, and to Bermuda. While attending a lecture by Professor John Merriam on paleontology at the University of California at Berkeley, she became fascinated with the subject. She offered to fund the lecturer's next expeditions to Fossil Lake in Oregon and to Mount Shasta, and she participated in both. Her father and his friend then took her on a big-game safari in East Africa. While the men hunted trophies, she collected fossils. Sadly, the two men died during the expedition in separate mishaps.

A year later she funded an expedition to search for dinosaur fossils in Nevada and again participated in the fieldwork. Workers discovered and collected several specimens of ichthyosaur. With a substantial inheritance from her father she was able to contribute even more in support of the research work in natural history at Berkeley. She proposed that Berkeley establish a museum of natural history and offered financial help for associated collecting and research. In addition, she established endowments for two museums, those of vertebrate zoology and paleontology.

In 1906 she funded and led a five-month expedition to collect mammals, birds, and other biota from the islands of the Alaskan Panhandle.[9] She did so again in 1907 and 1908. In 1909 she funded a fourth expedition but did not participate in it. Each time, starting from Seattle, members of the expeditions had steamed past Vancouver Island, outward and return, without stopping. Alexander and the zoologists wondered if different species or subspecies had evolved on the island from those on the mainland and Alaska.[10]

So in April 1910 they started out from Berkeley, travelling first to Vancouver, then Nanaimo, where they set out a line of traps for two days. From there, they moved on to spend two weeks in Parksville, where Edward Despard joined the party.

EDWARD "NED" DESPARD

Despard was an Irish-born settler, who had farmed at nearby French Creek for two decades. He was a skilled hunter and trapper, and supplemented his income by guiding hunting parties and expeditions. He claimed to have killed the largest-known elk on Vancouver Island, and its antlers adorned the wall of his house. Despard's task was to obtain specimens of mink, marten, racoon, and otter, while the women concentrated on birds and small mammals. By the end of the first week they had acquired 137 specimens, including a cougar.[11]

He joined Alexander and Kellogg in Parksville, and they made successive camps at Little Qualicum River, French Creek,

the Swain Ranch at Errington, and Beaver Creek in the wetlands just north of Great Central Lake.

HARRY SWARTH

In early June 1910, Alexander came to be under canvas in the Upper Stamp River wetland, 20 miles (32 kilometres) northwest of Port Alberni, when Harry Swarth joined the expedition. He had recently been appointed curator of birds at the zoology museum in Berkeley. To Alexander's annoyance, Swarth arrived a week ahead of his camp and collecting kit, as well as a sorely needed resupply of shotgun shells. Until these arrived, he was considered more of an encumbrance than a useful member of the team.

Swarth, born in 1878 in Chicago, moved to Los Angeles at age 13 with his parents. While at grammar school and college, he became interested in natural history, especially birds. He began collecting seriously and in 1896 joined an extended collecting expedition to Arizona, publishing the first distribution catalogue of the state's birdlife. In 1905 he joined the professional staff of the Field Museum in Chicago. Three years later he moved to a similar position at Berkeley, where he remained until 1927. He became a respected member of the Cooper Ornithological Club and the American and British Ornithologists' Unions. Annie Alexander's grants to the Museum of Vertebrate Zoology at Berkeley were paying for his services and those of the trapper Despard. The previous year, 1909, Swarth had been one of two salaried naturalists comprising the fourth Alexander expedition to Alaska.

All four members of the Vancouver Island expedition were together for the remaining three weeks of June 1910. Using the Beaver Creek camp as their base, they sought specimens around the lakes, rivers, and extensively cleared lands in the vicinity of Alberni. Here they found the birdlife plentiful, in marked

FIG. 20-3 Well protected from insect pests with a head net, ornithologist Harry Swarth inserts a bird he has collected into a paper sleeve before it is "bagged." The photographer is not known. *From author's collection.*

contrast to the areas of dense, still uncut forest. At the beginning of July, Alexander and Kellogg decided to return home, taking a steamer from Alberni to Victoria. They left Swarth and Despard to continue collecting for the rest of the season, wherever they saw fit. Swarth reported to his superior Joseph Grinnell that

> I believe so far Miss Alexander and Miss Kellogg have put up over a thousand specimens! They are wonders. You never saw anything like the way they work; I'm not in their class at all.[12]

The professionals opted to spend the next three weeks in the rugged area southeast of Alberni bounded by McLaughlin Ridge, Mount McQuillan,[13] and Douglas Peak. This had been a centre of mining activity known as China Creek and was well served by old miners' trails. They took advantage of an abandoned mine building in the Golden Eagle basin for their new base camp. The area provided a wide range of habitats from dense scrub through coniferous forests, alpine meadows, and rocky peaks. Even in July, the valley bottoms were still under deep snow. The two-man team found many bird species, but small mammals, such as mice and shrews, were significantly absent. On their first day there, Despard identified the tracks of a wolverine.

It was in this area that they made what proved to be the most important discovery of their collection: the Vancouver Island marmot. Swarth recorded:

> Wherever the ground was bare of timber, or but sparsely covered, as is the case over extensive areas at this point, the marmots had established themselves, burrowing under the rocks, and apparently never wandering very far from home. They were vigilant and unapproachable; all secured were shot by Despard with his 30-30 rifle, as we were never able to approach within shot-gun

FIG. 20-4   Wolverine tracks in the snow. *Photo courtesy of the Wolverine Foundation [image edited].*

FIG. 20-5   A Vancouver Island marmot on Mount Washington. Note the tag in its ear. The population is under threat and is the subject of intense recovery efforts. *Photo © courtesy of Mike Yip [image edited].*

range, and it was impracticable to use traps. . . . Their extreme wariness is correlated with conspicuousness, for the dark brown pelage shows in marked contrast against either gray rocks or green grass.[14]

They collected 11 specimens, all adults, and preserved 2 complete skeletons. Several other marmots that would have been shot managed to retreat into their burrows and were not retrievable. One of the skins acquired by Swarth became the type specimen, providing the description and name for the new species.

Swarth was not, however, the first naturalist to have observed this animal. The local people had hunted the marmots for meat for centuries. They did so while the giant ground squirrels were dormant in their burrows, according to BC's deputy minister of agriculture J.R. Anderson. He made two expeditions to climb and collect on Mount Arrowsmith, in 1901 and 1903. With Anderson on both trips were the Dominion Entomologist Dr. James Fletcher and the provincial entomologist, the Reverend George Taylor. All three were competent general naturalists as well as experts in their fields. On the 1901 trip, they were guided by Tseshaht guide John Clutesi[15] of Port Alberni and some local packers. Anderson later noted:

> Dr. Fletcher and I were regaled with a dinner of marmot, which our Indians cooked whole, with the skin on. When it was done, the skin came off easily and the flesh was well done underneath. . . . The flesh is not bad—something like rabbit—but tough unless properly and thoroughly cooked.[16]

Reporting on his 1903 trip, Anderson noted the differences between the marmots of Vancouver Island and those known from the mainland.

[The higher parts of Mt. Arrowsmith are] the home of the marmot, the specimen of which in the museum here [Victoria] is called the "Hoary Marmot." This I presume is a mistake, as the island variety is a very dark brown, nearly black, about double the size of a large cat, whilst those on the Mainland are grey properly, I should say, the "Hoary Marmot"; and in comparison as to size, I should think average a little smaller.[17]

While Swarth and Despard were in the mountains around the head of China Creek, they encountered and acquired many specimens of black bear busy filling their stomachs with the fresh new grass. Swarth noted that "these bears are in remarkably fine pelage, considering the season, being almost like winter skins."[18] He attributed it to the almost permanent snow of the area.

After three weeks in the hills, the two men descended to Port Alberni, where they took the coastal steamer *Tees* to Friendly Cove in Nootka Sound. Swarth had read accounts of the place, both historical and contemporary. He knew that it had played an important role during the age of maritime exploration, and that several naturalists had reported on the birds they had seen there. From reading the accounts, Swarth had misgivings about the "physical conditions on the west coast, the drawbacks of canoe travel and the impossibility of travel by land" so did not expect to have much collecting success.

He and Despard also spent a few days at Tahsis and found a homesteader (whom Swarth described as a "trapper") near there who eked out a living from government bounties for killing cougars and wolves. The man, Carl Leiner,[19] helped them search for the old Oolichan Trail across the island to Alert Bay, but without success. Nor did they have any luck locating the hoped-for bigger mammals. They found instead the forest of huge trees, with a matted tangle of salal beneath, every bit as impenetrable as had been reported.

Swarth was anxious to obtain topotypes[20] for four species of bird first reported at Nootka. They were the rufous hummingbird, red-breasted sapsucker, blue-fronted jay (now called Steller's jay), and varied thrush. The men found three of the species, and although they saw the typical lines of drill holes in trees made by the sapsucker, they did not see a single one.

He was most impressed with the situation of Friendly Cove (more correctly called Yuquot) and could understand how it must have been a favoured location for ages before the coming of the white man. He had read Robert Brown's edition of John Jewitt's journal of his time as a slave of the Mowachaht,[21] and was impressed with the accuracy of Jewitt's description of the place. Swarth had also read Brown's list of the birds of Vancouver Island.[22] In his report to the ornithology journal *The Condor*, Swarth listed 45 species of birds that they had observed during the 19 days they spent at Nootka Sound, and "beside these, numbers of gulls, scoters, and phalaropes were seen, but under circumstances not permitting of absolute specific identification."[23]

They returned to Alberni by steamer and Swarth recorded:

In the town of Alberni, and in the immediate vicinity, birds were numerous, and of many species. The open fields and meadows, the partly cleared woods nearby, and the maples along the roads, and shrubbery in the gardens, sheltered quantities of the smaller species, while the quiet waters of the harbor, with streams flowing into it, attract many water birds.[24]

After a few days they headed for Great Central Lake, a "narrow sheet of water, twenty-four miles in length. . . . The shores are precipitous for the most part, the only level ground being at the two ends." They made camp at the upper end but had great difficulty getting through the underbrush. Seeking ptarmigan, they decided to climb the mountain to the northwest, but

FIG. 20-6 Della Falls in Strathcona Park, with a vertical drop of 1,443 feet (440 metres), the highest waterfall in Canada. Swarth and Despard climbed to the lake at the top, seeking ptarmigan. *Photo from author's collection.*

FIG. 20-7 The white-tailed ptarmigan, a strong flyer, is present on most mountaintops on Vancouver Island. *Photo © courtesy of Karl Stevenson [image edited].*

the country was so rough that we were unable to transport enough camp equipage to enable us to remain more than a day or two. There are a number of streams to be crossed over very precarious bridges, some of them at dizzy heights above the water. At the farther end of the trail, which led to the base of a towering rocky cliff, over which a stream tumbled in a series of tremendous falls. The "trail" ascended, and the climb (of about 2000 feet) was a series of scrambles up the face of a cliff. Our dog was unable to follow and remained at the foot of the trail.[25]

At the top of Della Falls they found the lake, still full of snow in mid-August, and they managed to shoot six birds from a covey of nine white-tailed ptarmigan, all juveniles, before

the weather suddenly turned cloudy, and threatening fog banks settled over the peak, making traveling dangerous over the slippery, dripping ledges; so, while we could still distinguish directions and land marks, we hastily descended the mountain.[26]

Swarth noted that

a view from a mountain top in this region, even in mid-summer, gives one the impression that the island is mostly snow and glaciers, so wintry is the aspect, while from the warm valleys below, looking toward the mountains, there is but little of this to be seen.[27]

After retracing their route down Great Central Lake and to Alberni, they moved their equipment and collection back to Errington, where Alexander and Kellogg had previously camped. It was in an area of mixed woods interspersed with small patches cleared by settlers. In the distance to the southwest they could see Mount Arrowsmith. They spent three days getting to and climbing the mountain that Alexander and her friend had ascended earlier. At the Errington camp they saw numerous raptors, many of which appeared to be migrating south. They also noted a large number of ring-necked pheasants. These had been imported from England and seemed quite at home in the settlers' fields.

At the end of September they packed up camp to return to California via Nanaimo and Vancouver. In his report on the expedition, Swarth recorded having noted 111 species of birds, of which specimens from 89 were bought back, in many cases multiple individuals. They noted 20 species of mammals. Grinnell was reported to be delighted with the results. Swarth concluded his report with a cautious comment on the distribution:

> Vancouver Island is but slightly separated from the mainland and has but few species peculiar to it. There are no birds of this class, but the following mammals are not known to occur elsewhere: Microtus tetramerus [Vancouver Island meadow mouse], Marmota vancouverensis [Vancouver Island marmot], and Sorex vancouverensis [Vancouver Island shrew]. The marmot, singularly isolated in the centre of the island, is a strongly marked species. . . . In view of the presence of such genera as Marmota [marmots], Gulo [wolverine], Mustela [members of the weasel family],

and Felis [small-to-medium-sized cats, including cougars], the non-occurrence of Erethizon [porcupines], Lynx, and Evotomys [now Myodes, red-backed voles] seems rather remarkable. The presence of elk on Vancouver [Island] is also of interest.[28]

After the 1910 expedition, the participants went their separate ways. Harry Swarth remained at Berkeley, eventually being promoted to curator of vertebrate zoology, until he joined the California Academy of Sciences in 1927. He died at Berkeley in 1935. Ned Despard returned to his property, soon afterward marrying Maud, a schoolteacher. They sold the farm and bought a house with a fine garden at nearby Errington. He then devoted his time to gardening, woodcarving, and topiary. He died a popular and respected pioneer of the Parksville region in 1947, two weeks short of his 80th birthday.[29]

Annie Alexander and Louise Kellogg established and operated a successful asparagus farm in northern California. Alexander continued to finance expeditions and participate in fieldwork until her death, aged 83. One of the doctoral students at Berkeley whom she funded was a man who would become the foremost scientific naturalist in the history of British Columbia, Ian McTaggart Cowan.[30]

FIG. AW-0 *An Island in Bird's Eye Cove*, watercolour by E.J. Hughes, 1993. Robert Amos considered this to be "technically, one of the finest watercolours [Hughes] ever created."[1] The island is called Chisholm after the first settler of the area, William Chisholm.[2] *Used here and on the cover with the kind permission of the artist's executors. Photo courtesy of Robert Amos.*

AFTERWORD

THE MEN AND WOMEN WHO appeared in these pages were the first Europeans to investigate and record the natural history of what is now Vancouver Island. These naturalists, as we call them, included scientists and amateurs, some academically trained, others self-taught. They were interested in many different aspects of nature: plants, birds, insects, fish, and other marine life. They saw and wrote of the forests in their pristine state, immense runs of salmon ascending many streams, and butterflies in great numbers, and of how local peoples interacted with and used the flora and fauna of their region.

These naturalists' discoveries supplemented the sum of Europe's geographical and biological knowledge, developed over time and contact with many nearby cultures. Their findings were understood and recorded using frames of reference developed within an essentially European culture. They also offered a measure for assessing the depredations and impacts to the Indigenous population by the European arrival and the industrial age.

The work of these early naturalists provided a firm foundation for those who came after. In the decades that followed, the gap between natural history and the scientific disciplines of biology continued to widen. Government agencies and ministries established professionally staffed laboratories. Universities developed faculties dedicated to educating scientists, many of whom were also collectors and hobbyists. Museums employed specialized curators, technician-preparators, illustrators, and field staff.

While the early naturalists were mostly driven by their curiosity and desire to contribute to the body of knowledge as recorded in the European literature, they operated from and within a culture of social superiority. In many earlier cases, their presence and work were funded, directed, and exploited by entities less motivated by pure science than by imperial expansion and economic advantage. Also, societal pressures played an important role—there were very few women involved in the voyages of exploration or expeditions of discovery. Scant attention was paid to the Traditional Knowledge held by Indigenous women in the communities the naturalists encountered.

This process left wide and significant gaps in the body of knowledge, which are now starting to be filled in. Women are now involved at all levels of investigation and research, and the wisdom of women Traditional Knowledge Keepers is sought, respected, and incorporated into, and, at long last, is beginning to inform, government decision making. More, of course, needs to be done, but the signs are encouraging. A body of literature is building that seeks to bridge the divide between Traditional Knowledge and the world of published science.

This new genre is serving to reinforce the awareness and respect within the non-Indigenous population for the value of Traditional Knowledge. Both the "scientific" and Traditional Knowledge systems have value. Together they can, and must, be brought to bear on the many problems, errors, misguided policies, and actions-in-ignorance that plague the world today if we are to continue living in nature's realm. We can only hope that we are not too late!

GLOSSARY

accreted terrane A fragment of crustal material formed on, or broken off from, one tectonic plate and accreted or "sutured" to the crust lying on another plate.

anadromous Of fish that migrate up rivers from the sea to spawn in fresh water.

biota The total collection of animal and plant life of a particular region, habitat, or geological period.

Coleoptera The order of insects known as beetles, the largest order in the natural world, with about 400,000 species, 25 per cent of all known animal life forms.

fond(s) The archival term for a collection of documents accumulated from the same source.

Lepidoptera The order of insects that includes the butterflies and moths. About 180,000 species have been described, 10 per cent of known living organisms.

midden Material that accumulates about a dwelling place. A shell midden on the coasts of British Columbia is typically composed of shell, bone, fire-altered rocks, charcoal, decomposed plant and other organic matter, and even human remains. Midden material was often used for land-forming to level space for habitations.

pelage The fur, hair, or wool of a mammal.

preparator A person who prepares a specimen, such as an animal, for scientific investigation or exhibition.

refugium A location in which a population of organisms can survive through a period of unfavourable conditions, especially glaciation.

Salmonidae The family of fishes that includes salmon, trout, char, freshwater whitefishes, and graylings, collectively known as the salmonids.

taxon A group of one or more populations of an organism taxonomists consider to form a unit, such as species, family, or class.

taxonomy The practice and science of classification of biological organisms on the basis of shared characteristics.

topotype A biological specimen from the location where the species or subspecies was first reported to science.

type specimen The particular biological specimen or set of specimens to which the scientific name of that organism is formally attached. Such specimens are usually kept in a museum or herbarium.

NOTES

Citations give the creator's last name or names (and initials if the bibliography lists more than one author of the same name) and a shortened title of the work. Entries preceded by "See" are more general sources of information on the topic noted. Full information about each work cited appears in the Selected Bibliography on page 262.

Preface

1. Examples of such collaboration and transfer of Traditional Knowledge include works by Erna Gunther, Nancy Turner, Hilary Stewart, Robin Wall Kimmerer, Mary Siisip Geniusz, and David Ellis with Luke Swan.
2. From program notes by Phillip Huscher, Chicago Symphony Orchestra.

Chapter One

1. See Turner, *Ancient Pathways.*
2. Indications of even earlier human activity have been found in the Bluefish Caves in Yukon.
3. The Hakai Institute, part of the Tula Foundation, https://www.hakai. org/publications/; also Liverpool University Press Online, https://online. liverpooluniversitypress.co.uk/doi/abs/10.3828/hgr.2016.22.
4. Manis Mastodon Site, https://en.wikipedia.org/wiki/Manis_Mastodon_ Site.
5. Many North American archaeologists were convinced that finely worked stone points—found at Clovis, New Mexico, and carbon dated to 13,200 to 12,900 calendar years BP—had been made by the first humans in the Americas. However, later discoveries of evidence of earlier human activity challenged this theory.
6. Failing to recognize these extensive gardens of native food crops, the newly arrived Europeans dismissed the gardens when they marked out totally inadequate "Indian Reserves."
7. See Stewart, *Cedar: Tree of Life* and also *Indian Fishing.*
8. Thompson and Kinkade, *North American Indians,* p. 30.
9. In this book, the names used for communities and other groupings follow the *Indigenous Peoples Atlas of Canada,* 2018.
10. Dewhirst, *Origins of Nootkan Whaling,* p. 4.

11. See Borden, "Facts and Problems of Northwest Coast Prehistory."
12. Ibid., p. 41.
13. Monks, McMillan, and St. Claire, "Nuu-chah-nulth Whaling," p. 62.
14. This technique seems to have been used exclusively by the Central Coast Salish People and the adjacent people of the Skagit Delta and Puget Sound.
15. Wagner, *Spanish Explorations in the Strait of Juan de Fuca,* p. 99. The Spaniards thought they might be channel markers at the entrance to Puerto de Revilla Gigedo—Sooke Harbour.
16. Nelson, *John Scouler (c. 1804–1871), Scottish Naturalist,* p. 109.
17. Jenness, *The W̱SÁNEĆ and Their Neighbours,* p. 13.
18. See Coleman, "Mountaineering on the Pacific."
19. Earlier known as Songhees.
20. See Sprot, "Early Indian Wildfowler of Vancouver Island."
21. The gap was for a canoe passage, and to provide a drain for the outflowing tide.
22. Smith et al., "3,500 Years of Shellfish Mariculture."
23. Stern, *Lummi Indians of Northwest Washington,* p. 47.
24. An Elder and renowned carver, Kwaxistalla had the advantage that, as a young child, he had been designated as a keeper of knowledge by his parents. He was hidden from the authorities and so not put through the ordeal and brainwashing of a residential school. As a boy, he provided the basis for Jim, the young protagonist in Margaret Craven's novel *I Heard the Owl Call My Name.*
25. Deur et al., "Kwakwaka'wakw 'Clam Gardens,'" note 4, quotes Randy Bouchard, who also found an earlier article by Bernhard Stern briefly mentioning a clam garden on Orcas Island.
26. Ibid.
27. See The Clam Garden Network, https://clamgarden.com/.
28. See Pojar, MacKinnon, et al., *Plants of Coastal British Columbia.*

Chapter Two

1. See Hatler, Campbell, and Dorst, *Birds of Pacific Rim National Park.*
2. See chapter 20.

3. See Swarth, "Collection of Birds and Animals from Vancouver Island."

4. See Folan and Dewhirst, *Yuquot Project*.

5. See McAllister, "Avian Fauna from the Yuquot Excavation."

6. Ibid., fig. 8, p. 115.

7. A small stick of wood or bone, sharpened at both ends, with the line attached to its centre, was inserted into bait so that, when swallowed, the stick toggles to jam within the bird's throat.

8. Ornithologist Gary Kaiser informed the author that no albatross comes close to shore, except to breed or during exceptional weather. The birds found in the midden must have been taken at sea, 1–6 miles (2–10 kilometres) out—not a problem for fishermen in canoes habitually venturing such distances seeking halibut.

9. Pearse, *Birds of the Early Explorers*, pp. 156–57.

10. Drucker, "Northern and Central Nootkan Tribes," p. 61.

11. See McMillan and St. Claire, *Huu7ii Household Archeology*.

12. Ibid., Appendix A, by Gay Frederick.

13. Ibid., Appendix D, by Ian Sumpter, table 3.

Chapter Three

1. Beaglehole, *Voyage of the Resolution and Discovery*, p. ccxxiii.

2. James Cook's three voyages of global exploration were as follows: His first, between 1768 and 1771, made a circumnavigation westabout into the Pacific, to New Zealand, eastern Australia, Cape of Good Hope, returning to Britain. On his second, from 1772 to 1775, he also circumnavigated but sailed eastabout skirting Antarctica, around islands in the South Pacific, New Zealand, Cape Horn, and home. On the third, from 1776 to 1779, he sailed eastabout to New Zealand, Sandwich Isles (Hawaii), Nootka, Alaska, Bering Sea, Hawaii (where Cook was killed), Bering Sea, Kamchatka, Japan, and the ships returned westabout.

3. Beaglehole, *Life of Captain James Cook*, p. 502.

4. His published account of this was just a youthful hoax.

5. See Ellis, W., *Authentic Narrative*.

6. See Pearse, *Birds of the Early Explorers*.

7. See Stresemann, "Birds Collected in the North Pacific."

8. See Beaglehole, *Voyage of the Resolution and Discovery*.

9. Clerke's journal had not been available to Pearse.

10. Beaglehole, *Voyage of the Resolution and Discovery*, vol. 2, p. 1330.

11. Cook, *Voyage to the Pacific Ocean*, vol. 2, p. 296.

12. That name, colloquial Spanish for "bone breaker" and usually meaning the bearded vulture or lammergeier, also applied to the giant petrels of Patagonia and the islands around Antarctica. Pearse's speculation was proved correct by later archaeological work at Yuquot. The midden revealed a large quantity of albatross bones. See chapter 2, under McAllister.

13. Ellis, W., *Authentic Narrative*, p. 220.

14. A portfolio of John Ellis's work is in the Zoology Special Collections, Natural History Museum, London, RBR Shelf 322 and 323. Some of John Webber's are in the Department of Prints and Drawings, London 1998 b. 2, and others scattered.

15. He did keep a personal journal, but it was found only later.

16. Beaglehole, *Voyage of the Resolution and Discovery*, vol. 2, p. 1403. The deer was most likely the mule deer, the fox the red fox, the squirrel the red squirrel, the polecat the marten, and the wildcat the cougar.

17. Ledyard, *John Ledyard's Journal*, p. 70.

18. *Canis lupus crassodon*, known as the Vancouver Island wolf.

Chapter Four

1. Howay, *Voyages of the "Columbia,"* p. 60.

2. Theed Pearse, *Birds of the Early Explorers*, p. 254. Pearse suspected Haswell's bird list was not limited to the Nootka area, and so he had difficulty identifying the species Haswell mentioned, several of which could not have been seen there. He cautiously recognized the "snow bird" as the (dark-eyed) junco, the "yellow bird" as the (American) goldfinch, and the "Marsh lark" as the horned lark. The rest he left without comment or dismissed. Haswell made the mistake of classing cetaceans and pinnipeds as fish.

3. Howay, *Voyages of the "Columbia,"* p. 63.

4. Pearse noted the new species as barn swallow and pileated woodpecker.

5. Linnaeus divided nature into three broad groups, or kingdoms: animals, plants, and minerals.

6. Dunmore, *The Journal of Jean-François de Galaup de la Pérouse*, vol. 1, p. cxlv.

7. Ibid., p. 160. These are known among birders as "LBJs"—little brown jobs.

8. Colnett, *Voyage to the North West Side of America*, p. 113.

9. Engstrand, *Spanish Scientists in the New World*, p. 19.

10. Four years prior to Cook's visit to Nootka, a Spanish voyage out of San Blas in Mexico had reached the northern tip of Haida Gwaii. On their return, the voyagers briefly anchored off Nootka, which they marked as "San Lorenzo," and traded with the local people but did not land or comment on local natural history. See Layland, *Land of Heart's Delight*, chapter 3, and *Perfect Eden*, chapter 2.

11. Wagner, *Spanish Explorations in the Strait of Juan de Fuca*, p. 138.

12. Pearse reported C.F. Newcombe's theory that these *mojarras* were halibut, but Caamaño's later list included both halibut and *mojarras*; the latter Newcombe described as "Sea-Fish: about 8 inches long: broad head: large

eyes: black spot near tail: 2 blk. Spots on gills; dark in colour; oval shaped body: sides rather compressed." From the description, this fish could be the brown rockfish (see Eschmeyer, *Field Guide to Pacific Coast Fishes*, p. 134; the same reference at p. 215 indicates *mojarras* are not found north of southern California), but there are 68 species of "rock cod" on this coast.

13. Wagner, *Spanish Explorations in the Strait of Juan de Fuca*, pp. 128–31.
14. Pearse, *Birds of the Early Explorers*, identified this as the winter wren, p. 144.
15. The full name given to the feature was El Gran Canal de Nuestra Señora del Rosario la Marinera.
16. Juan Pantoja y Arriaga was a Spanish pilot who was a close associate of Bodega y Quadra and made three voyages out of San Blas north along the Pacific coast. He proved a skilled hydrographer, perceptive observer, and able chronicler. His journal is particularly valuable for its descriptions of local people encountered. See Inglis, *Historical Dictionary*, p. 251.
17. Wagner, *Spanish Explorations in the Strait of Juan de Fuca*, p. 160.
18. Pearse found the inclusion of swifts interesting and suggested the black swift and the sandhill crane, and that the "bees" were rufous hummingbirds.
19. Pearse, *Birds of the Early Explorers*, identified this as the ruffed grouse.
20. "Map that covers" followed by a subtitle detailing the area—the interior and the coastline of the northwest Pacific coast between 48° and 50° north—based on scrupulous examination by its leader Eliza, his rank, and his ships: *Carta que comprehende los interiores y veril de la Costa desde los 48° de Latitude Norte hasta los 50° examinados escrulosamente por el Teniente de Navíode la Rl. Armada Dn. Franco Eliza Comandante del Paquebot des S.M. Sn Carlos del porte 16 Cañones y Goleta Sta Saturnina (Alias la Orcasitas)* [. . .] *1791*. The map was drawn by Juan Carrasco, but often incorrectly attributed to Eliza or to Narváez. See Layland, *Land of Heart's Delight*, p. 50, and McDowell, *Uncharted Waters*, pp. 292–93.
21. Howay, *Voyages of the "Columbia."* Alange, perhaps a word with an Arabic root, refers to the Alangiaceae family of dicotyledon plants, synonymous with the Cornaceae, the dogwood family (see Wikipedia: Alangiaceae). A significant member of this group is the western flowering dogwood that so impressed subsequent botanist-explorers such as Archibald Menzies (see chapter 7) and Robert Brown (see chapter 12).

Chapter Five

1. Proclaimed by the Vatican in the Treaty of Tordesillas, 1494.
2. The Americas, as pronounced by Columbus.
3. Ibáñez, "Tadeo Haenke," pp. 32–33.
4. Wagner, "Journal of Tomás de Suría," p. 240.
5. David et al., *Malaspina Expedition*, vol. 2, p. 184.

6. Porrúa, *Diary of Antonio de Tova*, pp. 422–23.
7. During that time he reported two remarkable botanical species new to science: one was the enormous Amazonian water lily, *Victoria regia* (now *V. amazonica*); the other, the equally gigantic bromeliad queen of the Andes, *Puya raimondii*, 50 feet (15 metres) tall, of the frigid altiplano. Both of these, and many other species that he had been the first to report, were credited to later "discoverers," although they would have been well known to Indigenous Peoples in that area. He had earlier described and collected the seeds of yet another botanical giant, the coast redwood, *Sequoia sempervirens*, from California.
8. Ibáñez, "Tadeo Haenke," p. 187.
9. Ibid., pp. 66–87.
10. Cutter, *Malaspina & Galiano*, pp. 75–76.
11. Engstrand, *Spanish Scientists in the New World*, p. 63.
12. Wagner, "Journal of Tomás de Suría," p. 275.
13. Kendrick, *Voyage of* Sutil *and* Mexicana, p. 41.
14. Wagner, *Spanish Explorations in the Strait of Juan de Fuca*, p. 152.
15. For a full list and appreciation of the contents, see Higueras and Martin-Merás, eds., "Sources," pp. 53–59.
16. See Ibáñez, "Tadeo Haenke."

Chapter Six

1. There were various versions of this toponym, including Nuca. It is now called by its Indigenous name, Yuquot.
2. Moziño, *Noticias de Nutka*, p. 6.
3. Ibid., p. 4.
4. Ethnoecologist Nancy Turner has investigated the knowledge and use of locally available food and therapeutic resources by the Indigenous Peoples of Vancouver Island. She has clearly shown that this was far more extensive and sophisticated than even an observer with Moziño's learning could have appreciated. See Turner et al., *Ethnobotany of the Nitinaht*.
5. This was at today's Neah Bay, at the northwestern tip of the Olympic Peninsula.
6. Members of the Nuu-chah-nulth language group whose territory is in what is now Washington State.
7. See Layland, *Land of Heart's Delight*, p. 59.
8. Kendrick, *Voyage of* Sutil *and* Mexicana, p. 103.
9. Alcalá Galiano and Valdés y Flores, *Spanish Voyage to Vancouver*, p. 66.
10. Pearse, *Birds of the Early Explorers*, p. 148
11. Alcalá Galiano and Valdés y Flores, *Spanish Voyage to Vancouver*, pp. 96–97.
12. For an 1802 version of the published report, maritime historian Martín de Navarrete wrote a 167-page introduction providing a sweeping survey

of the voyages of exploration carried out by Spain up to 1792. See Inglis, *Spain and the North Pacific Coast*, appendix.

13. Wagner and Newcombe, "Journal of Jacinto Caamaño," p. 190.

14. This name is also given to the arbutus, which does occur at Nootka, though not in the region Maldonado visited with Caamaño.

15. This system, developed in 1735 by the great Swedish botanist Carolus Linnaeus, organized living organisms into a hierarchy, with levels called taxa: domain, kingdom, phylum, class, order, family, genus, and species. Linnaeus first addressed the plant kingdom, then extended the system to the animal kingdom. Initially written in Latin, the system had included only European species. Moziño's mentor, Martín Sessé, a follower of Linnaeus, had been working with fellow taxonomists to bring the New World species into the system. A creation of the Enlightenment, it remains an important worldwide structure for scientific nomenclature. Since its beginning, however, the system evolved as taxonomists progressively improved it. This has meant that many species, even genera, have been renamed.

16. Moziño, *Noticias de Nutka*, p. 6.

17. Ibid., pp. 20–21.

18. Ibid., p. xii.

Chapter Seven

1. Lamb, Menzies to Banks, August 21, 1786.

2. BC Archives, Add. MSS 1077, v. 49, f. 3.

3. So named by Charles Duncan, captain of *Princess Royal*, the second ship of the Etches-Colnett venture.

4. Colnett, *Voyage to the North West Side of America*, p. 18.

5. Not the same vessel as Cook's but of the same name, newly designed and built for the mission.

6. Just such an issue—modifications to the ship's superstructure for the purposes of the scientists, considered by the mariners to hinder effective handling of the vessel—had been the source of conflict between Banks and Cook before his second voyage. That time, the Admiralty had prevailed, withdrawing permission for Banks to participate. Having been a midshipman on that voyage, Vancouver was well aware of the issue, and he viewed the construction of the plant hutch as a continuation of that quarrel. By this time, 17 years later, Banks's standing in society had advanced considerably. He was founder and president of the Royal Society, a trustee of the British Museum, knighted, and a close confidant of the King—not a man to be crossed.

7. BC Archives, PR-1261.

8. Groves, "Archibald Menzies (1754–1842)," pp. 80–81.

9. Groves, *Archibald Menzies: An Early Botanist*, p. 24.

10. Lamb, Banks to Menzies, February 22, 1791.

11. See Lamb, "Banks and Menzies: Evolution of a Journal."

12. Groves, *Archibald Menzies: An Early Botanist*, p. 75.

13. Menzies, *Journal*, p. 30.

14. Ibid., p. 75.

15. Ibid., p. 71.

16. Ibid., pp. 73–74.

17. Ibid., p. 96.

18. Ibid., p. 22.

19. Ibid., p. 52.

20. Ibid., p. 23.

21. Ibid., p. 30.

22. Ibid., pp. 46–47.

23. This last, of course, was *Arbutus menziesii*, one of the few species discovered by him and acknowledged as such in the botanical taxonomic record.

24. Menzies, *Journal*, p. 20.

25. Ibid., p. 31.

26. See Groves, *Archibald Menzies: An Early Botanist*, for identifications.

27. Menzies, *Journal*, p. 49.

28. The previous head-person, also called Maquinna.

29. Menzies, *Journal*, p. 118.

30. Ibid., p. 128.

31. During the voyage, Menzies had treated Vancouver medically on a few occasions, and at Nootka even Bodega y Quadra consulted him about persistent headaches. This seems curious, since the Spanish surgeon Moziño was a fully qualified doctor, unlike Menzies. Bodega y Quadra was to die two years later of a brain tumour, respected and mourned by Vancouver and everyone who had met him.

32. Galloway and Groves, "Archibald Menzies [. . .] Aspects of His Life," "Menzies to Banks, April 28, 1795," p. 20.

33. Groves, *Archibald Menzies: An Early Botanist*, p. 25.

34. See Groves, *Archibald Menzies: An Early Botanist*.

35. See Gorsline, *Rainshadow*.

Chapter Eight

1. This was intended to present the animal life of all that portion of North America proper that, commencing with the extreme Arctic islands, stretches south to the boundary, so far as it has been ascertained, of the United States and California.

2. A highly prestigious academic appointment, unique to certain, select British universities. The monarch has established and appointed such "Chairs" since 1497.

3. This fur-trading post had been established by the American entrepreneur John Jacob Astor in 1811 in competition with the British. The outbreak of the War of 1812 caused the property to pass first to the North West Company, then, in 1821, to the HBC. The location is now called Astoria.

4. See Hooker, "On the Botany of America."

5. See sidebar "The Influence of London's Learned Societies," p. 99.

6. For a compilation of articles on the history of these groups, see Allen, *Naturalists and Society.*

7. Those lands of the colony not subject to treaty or declared as "Indian Reserves," and considered by the British colonial authorities to be "Crown" land and thus available for sale or grant to British settlers.

8. Younger sons of the gentry sent to the colonies with an allowance, on condition that they would not return to disrupt the process of primogeniture.

9. See Bosher, *Vancouver Island in the Empire,* p. 155.

10. These included fly-fishing and wildfowling, as well as the excitement of adding new specimens to their collections of plants, birds' eggs and skins, lepidoptera, fossils, and minerals, among many others. Vestiges of the style have even survived through to modern times. Victoria is regularly among the communities with greatest participation in the Christmas Bird Count throughout North America.

11. The venerable Royal Society is far older, founded in 1660. Fellowship is open only to the most eminent scientists in all fields, by election. It is the official national science academy of the United Kingdom. As such, it is distinct from the other London learned societies, although there has been much cross-membership.

12. Allen, *Naturalists and Society,* chapter 7.

13. Barber, *Heyday of Natural History,* p. 28.

14. Wikipedia: "List of Learned Societies, United Kingdom." https://en.wikipedia.org/wiki/Category:Learned_societies_of_the_United_Kingdom.

15. For an excellent recent compilation of stories on collecting birds' skins and eggs, see Brunner, *Birdmania.*

16. See chapter 16.

17. For articles related to such crazes, see Allen, *Naturalists and Society.*

18. In 1824 the HBC built its first regional base on the Pacific coast and named it after the well-known explorer. It was located on the north bank of the Columbia River, near today's city of Vancouver, Washington.

19. A type of brig, two-masted, square-rigged, with special adaptation for a gaff-rigged sail aft; speedy and manoeuvrable, favoured by privateers and fur traders.

20. Nelson, *John Scouler (c. 1804–1871), Scottish Naturalist,* p. 93. Ten years later, of course, just such an extended study did happen, when Charles Darwin aboard HMS *Beagle* spent five weeks in the archipelago during a charting mission. But that scientist would not publish the results of his visit, far-reaching in significance, until decades afterward.

21. Lindsay and House, *David Douglas: Explorer and Botanist,* p. 52.

22. Nelson, *John Scouler (c. 1804–1871), Scottish Naturalist,* p. 100.

23. For more on the British maritime fur trade, see Gough, *Distant Dominion,* pp. 41–71.

24. Gibson, *Otter Skins, Boston Ships and China Goods,* p. 315.

25. Ford, *Marine Mammals of British Columbia,* p. 401.

26. Nelson, *John Scouler (c. 1804–1871), Scottish Naturalist,* p. 28.

27. Ibid., p. 106. This situation was not helped by an attack, massacre, looting, and destruction of an American trading vessel, *Tonquin,* in 1811, attributed unjustly to the Mowachaht, but more likely the actions of a group of renegades from the nearby Wikinanish clan.

28. Ibid., p. 30.

29. Ibid., p. 107.

30. Ibid.

31. Ibid.

32. Ibid., p. 109.

33. Some of the regional Indigenous Peoples bound boards to the heads of infants in order to flatten and elongate the skulls.

34. Related to the Clatsop, Salishan speakers living along the lower Columbia River.

35. This is the correct title of the research and educational organization. The botanical gardens are usually called "Kew Gardens," or just "Kew."

36. Davies, *Douglas of the Forests,* p. 164.

37. Douglas, *Journal Kept by David Douglas,* p. 297.

Chapter Nine

1. See Harvey, "Meredith Gairdner: Doctor of Medicine."

2. See Tolmie, *Journals.*

3. Ibid., p. 171.

4. In 1836, Sir John Richardson, naturalist on the first Franklin Expedition, named the popular sporting fish *Salmo gairdneri* in honour of Gairdner, who had sent him specimens in connection with Richardson's *Fauna Boreali-Americana.* The steelhead is anadromous, that is, it spends two to three years in the ocean. A related form, the rainbow trout, *Oncorhynchus*

mykiss, spends its life in freshwater streams and lakes. The name *S. gairdneri* was later restricted to just the Columbia River subspecies.

5. Among the mammals associated with Townsend's name are a ground squirrel, a chipmunk, a vole, a bat, and a white-tailed jackrabbit. So, too, are a thrush, a warbler, a solitaire, a longspur, Brandt's cormorant, water ouzel (dipper), surfbird, chestnut-backed titmouse (chickadee), and western bluebird—among the 94 species of birds he "found in the Territory of Oregon" (Townsend, pp. 331–33). Many of these species are encountered on Vancouver Island, although Townsend did not visit the island. He had been a member of the second Wyeth expedition to Oregon, as had the renowned naturalist Thomas Nuttall.

6. See Layland, *Land of Heart's Delight*, pp. 63–70.

7. Tolmie, *Journals*, p. 391.

8. Mackie, "Skylark: Old Friend in a New Land," p. 29.

9. See Layland, *Land of Heart's Delight*, p. 78.

10. Grant, W.C., "Description of Vancouver Island," p. 289.

11. Among the crops brought to Nootka by Pedro de Alberni and other Spaniards. Originally from the Andes, it had been propagated in Mexico. It thrived and spread throughout the region through trade.

12. Grant, W.C., "Description of Vancouver Island," pp. 291–92.

13. Ford, *Marine Mammals of British Columbia*, p. 398, gives maximum length at 4.9 feet (1.49 metres).

14. Grant, W.C., "Description of Vancouver Island," p. 290.

15. The Atlantic white cedar, not native to the island. Probably he refers to the yellow cedar.

16. The European cork oak, not found on the island. Grant probably meant the Garry oak.

17. Western white pine.

18. Grant, W.C., "Description of Vancouver Island," pp. 292–93.

19. Later, and for a few years, called the Geological and Natural History Survey of Canada. See chapters 14 and 15.

20. For detailed accounts of this botanical expedition, see Johnstone, J.T., "John Jeffrey and the Oregon Expedition"; Harvey, A.G., "John Jeffrey: Botanical Explorer"; and Lange, "John Jeffery [*sic*]."

21. This refers to the Oregon Territory, the region west of the crest of the Rockies, between latitudes 42° and 54°40' north, including Vancouver Island, and subject to the Anglo-American Convention of 1818 for joint occupancy. The Treaty of 1846 establishing the boundary at 49° superseded the convention, but the Edinburgh groups seem to have disregarded this development.

22. In current-day northeastern Manitoba.

23. Father of Adolphus, the young cartographer who accompanied James Douglas on his 1842 reconnaissance for a new establishment that became Fort Victoria.

24. Johnstone, J.T., "John Jeffrey and the Oregon Expedition," p. 9.

25. Son of the renowned HBC trailblazer Alexander Caulfield Anderson, who had escorted Jeffrey earlier.

26. Johnstone, J.T., "John Jeffrey and the Oregon Expedition," p. 38.

27. Ibid., p. 13.

Chapter Ten

1. For full accounts of the expedition, see Stanton, *United States Exploring Expedition*, and also Tyler, *The Wilkes Expedition*.

2. Wilkes, *Narrative of the United States Exploring Expedition*, vol. 4, May 4, 1841.

3. The ethnographic cultural objects and natural history specimens collected by the expedition and that that survived included over 60,000 plant and bird specimens, seeds from 648 species, and 254 live plants. They would form the basis of the collections for many branches of the new Smithsonian Institution. Through mismanagement, however, many more were damaged or lost, or lacked identification. Even so, 19 out of a planned 28 volumes of the expedition report were published and made a fundamental contribution to the growth of science in the United States. Tyler's appendix describes the convoluted saga of producing the natural history reports.

4. The first to visit "Wilkes Land," on January 16, 1840.

5. Evidently, he had not been exposed to the steelhead. For more detail, see Layland, *Perfect Eden*, pp. 104–6.

6. Warre and Vavasour, "Extract from a report [. . .] October 1845."

7. Samson, "That Extensive Enterprise," p. 287.

8. Not yet granted Royal Charter.

9. An Englishman, trained at the Royal Military Academy, Woolwich, but whose career had been with the Russian Imperial Army Staff. He was then living in London as a trade commissioner for the Russian Empire.

10. Seemann, *Voyage of HMS Herald*, pp. 101–2.

11. Euryalus, *Tales of the Sea*, p. 172.

12. Significantly shorter than estimated by Vancouver.

13. Seemann, *Voyage of HMS Herald*, p. 110. They lacked local informants to explain that the tall poles were used to support nets for catching ducks and geese.

14. Sclater published the list in the 1859 issue of the society's *Proceedings*.

15. See Washington, *Hydrographic Instructions for Capt. George Richards*.

16. Mayne, *Four Years in British Columbia*, p. 11.

Chapter Eleven

1. Mayne, *Four Years in British Columbia*, pp. 195, 371.
2. Richards, *Private Journal of Captain G.H. Richards*, p. 190.
3. See Wood, manuscript report to Capt. G.H. Richards.
4. See Mayne, *Four Years in British Columbia*.
5. Ibid., pp. 413–22.
6. At the time of Colnett's voyage, 90 years earlier, a "good" sea otter skin was valued at 25 Spanish dollars, equivalent to 6 pounds. Colnett, *Voyage to the North West Side of America*, p. 18.
7. Mayne, *Four Years in British Columbia*, p. 398.
8. See chapter 16.
9. See Lyall, A., "David Lyall (1817–1895)."
10. Harvey was a medical doctor, Fellow of the Royal Society (FRS), Fellow of the Linnean Society (FLS), and professor of botany, University of Dublin.
11. Bull kelp.
12. Harvey, W.H., "Collection of Algae," p. 162.
13. Ibid., p. 163.
14. Lyall, D., "Botanical Collections Made by David Lyall."
15. Ibid., p. 131.
16. See Lord, *Naturalist in Vancouver Island*.
17. Ibid., vol. 2, p. 263.
18. Ibid., vol. 1, p. 135.
19. Ibid., vol. 2, pp. 12–13.
20. Ibid., p. 32.
21. Ibid., p. 289.
22. *Dictionary of Canadian Biography*.
23. See Akrigg, P., and H. Akrigg, *Gold and Colonists*.
24. *Daily British Colonist*, June 20, 1862.
25. Forbes, *Vancouver Island: Its Resources*, p. 60.
26. *Reports of Explorations and Surveys* [. . .] *Railroad from the Mississippi River to the Pacific Ocean* [. . .] *in 1853–54*. Washington: Government Printing Office, 1855–61.
27. The grizzly, now known as the North American brown bear (*Ursus americanus* ssp.), was not found on the island.
28. Mayne, *Four Years in British Columbia*, pp. 455–56.
29. Markham, M.E., and F.A. Markham, *Sir Albert Hastings Markham*, pp. 149–65.
30. This is particularly remarkable, since at the time they were on active service. The maritime War of the Pacific between Chile and Peru was in progress. Also, there were fears of Russian threats to Esquimalt.
31. Including Markham's storm petrel collected in Galapagos.
32. *Ossifraga gigantea*. The genus name is Latin for "bone breaker"—which is also the meaning of "Quebrantahuessos."
33. Dubious, possibly mislabelled from "Esquimalt," or a misidentified Swainson's thrush.
34. Markham, M.E., and F.A. Markham, *Sir Albert Hastings Markham*, p. 177.
35. Salvin, "Birds collected by Captain A.H. Markham," p. 419.

Chapter Twelve

1. Brown, *Journal of B.C. Bot'l Expedition*, p. 38.
2. It was of immense medicinal significance to Indigenous Peoples.
3. *Edinburgh New Philosophical Journal*, vol. 19, p. 167.
4. The *Chronicle* published Brown's article, "The Land We Live In," in two parts, on May 8 and two days later, the day of a public meeting, to announce the plan.
5. See Layland, *Perfect Eden*, pp. 168–76.
6. See Ludvigsen and Beard, *West Coast Fossils*.
7. He had been the official artist on the Vancouver Island Exploring Expedition three years earlier.
8. Brown, "Synopsis of the Birds of Vancouver Island," pp. 415–16.
9. BC Archives, MS-0794, v. 3, f. 11.

Chapter Thirteen

1. For a biography, see Larrison, "James Hepburn."
2. Carter and Sealy, "Short-tailed Albatross," p. 27.
3. *Daily British Colonist*, April 17, 1879.
4. *British Columbian*, April 17, 1879.
5. Larrison, "James Hepburn," pp. 249–50.
6. Larrison based his article on reports from Swarth and Kinnear in *The Condor*.
7. BC Archives, PR-0365, vol. 30, f. 2.
8. This last seems to be in error, as it is not "on or near Vancouver Island."
9. Possibly Billy, Dr. Charles F. Newcombe's son.
10. Brown's list included neither species.
11. Brown described the specimen as taken by P.N. Compton at Fort Rupert.
12. Near today's Port Hardy on northern Vancouver Island.
13. Compton, *Early Trip to Fort Victoria*, pp. 2–3.
14. The village that grew around Fort Simpson later became known as Port Simpson, and in 1986 the name was officially changed to Lax Kw'alaams.
15. BC Archives, MS-0918.
16. Compton, *Early Trip to Fort Victoria*, p. 43.
17. *British Colonist*, February 2, 1866.
18. Compton, *Early Trip to Fort Victoria*, p. 20.

19. Ibid., p. 51.
20. By Dr. William Hornaday of the New York Zoo.
21. Compton, *Early Trip to Fort Victoria*, p. 52.
22. BC Archives, see in "Photographs and Documentary Art collection" (call code: Pdp) under "Compton, Pym Nevins."

Chapter Fourteen

1. Macoun, John, *Autobiography*, p. 9.
2. Waiser, *The Field Naturalist*, pp. 8–12, has an in-depth review of this conflict.
3. Ibid., p. 14.
4. A Scottish engineer and surveyor who had come to Canada in 1845 and was influential in building railways and international telegraph cables, and even created the North American time zones. A charter member and an early president of the Royal Society of Canada, he was knighted in 1897.
5. Macoun, John, *Autobiography*, p. 47.
6. Grant, Rev. G., *Ocean to Ocean*, p. 24
7. Waiser, *The Field Naturalist*, p. 86.
8. Of the Royal Geographical Society expedition of 1856–60.
9. Macoun, John, *Autobiography*, pp. 92–94.
10. John Macoun's report in the Geological Survey of Canada's *Summary Report for 1875–76*, pp. 110–14.
11. Letter, Macoun to Hooker, September 5, 1876, Royal Botanic Gardens, Kew, Archives: Directors' Correspondence 195.
12. Macoun, John, *Autobiography*, p. 217.
13. In it, and afterward, he retained a stubborn but misguided enthusiasm for the potential of the region, despite significant disagreement from several eminent scientists, including the geologist George M. Dawson. The result was that when many settlers faced severe hardship after the rains failed, the government, following Macoun's opinions, offered little assistance.
14. Published 1883–1902, to be later followed by the *Catalogue of Canadian Birds*, published 1887–1909, co-written with his son James.
15. Founded in 1831, its full title was the British Association for the Advancement of Science.
16. Macoun, John, *Autobiography*, p. 224.
17. Including Hooker and the explorer John Rae.
18. Lorne's father.
19. Founded in 1879. Macoun immediately became a corresponding member until he moved to Ottawa, then continued as a full member for the remaining 38 years of his life.

Chapter Fifteen

1. By this time, the elder son, James, had joined the department to spend the summers assisting expeditions and the winters organizing the herbarium.
2. The Provincial Museum of Natural History and Anthropology had opened a few months earlier. See Corley-Smith, *The Ring of Time*, p. 20.
3. *Daily Colonist*, April 16, 1887.
4. Master of arts, Fellow of the Royal Society of Canada, and Fellow of the Zoological Society of London. For more details, see Taylor, Edward D., *A Very Gentle Man*.
5. Elizabeth Williams, the cathedral's organist and headmistress of Victoria's Girls' Central School.
6. The first was entitled "Notes on the Entomology of Vancouver Island."
7. See Taylor, Rev. G., "A Plea for a Biological Station."
8. Taylor listed 30 species of edible molluscs on the coast, only three of which were being used for food.
9. Johnstone, K., *Aquatic Explorers*, p. 61.
10. Sir Mackenzie Bowell, a friend and early mentor to Professor Macoun.
11. Probably following Alexander von Humboldt's precedent on Chimborazo in the Andes of Ecuador in 1802. Macoun had read the great scientist's works avidly while still in Belleville.
12. *Geological and Natural History Survey of Canada Annual Report* 1887–88, pp. 53–55.
13. Macoun, John, *Autobiography*, p. 249.
14. The height is 5,962 feet (1.3 miles or 1,616 metres).
15. Macoun, John, *Autobiography*, p. 251.
16. Letter to Newcombe, March 18, 1890, BC Archives, A1749-4-97. The new fish was a scalyhead sculpin, but the report—and attribution to Macoun—was preceded by a specimen found later but named *harringtoni*, after the president of the University of Washington.
17. He collected 1,100 species of plants during his sojourn.
18. For a more detailed reminiscence, see Taverner, "William Spreadborough."
19. Percy Taverner, the ornithologist who benefited from Bill's skills during a survey of the Grand Trunk Railway route from Prince Rupert to Jasper, noted, "His energy was inexhaustible and no mountain was too steep or way too rough for him to face if a desirable specimen were the objective."
20. On page 7.
21. Waiser, *Saskatoon Star Phoenix*, March 18, 2016.
22. These would have included the George Taylors and Dr. Newcombe, both of whom had been sending him specimens.
23. An expert in shells and crabs, and one of the founders of the Natural History Society of British Columbia, he was, at the time, a collector on

commission to the Geological Survey of Canada and other museums. See chapter 17.

24. Non-seed-bearing plants such as algae, lichens, mosses and ferns, and perhaps fungi, which are not plants.

25. Owned by Mr. Sutton, a storekeeper.

26. Now Haida Gwaii.

27. After 1927, the National Museum of Canada.

28. See Layland, *Land of Heart's Delight*, pp. 207–11.

29. Oliver, Macoun's grandson, was at the time a second lieutenant with the Royal Engineers. He would serve with great distinction in the war to come, and gain renown as an explorer and surveyor of Everest, concluding his career as a brigadier general and the surveyor general of India, and receiving a knighthood.

30. For details of the expedition, see Wheeler, A., "Alpine Club of Canada in Strathcona Park"; Wheeler, E., "Mount Elkhorn, Strathcona Park"; and Foster, "Strathcona Park."

31. Macoun, James, "Flora of Strathcona Park," p. 68.

32. Macoun, James, "List of Birds," p. 71.

33. Waiser, *The Field Naturalist*, p. 195.

34. South of the border, in the US San Juan group.

35. Later surf birds were found to breed in Alaska and Yukon.

36. Geological Survey of Canada *Summary Report for 1916*, pp. 347–57.

37. BC Provincial Museum annual report for 1917, pp. 17–28.

38. This catalogue was compiled by the museum's director, Francis Kermode.

39. Henry had published his own book in 1915.

Chapter Sixteen

1. See Ben-Ari, "Better Than a Thousand Words."

2. See Newberry House, *200 Years of Botanical Art*.

3. Lindley was one of Britain's most respected scientists. As a young man he had been a protegé of Hooker and an assistant to Banks. He was appointed the first Chair of Botany at the new University College, London, and served for 36 years in key capacities with the Royal Horticultural Society. His vigorous promotion of the Royal Botanic Gardens at Kew saved them, and led to their worldwide pre-eminence.

4. See Lindley, "Introductory Lecture."

5. Stearn, *John Lindley*, p. 40.

6. The BC Archives holds a large collection of her botanical artwork and prints from this stage of her life.

7. The only thing she might have discovered would have been Grant's article in the Royal Geographical Society's journal.

8. Bridge, *Henry & Self*, p. 59.

9. Later renamed Birr, in County Laois.

10. Named after a place near Parsonstown, the seat of the Woods family.

11. *Daily British Colonist*, September 27, 1884, p. 3.

12. Finlay, *A Woman's Place*, p. 79. Josephine Crease, Sarah's daughter, was another classmate.

13. This would have been Mrs. Frazer's at Marifield cottage. Carr called it "the nicest school I ever went to" in the essay "Mint" in her book *Wild Flowers*.

14. Carr, *Growing Pains*, p. 14.

15. See Carr, *Wild Flowers*.

16. Carr, *Hundreds and Thousands*, p. 21.

17. A few years later, Edward Wallace of the Natural History Society lobbied the mayor of Victoria to discourage the public's widespread practice of gathering these flowers as it was detrimental to their continued presence. See chapter 17.

18. The Sisters of Saint Ann have most generously permitted the inclusion of *Wild Lilies* in this book.

19. It is not a bound album, but a series of plates now mounted and framed.

20. Cousin of the Duke of Edinburgh.

21. Royal Horticultural Society, "Royal Autographs," pp. 94–104.

22. Newberry House, *200 Years of Botanical Art*, p. 36.

23. Ibid., p. 24.

24. Tuele, "Sophia Theresa Pemberton: Her Life and Art" (MA thesis), p. 7.

25. Tuele, *Sophia Theresa Pemberton (1869–1959)*, p. 24.

26. From 1890, Beanlands was active in the Natural History Society of BC.

27. Incidentally, it was not until 1903 that the Natural History Society of BC revised its constitution to admit women, but as second-class members. They were then allowed to attend meetings and field excursions, but not to vote or serve on committees.

28. Tuele, *Sophia Theresa Pemberton (1869–1959)*, p. 27.

29. In 1978, the Vancouver Art Gallery held a retrospective exhibition of 80 of her paintings, curated by Nicholas Tuele, whose master's thesis, two years later, was on Sophie Pemberton's life and work.

30. Shteir, *Cultivating Women*, p. 182.

31. The sisters, with their brother William, also brought up an infant whose mother had died in childbirth. They raised the boy, William Towle Taylor, through University School and training as a land surveyor, but as an early volunteer for the military, he was killed in action. He had been the second son of the Reverend George Taylor, the noted entomologist.

32. See Blachford, "History of Women in Botany."

33. Trained in Aberdeen, Davidson founded the UBC Botanical Garden and between 1911 and 1916 was provincial botanist in charge of the Botanical Survey of British Columbia. During the war, politics created unseemly conflict between him and J.R. Anderson, by then elderly.

34. *Daily Colonist*, December 30, 1904.

35. Ibid., August 10, 1893.

Chapter Seventeen

1. See Wade, *Overlanders of '62*.

2. See Grahame, "John Fannin, Naturalist."

3. Lieutenant-governor's memorandum to Executive Council, January 26, 1886.

4. Corley-Smith, *White Bears*, p. 142.

5. Mayse, *Our First 125 Years*, p. 46.

6. Many of the trophies were from a single source, A.S. Reed. He was a member who later claimed that they were there on loan only, and acrimoniously sold his collection to the New York Zoological Society for $6,000, but the display was soon rebuilt by other members. Bissley, p. 71.

7. Many of these specimens were later donated to the provincial museum. Currently, there are initiatives to repatriate the cultural treasures to their Indigenous sources.

8. In 1965, the museum was officially renamed the British Columbia Museum of Natural and Human History, and in 1987, Queen Elizabeth II conferred the title of the Royal British Columbia Museum. In 2003, the Royal BC Museum was joined with the BC Archives, without a name change for either, although for a time it was also known as the Royal British Columbia Museum and Archives. During the period covered in this book, it was generally referred to as the provincial museum. See Corley-Smith, *White Bears*, and Roy, *The Collectors*.

9. Apparently, the first signature in the visitors' book was dated October 25, 1887. This could mean that an earlier book has been lost, or that the existing book was provided belatedly.

10. Low, "Dr. Charles Frederick Newcombe," p. 34.

11. Natural History Society of British Columbia, *Papers*, p. 3.

12. Lopatecki, originally from Poland, was a colourful, multilingual journalist and amateur botanist. Worsfold was an accountant. Deans was a realtor and property speculator who owned acreage on Mount Newton, later a provincial park. Fielding was a recently arrived junior land surveyor. Born in Canterbury, England, the son of a lawyer, he graduated with distinction in mathematics from Kings College, London. After qualifying as provincial land surveyor number 3, he left Victoria for Kaslo, Spokane (Washington), and Grand Forks. Deveraux had been a merchant naval officer and was superintendent of Esquimalt graving dock. Wooton seems to have been one of the sons of an HBC ship's officer who arrived in 1856 and served variously as postmaster and harbourmaster.

13. Some years later, Beanlands, by then the canon of the cathedral, courted and married artist Sophie Pemberton.

14. He later reported that he had inherited $10 million from the Polish Duke of Fedorowitz, but because of Russian objections expected to be able to collect only $2.5 million of it. *Daily Colonist*, June 21, 1891, p. 5.

15. Green served as president for 10 years.

16. The museum's collection of reference books was growing and seen to be of increasing importance.

17. Natural History Society of British Columbia, *Papers*.

18. See Fannin and Thayer, *Check List of British Columbia Birds*.

19. The two Newcombes were also trusted confidants of Emily Carr, and their collection included 123 of her works of art, now in the custody of BC Archives.

20. Natural History Society of British Columbia, *Bulletin*.

21. Born 1863, in Cambridgeshire, England, the son of a parson and trained as a land surveyor, de Blois Green came to Canada in 1888 and settled in the Okanagan. In the course of his work in the surrounding mountains, he collected birdskins, eggs, and lepidoptera. He discovered several new bird species and the distribution and nesting habits of many more. See Riegert, *Entomologists of British Columbia*, p. 23.

22. Captain of the government vessel SS *Quadra*, who, in 1909, published the popular and informative *British Columbia Coast Names*.

23. He had been appointed superintendent of the Royal Jubilee Hospital in 1897, a post he held with distinction for 19 years.

24. Apparently, all documents related to Kermode's early years with the museum, including his appointment as curator, are missing, suspected destroyed. See Corley-Smith, *White Bears*, p. 45.

25. Penn, pp. 204–5.

26. Kermode, *Catalogue of British Columbia Birds*.

27. See Menzies, *Journal*.

28. *Daily Colonist*, March 31, 1905.

29. Edward Wallace, a nurseryman and seller of bulbs (including cultivated "Easter" lilies) in Victoria.

30. Judging by their current abundance in Beacon Hill and other parks, Wallace's letter seems to have been effective.

31. *Daily Colonist*, March 21, 1914.

32. In 1944, a new organization, the Victoria Natural History Society, began to function, and it flourishes to this day. Membership in 2018 stood at 750.

"Some members are professional biologists, others are students, but most are amateur or volunteer naturalists." See http://www.vicnhs.bc.ca/.

Chapter Eighteen

1. See Williams, M., "Game Bird Imports."
2. *Daily Colonist*, February 16 and 17, and March 4, 1882.
3. Ibid., October 11, 1884.
4. Although they called them "English," the Eurasian skylark is now known to breed from the British Isles to Scandinavia to Siberia, and south to the Mediterranean and Japan.
5. *Daily Colonist*, August 25 and 26, 1886.
6. Ibid., August 25, 1897.
7. Just as is being done currently with Vancouver Island marmots.
8. *Daily Colonist,* November 7, 1897.
9. Ibid., December 25, 1898.
10. *Daily Colonist*, April 6, 1902.
11. Ibid., December 15, 1903.
12. BC Archives, Add. MSS 284, v. 18, f. 1, letter from E.P. Michell, November 4, 1963.
13. Minutes of the Natural History Society of British Columbia, January 21, 1904.
14. *Daily Colonist*, December 29, 1903.
15. Ibid., June 4, 1904.
16. Ibid., March 21, 1905.
17. Ibid., June 2, 1907.
18. Ibid., August 11, 1909.
19. *Daily Colonist*, March 12, 1911.
20. Ibid., May 14, 1911.
21. Ibid., February 28 and 29, 1912.
22. Ibid., May 26, 1913.
23. Minutes of the Natural History Society of British Columbia, April 12, 1912.
24. Ibid., March 10, 1913.
25. *Daily Colonist*, April 7, 1913.
26. Minutes of the Executive Committee, Natural History Society of British Columbia, March 28, 1913.
27. Ibid., October 23, 1913.
28. BC Archives, Add. MSS 284, v. 19, f. 1, letter, June 16, 1913.
29. *Daily Colonist*, April 9, 1913.
30. Ibid., April 21, 1914.
31. Minutes of the Executive Committee, Natural History Society of British Columbia, March 31, 1913.
32. Minutes of the annual general meeting, Natural History Society of British Columbia, March 24, 1914.
33. This species is also native to the region. The contribution, if any, by imported birds to the current gene pool is not known.
34. From *In Flanders Fields*, by Lieutenant Colonel John McCrae, May 1915.
35. Sprot, "Notes on the Introduced Skylark."
36. A small street nearby, in a later development, bears the name Skylark Place.
37. Toochin and Meredith, "Eurasian Skylark."
38. Author's discussion with Ann Nightingale.
39. See Mackie, "Skylark."

Chapter Nineteen

1. *Stoop* was the collective noun proposed by author Richard Jones, a.k.a. "Bugman," because of entomologists' habit of "stooping over glass-topped display boxes showing their latest finds or discoveries."
2. See chapter 11.
3. As had been their father, the Reverend Andrew Hughes Matthews. All four shared a deep, lifelong interest in ornithology and entomology.
4. See LeConte, "List of Coleoptera."
5. Hatch, *A Century of Entomology*, p. 4.
6. See chapter 15, sidebar "The Reverend George W. Taylor," p. 174.
7. The common name of *Colias* is clouded sulphur, *Papilio* is swallowtail, *Vanessa* is painted lady, *Chrysophanus* is copper or hairstreak, *Pamphila* is skipper, and *Limenitis* is admiral.
8. *Canadian Entomologist* 16, no. 4 (April 1884): 61–62.
9. "Visit to the home of Chionobas Gigas Butler," *Annual Report*, Entomological Society of Ontario, 1885, p. 24.
10. See chapter 17.
11. Originally *Melia danbyi* (1892).
12. Riegert, *From Arsenic to DDT*, pp. 46–47.
13. Elms, *Beyond Nootka*, pp. 73–77.
14. See Anderson, J.R., "Climbing Mt. Arrowsmith."
15. Hopping, "Entomological Society of British Columbia," p. 31.
16. One of his new partners, the Reverend W.W. Bolton, had recently completed an exploration of the northern end of Vancouver Island. See Layland, *Land of Heart's Delight*, pp. 187–92.
17. See Glendenning, "Notes on the Life History."
18. Perhaps best known as the author of *Westward Ho!* and *The Water Babies*, Kingsley was a distinguished scholar and friend of Charles Darwin.
19. From Day, "Presidential Address to the Entomological Society."
20. Those difficult-to-distinguish small moths, some of which, as larvae, eat holes in woollen clothing or carpets.

21. Riegert, *Entomologists of British Columbia.*

Chapter Twenty

1. See Chapman, "Clark P. Streator."
2. *Santa Cruz Sentinel* (California), December 10, 1943.
3. See Chapman, "Clark P. Streator."
4. This was no relation to the Henry Wickham who, in 1876, smuggled 70,000 seeds of *Hevea brasiliensis*, the wild rubber tree of Amazonia, out of Brazil. He brought them to Kew Gardens where they were propagated, and then were cultivated in plantations in Malaya, which eventually caused the collapse of Brazil's rubber boom.
5. 1890, no. 22, pp. 169–72.
6. This story has been well recounted several times. See MacMillan, "Marine Botanical Seaside Station"; Nicholson, *Vancouver Island's West Coast*; Moore and Toov, "Minnesota Seaside Station"; and Horsfield, "Enduring Legacy of Josephine Tilden."
7. One of the Nuu-chah-nulth First Nations.
8. See Moore and Toov, "Minnesota Seaside Station."
9. See Grinnell, *Birds and Mammals of the 1907 Alexander Expedition.*
10. Stein, *On Her Own Terms*, p. 138.
11. Ibid.
12. Ibid., p. 141.
13. Called by Swarth "Mt. Saunders."
14. Swarth, "Collection of Birds and Animals," pp. 89–90.
15. John's son, George Clutesi, became a renowned artist, author, broadcaster, and folklorist.
16. See Anderson, J.R., "Climbing Mt. Arrowsmith," p. 21.
17. Ibid.

18. Swarth, "Collection of Birds and Animals," p. 107.
19. Leiner pre-empted land at the mouth of the secondary river (now the Leiner River) flowing into the head of Tahsis Inlet.
20. Biological specimens from the location where the species or subspecies were first reported to science.
21. See Brown, *Adventures of John Jewitt.*
22. Brown, "Synopsis of the Birds of Vancouver Island."
23. Swarth, "Collection of Birds and Animals," p. 21.
24. Ibid., pp. 5–6.
25. Ibid., p. 11.
26. Ibid., p. 24.
27. Ibid., p. 12.
28. Ibid., p. 113.
29. *Courtenay-Comox Argus*, December 18, 1947.
30. Penn, *The Real Thing*, p. 134.

Afterword

1. Amos, *E. J. Hughes Paints Vancouver Island*, p. 94.
2. BC *Geographical Names*. BC Government website: http://apps.gov.bc.ca/pub/bcgnws/

SELECTED BIBLIOGRAPHY

Akrigg, Philip. "The Naturalists Discover British Columbia." *BC Historical News* (November 1972).

Akrigg, Philip, and Helen B. Akrigg. *British Columbia Chronicle 1847–1871: Gold and Colonists.* Vancouver, BC: Discovery Press, 1977.

Alcalá Galiano, Dionisio, and Cayetano Valdés y Flores. *A Spanish Voyage to Vancouver and the North-West Coast of America.* Edited by Cecil Jane. Amsterdam: N. Israel, Argonaut Press #10, 1971.

Allen, David E., ed. *Naturalists and Society: The Culture of Naturalists in Britain 1700–1900.* Variorum Collected Studies Series CS724. Aldershot, UK: Ashgate Publishing, 2001.

Amos, Robert. *E.J. Hughes Paints Vancouver Island.* Victoria, BC: TouchWood Editions, 2018.

Anderson, Bern. *Surveyor of the Sea: The Life and Voyages of Captain George Vancouver.* Toronto, ON: University Press, 1960.

Anderson, J.R. "Climbing Mt. Arrowsmith 25 Years Ago." *Daily Colonist,* Sunday, October 27, 1927.

Arima, E.Y. *The West Coast People: The Nootka of Vancouver Island and Cape Flattery.* Special Publication No. 6. Victoria: BC Provincial Museum, 1983.

Arima, Eugene, and Alan Hoover. *The Whaling People of the West Coast of Vancouver Island and Cape Flattery.* Victoria: Royal BC Museum, 2011.

Barber, Lynn. *The Heyday of Natural History, 1820–1870.* London: Jonathan Cape, 1980.

Barneveld, J.W. van, M. Rafiq, G.F. Harcombe, and R.T. Ogilvie. *An Illustrated Key to Gymnosperms of British Columbia.* Victoria, BC: Terrestrial Studies Branch and British Columbia Provincial Museum, 1980.

Bartroli, Tomás. *Brief Presence: Spain's Activity on America's Northwest Coast (1774–1796).* Burnaby, BC: Tomás Bartroli, 1991.

Beaglehole, J.C., ed. *The Life of Captain James Cook.* Stanford, CA: Stanford University Press, 1974.

——. *The Voyage of the Resolution and Discovery 1776–1780.* London: The Hakluyt Society, 1967.

Ben-Ari, Elia T. "Better Than a Thousand Words: Botanical Artists Blend Science and Aesthetics." *BioScience* 49, no. 8 (August 1, 1999): 602–98.

Bissley, Paul L. *The Union Club of British Columbia: 100 Years 1879–1979.* Vancouver: Evergreen Press, 1979.

Blachford, Brittany, "Exploring the History of Women in Botany," GEOG 429, 2013, https://open.library.ubc.ca/cIRcle/collections/undergraduateresearch/52966/items/1.0075696.

Bodega y Quadra, Juan Francisco. *Voyage to the Northwest Coast of America, 1792.* Translated and edited by Freeman Tovell. Norman, OK: Arthur H. Clark Co., 2012.

Borden, Charles E. "Facts and Problems of Northwest Coast Prehistory." *Anthropology in BC,* no. 2. Victoria, BC: British Columbia Provincial Museum, 1951.

Bosher, John F. *Vancouver Island in the Empire.* Tamarac, FL: Llumina Press, 2012.

Bridge, Kathryn. *Henry & Self: The Private Life of Sarah Crease, 1826–1922.* Victoria, BC: Sono Nis Press, 1996.

Brody, Hugh. *The Washing of Tears.* Montreal: National Film Board of Canada, 1994.

Brown, Robert. *Abstract of Journal of B.C. Bot'l Expedition 1863–4–5 (partly).* BC Archives MS-0794 (Robert Brown Fonds), vol. 2, file 2.

——. *The Adventures of John Jewitt* [. . .]. London: C. Wilson, 1896.

——. "Synopsis of the Birds of Vancouver Island." *Ibis* 4 (1868): 414–28.

Brunner, Bernd. *Birdmania: A Remarkable Passion for Birds.* Translated from German by Jane Billinghurst. Vancouver, BC: Greystone Books, 2017.

Carr, Emily. *Growing Pains: The Autobiography of Emily Carr.* Toronto: Oxford University Press, 1946.

——. *Hundreds and Thousands: The Journals of Emily Carr.* Toronto: Clarke, Irwin, 1966.

——, with illustrations by Emily Woods and notes by Kathryn Bridge. *Wild Flowers.* Victoria: Royal BC Museum, 2006.

Carter, H.R., and S.G. Sealy. "Historical Occurrence of the Short-tailed Albatross in British Columbia and Washington, 1841–1958." *Wildlife Afield* 11, no. 1. Winnipeg, MB: Biodiversity Centre for Wildlife Studies, University of Manitoba, 2014.

Castile, G.P., ed. *The Indians of Puget Sound: Notebooks of Myron Eells*. Seattle, WA: University of Washington Press, 1985.

Chapman, Frank M. "On a collection of birds made by Mr. Clark P. Streator in British Columbia." *Bulletin of the American Museum of Natural History* 3, art. 7, 1890.

Chaster, G.D., W.R. Douglas, W.H. Warren, and J.W. Neill. *Trees of Greater Victoria: A Heritage. A Field Guide to Arboreal Riches of Greater Victoria*. Victoria: Heritage Tree Book Society, 1988.

Clemens, W.A., and G.V. Wilby. *Fishes of the Pacific Coast of Canada*. Ottawa: Fisheries Research Board of Canada Bulletin, 1946.

Coleman, Edmund T. "Mountaineering on the Pacific." *Harper's New Monthly Magazine*, vol. 39, pp. 793–817, 1869.

Colnett, James. *A Voyage to the North West Side of America: The Journals of James Colnett, 1786–89*. Edited by Robert Galois. Vancouver, BC: University of British Columbia Press, 2004.

Compton, P.N. *Early Trip to Fort Victoria and Life in the Colony*. BC Archives, MS-2778 (transcript), ca. 1869.

Cook, James. *A Voyage to the Pacific Ocean Undertaken by the Command of His Majesty [. . .]*, vol. 3. Edited by James King. London: G. Nichol and T. Cadell, 1784.

Corley-Smith, Peter. *The Ring of Time: The Story of the British Columbia Provincial Museum*. Victoria: British Columbia Provincial Museum Special Publication No. 8, 1984.

——. *White Bears and Other Curiosities: The First 100 Years of the Royal BC Museum*. Victoria: Crown Publications, 1989.

Craven, Margaret. *I Heard the Owl Call My Name*. Markham, ON: Fitzhenry & Whiteside, 1967.

Cutter, Donald C. "Early Spanish Artists on the Northwest Coast." *The Pacific Northwest Quarterly* 54, no. 4 (October 1963).

——. *Malaspina & Galiano: Spanish Voyages to the Northwest Coast, 1791 & 1792*. Vancouver, BC: Douglas & McIntyre, 1991.

——. *Malaspina in California*. San Francisco, CA: John Howell, 1960.

Danby, W.H., and C. de B. Green. "Report on the Entomology of British Columbia." *Bulletin of the Natural History Society of British Columbia*, art. 3. Victoria: 1893.

David, Andrew, Felipe Fernández-Armesto, Carlos Novi, and Glyndwr Williams, eds. *The Malaspina Expedition 1789–1794: Journal of the Voyage by Alejandro Malaspina*. 3 vols. London: The Hakluyt Society, 2001, '03, '04.

Davies, John. *Douglas of the Forests*. Seattle: University of Washington Press, 1980.

Day, George O. "Presidential Address to the Entomological Society of British Columbia." *Proceedings*, 1914.

Deur, Douglas, Adam Dick, Kim Recalma-Clutesi, and Nancy Turner. "Kwakwaka'wakw 'Clam Gardens': Motives and Agency in Traditional Northwest Coast Mariculture." *Human Ecology* 43, no. 2 (April 2015).

Dewhirst, John. "Nootka Sound: A 4,000 Year Perspective." *Nutka: The History and Survival of Nootkan Culture. Sound Heritage* 7, no. 2. Victoria: Provincial Archives of BC, 1978.

——. *The Origins of Nootkan Whaling*, Nortoft, Germany: Abhandlungen der Völkerkundlichen Arbeitsgemeinerschaft, no. 33, 1982.

Dictionary of Canadian Biography. University of Toronto/Université Laval, online version: www.biographi.ca.

Doe, Nick. "The *tabla* of Toba Inlet." *SHALE* 11 (May 2005): 22–36. Gabriola, BC: Gabriola Historical & Museum Society. See also http://www.nickdoe.ca/pdfs/Webp28c.pdf.

Dorst, Adrian. *The Birds of Vancouver Island's West Coast*. Vancouver: UBC Press, 2018.

Douglas, David. *Journal Kept by David Douglas during His Travels [. . .] Death in 1834*. London: William Wesley & Son, 1914.

Downes, W. "Fifty Years of Entomology on Vancouver Island." *Proceedings, Entomological Society of BC (1951)* 48 (August 15, 1952).

Drucker, P. "The Northern and Central Nootkan Tribes." *Smithsonian Institution Bureau of American Ethnology Bulletin* 144. Washington: Smithsonian Institution, 1951.

Duff, Wilson. *The Indian History of British Columbia: The Impact of the White Man*. Victoria: Royal BC Museum, 1964. New edition 1997.

Dunmore, J., ed. *The Journal of Jean-François de Galaup de la Pérouse 1785–1788*. London: The Hakluyt Society, 1994.

Edwards's Botanical Register (also ed. by Lindley, John). London: James Ridgeway (series).

Efrat, Barbara S., and W.J. Langlois. *Nutka: The History and Survival of Nootkan Culture. Sound Heritage* 7, no. 2. Victoria: Provincial Archives of BC, 1978.

Ellis, David, and Luke Swan. *Teachings of the Tides: Uses of Marine Invertebrates by the Manhousat People*. Nanaimo, BC: Theytus Books, 1981.

Ellis, W. *An Authentic Narrative of a Voyage Performed by Captain Cook and Captain Clerke*. Amsterdam: N. Israel, 1969.

Elms, Lindsay. *Beyond Nootka: A Historical Perspective of Vancouver Island Mountains*. Courtenay, BC: Misthorn Press, 1996.

Emmerson, John, of Wolsingham. *British Columbia and Vancouver Island: Voyages, Travels and Adventures*. Durham, UK: Wm. Ainsley, 1865.

Engstrand, Iris H.W. "José Moziño and Archibald Menzies: Crossroads of the Enlightenment in the Pacific Northwest." *Columbia: The Magazine of Northwest History* 24 (Spring 2004).

——. "Mexico's Pioneer Naturalist and the Spanish Enlightenment." *The Historian* 53, no. 1 (1990).

——. "Of Fish and Men: Spanish Marine Science During the Late Eighteenth Century." *Pacific Historical Review* 69 (February 2000).

——. "Pictures from an Expedition." *The Sciences* 23, no. 5. New York: New York Academy of Sciences, 1983.

——. *Spanish Scientists in the New World: The Eighteenth-Century Expeditions.* Seattle, WA: University of Washington Press, 1981.

Eschmeyer, W.N., and Earl Herald. *A Field Guide to Pacific Coast Fishes.* Boston, MA, Peterson Field Guide, 1983.

Euryalus (probably Pim, Midshipman Bedford). *EURYALUS: Tales of the Sea.* London: J.D. Potter, 1860.

Fannin, John, and John Eliot Thayer. *Check List of British Columba Birds.* Victoria: Queen's Printer, September 1891.

Finlay, Karen. *A Woman's Place: Art and the Role of Women in the Cultural Formation of Victoria, BC, 1850s–1920s.* Victoria: Maltwood Art Museum and Gallery, University of Victoria, 2004.

Folan, William J., and John Dewhirst, eds. *The Yuquot Project,* vol. 2. Ottawa, ON: Parks Canada, 1980.

Forbes, Charles. "Notes on the Physical Geography of Vancouver Island." *Journal of the Royal Geographical Society,* 1865.

——. *Prize Essay: Vancouver Island: Its Resources and Capabilities as a Colony.* Victoria, BC: Colonial Government, 1862.

Ford, John K.B. *Marine Mammals of British Columbia.* Victoria: Royal BC Museum Press, 2014.

Foster, W.W. "Strathcona Park." *Canadian Alpine Journal* 5 (1913): 96–99.

Galloway, D.J., and E.W. Groves. "Archibald Menzies MD FLS (1754–1842), Aspects of His Life, Travels and Collections." *Archives of Natural History* 14, no. 1 (1987).

Geniusz, Mary Siisip. *Plants Have So Much to Give Us, All We Have to Do Is Ask: Anishinaabe Botanical Teachings.* Minneapolis: University of Minnesota Press, 2015.

Gibson, James R. *Otter Skins, Boston Ships and China Goods: The Maritime Fur Trade of the Northwest Coast, 1785–1841.* Montreal: McGill-Queen's University Press, 1992.

Glendenning, R. "Notes on the Life History of the Entomological Society of British Columbia." *Proceedings.* BC Entomological Society, 1933, pp. 3–7.

Godman, John D. *American Natural History.* 2 vols. Philadelphia: Uriah Hunt & Son, 1860.

Gorsline, Jerry. *Rainshadow: Archibald Menzies and the Botanical Exploration of the Olympic Peninsula.* Port Townsend, WA: Jefferson County Historical Society, 1992.

Gough, Barry M. *Britannia's Navy on the West Coast of North America 1812–1914.* Victoria, BC: Heritage House, 2016.

——. *Distant Dominion: Britain and the Northwest Coast of North America, 1579–1809.* Vancouver: University of British Columbia Press, 1980.

Grahame, Annie. "John Fannin, Naturalist." *Victoria Daily Colonist,* June 26, 1904, p. 9.

Grant, Rev. George M. *Ocean to Ocean: Sandford Fleming's Expedition through Canada in 1872.* Rev. ed. Toronto: Radisson Society of Canada, 1925.

Grant, W. Colquhoun. "Description of Vancouver Island, by Its First Colonist." *Journal of the Royal Geographical Society* 27 (1857): 268–320.

Graustein, Jeanette E. *Thomas Nuttall, Naturalist: Explorations in America, 1808–1841.* Cambridge, MA: Harvard University Press, 1967.

Grinnell, Joseph, et al. *Birds and Mammals of the 1907 Alexander Expedition to Southeastern Alaska.* Berkeley: University Press, 1909.

Groves, Eric W. *Archibald Menzies: An Early Botanist on the West Coast of North America. His Flowering Plant Observations and Collections Made during the Years 1787–8 and 1792–4.* Burnaby, BC: Simon Fraser University, 1992.

——. "Archibald Menzies (1754–1842), an early Botanist on the Northwestern Seaboard of North America, 1792–1794, with Further Notes on His Life and Work." *Archives of Natural History* 28, no. 1 (2001).

Gunther, Erna. *Indian Life on the Northwest Coast of North America.* Chicago: University of Chicago Press, 1972.

——. *Klallam Ethnography.* Seattle, WA: University of Washington Press, 1927.

Harbo, Nick. *Whelks to Whales: Coastal Marine Life of the Pacific Northwest.* 2nd ed. Madeira Park, BC: Harbour Publishing, 2011.

Harvey, Athelstan G. *Douglas of the Fir: A Biography of David Douglas, Botanist.* Cambridge, MA: Harvard University Press, 1947.

——. "John Jeffrey: Botanical Explorer." *British Columbia Historical Quarterly* 10, no. 4 (October 1946).

——. "Meredith Gairdner: Doctor of Medicine." *British Columbia Historical Quarterly* 9 (April 1945).

Harvey, William H. "Notice of a collection of Algae made on the North-West Coast of America, chiefly at Vancouver's Island, by David Lyall Esq. MD, RN, in the years 1859–61." *The Linnean 2010* 26, no. 2 (1862): 157–77.

Hatch, Melville H. *A Century of Entomology in the Pacific Northwest,* 1898. Reissued Seattle: University of Washington Press, 1949 (print-on-demand versions also available).

Hatler, David F., R. Wayne Campbell, and Adrian Dorst. *Birds of Pacific Rim National Park*. Victoria, BC: British Columbia Provincial Museum, Occasional Paper no. 20, 1978.

Hayman, John, ed. *Robert Brown and the Vancouver Island Exploring Expedition*. Vancouver: University of Vancouver Press, 1989.

Hazlitt, William Carew. *British Columbia and Vancouver Island: Comprising a Historical Sketch [. . .] Compiled from Official and Other Authentic Sources*. London: G. Routledge, ca. 1858.

Henry, Joseph K. *Flora of Southern British Columbia and Vancouver Island*. Toronto: W.J. Gage & Co., 1915.

Henshaw, Julia. *Mountain Wild Flowers of Canada*. Toronto: William Briggs, 1906.

——. *Wild Flowers of the North American Mountains*. New York: Robert McBride & Co., 1917.

Higueras, María Dolores, and María Luisa Martín-Merás, eds. *Relación del Viaje Hecho por Las Goletas Sutil y Mexicana en el Año 1792 para Reconocer El Estrecho de Juan De Fuca*. Madrid: Museo Naval, 1991.

——. "Sources for Assessing the Contribution of the Malaspina Expedition to the History of the Northwest Coast." In *Spain and the North Pacific Coast*, edited by R. Inglis. Vancouver, BC: Vancouver Maritime Museum, 1992.

Hooker, W.J. *Curtis's Botanical Magazine*. London: Royal Botanic Gardens, Kew (series).

——. "On the Botany of America." *Edinburgh Journal of Science* 2, no. 1 (1825): 108.

Hopping, Geo. R. "The Entomological Society of British Columbia." *Canadian Entomologist* 71 (January 1939): 31–33.

Horsfield, Margaret. "The Enduring Legacy of Josephine Tilden." *Hakai Magazine*, June 13, 2016.

Howay, F.W., ed. *Voyages of the "Columbia" to the Northwest Coast*. Portland, OR: Oregon Historical Society Press, 1990.

Ibáñez Montoya, M. Victoria, "Trabajos Científicos y Correspondencia de Tadeo Haenke." *Expedición Malaspina 1789–1794 (Edición Crítica)*, Tomo IV. Madrid: Museo Naval, 1987.

Indigenous Peoples Atlas of Canada. Ottawa: Royal Canadian Geographical Society; National Centre for Truth and Reconciliation; Assembly of First Nations; Métis National Council; Indspire, 2018.

Inglis, Robin. *Historical Dictionary of the Discovery and Exploration of the Northwest Coast of America*. Lanham, MD: Scarecrow Press, 2008.

——. *Spain and the North Pacific Coast: Essays in Recognition of the Bicentennial of the Malaspina Expedition, 1791–1792*. Vancouver, BC: Vancouver Maritime Museum, 1992.

Jackson, Colonel Julian R. *What to Observe; or The Traveller's Remembrancer*. London: Madden & Malcolm, 1841.

Jenness, Diamond. *The W̱SÁNEĆ and Their Neighbours: Diamond Jenness on the Coast Salish of Vancouver Island, 1935*. Edited by Barnett Richling. Oakville, ON: Rock's Mills Press, 2016.

Johns, Rev. C.A. *British Birds in Their Haunts*. Edited by J.A. Owen, illustrated by William Foster. London: George Routledge & Sons, 1909 (eighth edition, 1925).

Johnstone, James Todd. "John Jeffrey and the Oregon Expedition." *Notes from the Royal Botanic Garden Edinburgh*, vol. 20, July 1939. Edinburgh: His Majesty's Stationery Office, 1950.

Johnstone, Kenneth. *The Aquatic Explorers: A History of the Fisheries Research Board of Canada*. Toronto: University of Toronto Press, 1977.

Jonaitis, Aldona, with Richard Inglis. *The Yuquot Whalers' Shrine*. Seattle: University of Washington Press, 1999.

Justice, Clive. *Mr. Menzies' Garden: Plant Collecting on the Northwest Coast*. Vancouver, BC: Cavendish Press, 2000.

Keddie, Grant. "Victoria—Place of the Strong Fibre." *Discovery* (Summer 1993). Royal BC Museum.

Kendrick, John. *Alejandro Malaspina: Portrait of a Visionary*. Montreal and Kingston: McGill-Queen's University Press, 1999.

——. *The Men with Wooden Feet: The Spanish Exploration of the Pacific Northwest*. Toronto, ON: NC Press, 1986.

——. *The Voyage of Sutil and Mexicana 1792*. Spokane, WA: Arthur H. Clark Co., 1991.

Kermode, Francis. *Catalogue of British Columbia Birds,* Victoria: Provincial Museum, BC, King's Printer, 1904.

——. *A Preliminary Catalogue of the Flora of Vancouver and the Queen Charlotte Islands*. Victoria: Provincial Museum of Natural History, 1921.

Kimmerer, Robin Wall. *Braiding Sweetgrass*. Minneapolis: Milkweed Editions, 2013.

Kinnear, N.B. "Some Additional Notes on James Hepburn." *The Condor* 33 (July 1931): 169–71.

Kluckner, Michael. *Julia: A Biography of Julia Henshaw*. Vancouver: Midtown Press, 2018.

Lamb, Andy, and Phil Edgell. *Coastal Fishes of the Pacific Northwest, revised and expanded edition*. Madeira Park, BC: Harbour Publishing, 2015.

Lamb, W. Kaye. "Banks and Menzies: Evolution of a Journal." In *From Maps to Metaphors: The Pacific World of George Vancouver*. Edited by Robin Fisher and Hugh Johnston. Vancouver, BC: University of British Columbia Press, 1993.

Lang, William, and James Walker. *Explorers of the Maritime Pacific Northwest: Mapping the World Through Primary Documents*. Santa Barbara, CA: ABC-CLIO, 2016.

Lange, Erwin F. "John Jeffery [*sic*] and the Oregon Botanical Expedition." *Oregon Historical Quarterly* 68, no. 2 (June 1967): 111–24.

Larrison, Earl J. "James Hepburn Early Resident Naturalist in the Pacific Northwest." *Pacific Northwest Quarterly* 38, no. 3 (July 1947): 243–59.

Layland, Michael. *The Land of Heart's Delight: Early Maps and Charts of Vancouver Island*. Victoria, BC: TouchWood Editions, 2013.

——. *A Perfect Eden: Encounters by Early Explorers of Vancouver Island*. Victoria, BC: TouchWood Editions, 2016.

LeConte, John L. "List of Coleoptera collected in Vancouver's Island by Henry and Joseph Matthews, with Descriptions of some new Species." *The Annals and Magazine of Natural History* 4, no. 24, Fourth Series, December 1869.

Ledyard, John. *John Ledyard's Journal of Captain Cook's Last Voyage*. Edited by J.K. Munford. Corvallis, OR: Oregon State University Press, 1963.

Lepofsky, Dan, Nichole F. Smith, Nathan Cardinal, John Harper, Mary Morris, Gitla (Elroy White), Randy Bouchard, Dorothy I.D. Kennedy, Anne K. Salomon, Michelle Puckett, Kirsten Rowell and Eric McLay. "Ancient Shellfish Mariculture on the Northwest Coast of North America." *American Antiquity* 80, no. 2 (2015).

Lindley, John. "Introductory Lecture." *Ten Introductory Lectures Delivered at the Opening of the University of London*. London: John Taylor, 1829, p. 17.

——. *Ladies' Botany, or, a Familiar Introduction to the Study of the Natural System of Botany*. London: James Ridgeway & Sons, 1834.

Lindsay, Ann, and Syd House. *David Douglas: Explorer and Botanist*. London: Aurum Press, 1999.

Lord, John Keast. *The Naturalist in Vancouver Island and British Columbia*. London: Richard Bentley, 1866.

Low, Jean. "Dr. Charles Frederick Newcombe." *The Beaver* (Spring 1982).

Ludvigsen, Rolf, and Graham Beard. *West Coast Fossils: A Guide to the Ancient Life of Vancouver Island*. Vancouver: Whitecap Books, 1994.

Lyall, Andrew. "David Lyall (1817–1895): Botanical Explorer of Antarctica, New Zealand, the Arctic and North America." *The Linnean 2010* 26, no. 2.

Lyall, David. "Account of the Botanical Collections Made by David Lyall, MD, RN, FLS, Surgeon and Naturalist to the North American Boundary Commission." *Botany, Proceedings of the Linnean Society*, vol. 7, read June 18, 1863.

MacFie, Matthew. *Vancouver Island and British Columbia: Their History, Resources, and Prospects*. London: Longman Roberts & Green, 1865.

Mackay, David. *In the Wake of Cook: Exploration, Science & Empire, 1780–1801*. Wellington, NZ: Victoria University Press, 1983.

Mackie, Richard Somerset. "Skylark: Old Friend in a New Land: English Songbirds in British Columbia." Essay no. 459. *The Ormsby Review*, January 2, 2019.

——. *Trading Beyond the Mountains: The British Fur Trade on the Pacific 1793–1843*. Vancouver BC: University of British Columbia Press, 1997.

MacMillan, Conway. "A Marine Botanical Seaside Station on the Straits of Juan de Fuca." *Journal of Geography* 1 (June 1902): 263.

Macoun, James M. "The Flora of Strathcona Park." *Canadian Alpine Journal* 5 (1913): 62–70.

——. "List of the Birds Noted in Strathcona Park, July and August 1912." *Canadian Alpine Journal* 5 (1913): 71–72.

Macoun, John. *Autobiography of John Macoun, Canadian Explorer and Naturalist, 1831–1920*. 2nd ed. Ottawa: Ottawa Field Naturalists Club, 1979.

——. *Manitoba and the Great North-west: The Field for Investment; the Home of the Emigrant*. Guelph, ON: World Publishing Company, 1882.

Markham, M.E., and F.A. Markham. *The Life of Sir Albert Hastings Markham*. Cambridge, UK: At the University Press, 1927.

Mayne, Commander Richard Charles, RN. *Four Years in British Columbia and Vancouver Island*. London: John Murray, 1862.

Mayse, Susan. *Our First 125 Years: The Union Club of British Columbia*. Victoria: Union Club of BC, 2004.

McAllister, Nancy M. "Avian Fauna from the Yuquot Excavation." *The Yuquot Project*, vol. 2, 1979, pp. 103–74.

McCarthy, James. *Monkey Puzzle Man: Archibald Menzies, Plant Hunter*. Edinburgh: Whittles Publishing, Royal Botanic Garden, Edinburgh, 2008.

McDowell, Jim. *Uncharted Waters: The Explorations of José Narváez (1768–1840)*. Vancouver, BC: Ronsdale Press, 2015.

McLynn, Frank. *Captain Cook: Master of the Seas*. New Haven, CT: Yale University Press, 2011.

McMillan, Alan D. *Alberni Prehistory: Archeological and Ethnographic Investigations on Western Vancouver Island*. Nanaimo, BC: Theytus Books, 1982.

——. *Since the Time of the Transformers: The Ancient Heritage of the Nuu-chah-nulth, Ditidaht, and Makah*. Vancouver: University of British Columbia Press, 1999.

McMillan, Alan D., and Denis E. St. Claire. *Huu7ii Household Archeology at a Nuu-chah-nulth Village Site in Barkley Sound*. Burnaby, BC: Archeology Press, Simon Fraser University, 2012.

McMillan, Alan D., and Eldon Yellowhorn. *First Peoples of Canada*. Vancouver: Douglas & McIntyre, 2004.

McVaugh, Rogers. "Mociño, José Mariano." In *Dictionary of Scientific Biography*, vol. 9. New York: Scribner, 1974.

Meany, Edmond S. *Vancouver's Discovery of Puget Sound: Portraits and Biographies* [. . .]. New York: MacMillan & Co., 1907.

Menzies, Archibald. *Journal Written on Captain George Vancouver's Voyage to the Northwest Coast*. BC Archives, PR-1261.

Monks, Gregory G., A.D. McMillan, and D.E. St. Claire. "Nuu-chah-nulth Whaling: Archaeological Insights into Antiquity, Species Preferences, and Cultural Importance." *Arctic Anthropology* 38, no. 1 (2001).

Moon, Barbara J. "Vanished Companions: The Changing Relationship of the West Coast People to the Animal World." *Sound Heritage* 7, no. 1. Victoria: Provincial Archives of BC, 1978.

Moore, Eric A., and Rebecca Toov. "The Minnesota Seaside Station Near Port Renfrew, BC: A Photo Essay." *BC Studies* 187 (Autumn 2015).

Morton, Alexandra, and Billy Proctor. *Heart of the Raincoast: A Life Story.* Victoria: Horsdal & Schubart, 1998.

Moziño, José Mariano. *Noticias de Nutka.* Translated and edited by I.H. Wilson. Toronto: McClelland and Stewart, 1970.

Naish, John M. *The Interwoven Lives of George Vancouver, Archibald Menzies, Joseph Whidbey, and Peter Puget: Exploring the Pacific Northwest Coast.* Lampeter, Wales, UK: Edwin Mellen Press, 1996.

Natural History Society of British Columbia. *Bulletin of the Natural History Society of British Columbia.* Victoria, BC: Queen's Printer, 1893.

——. *Papers and Communications Read Before the Natural History Society of British Columbia,* vol. 1, no. 1. Victoria: Jas. A. Cohen,1891.

Nelson, E. Charles. *John Scouler (c. 1804–1871), Scottish Naturalist: A Life, with Two Voyages.* Glasgow: Glasgow Natural History Society, 2014.

Newberry House, Maria, with Susan Munro. *200 Years of Botanical Art in British Columbia.* Botanical Garden, University of British Columbia Technical Bulletin No. 11, Vancouver, 1979.

Newcombe, C.F. "List of Crustacea (Brachyura and part of Anomura) in the Provincial Museum of British Columbia." *Bulletin of the Natural History Society of British Columbia,* art. 4, Victoria, 1893.

Nicholson, George. *Vancouver Island's West Coast, 1762–1962.* Victoria: Morriss Printing, 1962.

Palau, Mercedes. *NUTKA 1792: Viaje a la costa Noroeste de la América Septentrional por Juan Francisco de la Bodega y Quadra.* Madrid: Ministerio de Asuntos Exteriores de España, 1998.

Palau, Mercedes, Carmen Fauria, and Marisa Cales y Araceli Sánchez. *Nootka: regreso a una historia olvidada.* Madrid: Ministerio de Asuntos Exteriores de España, 2000.

Palau, Mercedes, et al. *To the Totem Shore: The Spanish Presence on the Northwest Coast.* Madrid: Ministerio de Asuntos Exteriores de España, Ediciones El Viso, 1986.

Pearse, Theed. *Birds of the Early Explorers in the Northern Pacific.* Comox, BC: Theed Pearse, 1968.

Pemberton, Joseph Despard. *Facts and Figures Relating to Vancouver Island and British Columbia.* London, UK: Longman, Green, Longman, and Roberts, 1860.

Penn, Briony. *The Real Thing: The Natural History of Ian McTaggart Cowan.* Victoria: Rocky Mountain Books, 2015.

Pojar, Jim, Andy MacKinnon, et al. *Plants of Coastal British Columbia.* Victoria, BC: Ministry of Forests and Lone Pine Publishing, 1994.

Porrúa, Enrique J., ed. *The Diary of Antonio de Tova on the Malaspina Expedition (1789–1794).* Lewiston, NY: Edwin Mellen Press, 2001.

Proctor, Billy, and Yvonne Maximchuk. *Full Moon, Flood Tide: Bill Proctor's Raincoast.* Madeira Park, BC: Harbour Publishing, 2003.

Rattray, Alexander, MD Edin., RN. *Vancouver Island and British Columbia: Where They Are, What They Are [. . .] Especially as Colonies for Settlement.* London, UK: Smith Elder & Co., 1862.

Richards, Captain G.H. *The Private Journal of Captain G.H. Richards: The Vancouver Island Survey (1860–1862).* Edited by Linda Dorricott and Deidre Cullon. Vancouver, BC: Ronsdale Press, 2012.

Riegert, Paul W. *Entomologists of British Columbia.* Regina, SK: Entomological Society of Canada and Entomological Society of British Columbia, 1991.

——. *From Arsenic to DDT: A History of Entomology in Western Canada.* Toronto: University of Toronto Press, 1980.

Royal Horticultural Society (RHS). "The Royal Autographs of the Horticultural Society." *Occasional Papers from the Royal Horticultural Society Lindley Library,* vol. 8, April 2012.

Roy, Patricia E. *The Collectors: A History of the Royal British Columbia Museum and Archives.* Victoria, BC: Royal BC Museum, 2018.

Salvin, Osbert. "A list of the birds collected by Captain A.H. Markham on the west coast of America." *Proceedings of the Zoological Society of London,* no. 3, June 1883, pp. 419-32.

Samson, Jane. "'That Extensive Enterprise': HMS *Herald*'s North Pacific Survey, 1845–1851." *Pacific Science* 52, no. 4, 287–93.

Saunders, Howard. *An Illustrated Manual of British Birds.* 2nd ed. London, UK: Gurney & Jackson, 1899.

——. "On some *Laridae* from the coasts of Peru and Chili, collected by Capt. Albert H. Markham, RN, with Remarks on the Geographical Distribution of the Group in the Pacific." *Proceedings of the Zoological Society of London* 50, no. 3 (1882).

Say, Thomas. *A Description of the Insects of North America.* Edited by John L. Le Conte. New York: J.W. Bouton, 1869.

Sclater, Philip Lutley. "On a Collection of Birds from Vancouver's Island." *Proceedings,* Zoological Society of London, 1859, pp. 235–37.

Scouler, John. "Dr. John Scouler's Journal of a Voyage to N.W. America [1824–'25–'26] II: Leaving the Galapagos for the North Pacific Coast." *Quarterly of the Oregon Historical Society* 6, no. 2 (June 1905).

Seemann, Berthold. *Narrative of the Voyage of HMS Herald*. 2 vols. London: Lovell Reeve, 1853.

Shteir, Ann B. *Cultivating Women, Cultivating Science: Flora's Daughters and Botany in England, 1760–1860*. Baltimore: Johns Hopkins University Press, 1996.

Smith, Nicole F., Dana Lepofsky, Ginevra Toniello, Keith Holmes, Louie Wilson, Christine M. Neudorf, and Christine Roberts. "3,500 Years of Shellfish Mariculture on the Northwest Coast of North America." *PLoS ONE* 14, no. 2 (February 2019): e0211194. https://doi.org/10.1371/journal.pone.0211194.

Society for the Diffusion of Useful Knowledge (SDUK). *Insect Architecture*. Library of Entertaining Knowledge, Society for the Diffusion of Useful Knowledge. London: Charles Knight, 1830.

——. *Insect Transformations*. Library of Entertaining Knowledge, Society for the Diffusion of Useful Knowledge. London: Charles Knight, 1830.

Sprot, G.D. "The Early Indian Wildfowler of Vancouver Island." *Canadian Field-Naturalist* 42, (September 1928): 139–43.

——. "Notes on the Introduced Skylark in the Victoria District of Vancouver Island." *The Condor* 39, no. I, 24–36. American Ornithological Society, 1937.

Stanton, William Ragan. *The Great United States Exploring Expedition of 1838–1842*. Berkeley, CA: University of California Press, 1975.

Stearn, William T., ed. *John Lindley, 1799–1865: Gardener-Botanist and Pioneer Orchidologist: Bicentenary Celebration Volume*. Woodbridge, UK: Antique Collectors' Club in association with the Royal Horticultural Society, 1999.

Stein, Barbara. *On Her Own Terms: Annie Montague Alexander and the Rise of Science in the American West*. Berkeley, CA: University of California Press, 2001.

Stern, Bernhard J. *Lummi Indians of Northwest Washington*. New York: Columbia University Press, 1934.

Stewart, Hilary. *Cedar: Tree of Life to the Northwest Coast Indians*. Vancouver: Douglas & McIntyre, 1984.

——. *Indian Fishing: Early Methods on the Northwest Coast*. Vancouver: Douglas & McIntyre, 1977 (reprinted Quadra Recreation Society, 2018).

Stresemann, Erwin. "Birds Collected in the North Pacific Area during Captain James Cook's Last Voyage (1776–1779)." *Ibis* 91, no. 2 (1949): 244.

Suttles, Wayne. *Coast Salish Essays*. Vancouver: Talon Books, 1987.

——. *The Economic Life of the Coast Salish of Haro and Rosario Straits*. New York: Garland Publishing, 1974.

——, ed. *Northwest Coast, Handbook of North American Indians*, vol. 7. Washington, DC: Smithsonian Institution, 1990.

——. "Notes on Coast Salish Sea-Mammal Hunting." *Anthropology in BC*, no. 3. Victoria BC: Provincial Museum of BC, 1952.

Swarth, Harry S. "James Hepburn, a Little-known Californian Ornithologist." *The Condor* 27 (November–December 1926): 240–53.

——. "Report on a Collection of Birds and Animals from Vancouver Island." *University of California Publications on Zoology* 10, no. 4 (February 13, 1912). Berkeley, CA: University of California Press.

——. "A Visit to Nootka Sound." *The Condor* 14 (January 1912): 15–20.

Taverner, Percy A. *Birds of Western Canada*. Ottawa: Victoria Memorial Museum Bulletin no. 41, 1926.

——. "William Spreadborough—Collector." *Canadian Field-Naturalist* 47, no. 3 (March 1933).

Taylor, Edward D. *A Very Gentle Man* (biography of the Reverend George W. Taylor by his grandson). Typescript in BC Archives, MS-2812.

Taylor, Rev. George W. "A Plea for a Biological Station on the Pacific Coast." *Transactions of the Royal Society of Canada, 1907*, pp. 203–7, 1908.

Taylor, Leona, and Dorothy Mindenhall, compilers. *Victoria's Victoria*. "Index of Historical Victoria Newspapers." History Departments, University of Victoria. http://web.uvic.ca/~hist66/vicvic/.

Thompson, L.C., and M.D. Kinkade. "Languages." *Handbook of North American Indians*, vol. 7. Washington, DC: Smithsonian Institution, 1990, p. 30.

Thurman, Michael E. *The Naval Department of San Blas*. Glendale, CA: Arthur H. Clark Co., 1967.

Tolmie, William Fraser. *The Journals of William Fraser Tolmie, Physician and Fur Trader*. Vancouver, BC: Mitchell Press, 1963.

Toochin, Rick, and Mitch Meredith. "Status and Occurrence of Eurasian Skylark (*Alauda arvensis*) in British Columbia." *Ibis* (submitted April 15, 2018).

Torner Collection of Sessé & Mociño Biological Drawings. Pittsburgh, PA: Hunt Institute, Carnegie Mellon University.

Townsend, John K. *Narrative of a Journey across the Rocky Mountains to the Columbia River* [. . .]. Philadelphia, PA: Henry Perkins, 1839.

Tuele, Nicholas. *Sophia Theresa Pemberton (1869–1959)*. Vancouver: Art Gallery of Greater Vancouver, 1978.

——. "Sophia Theresa Pemberton: Her Life and Art." Master of arts thesis, University of British Columbia, 1980.

Turner, Nancy J. *Ancient Pathways, Ancestral Knowledge: Ethnobotany and Ecological Wisdom of Indigenous Peoples of Northwestern North America*. Montreal: McGill-Queen's University Press, 2014.

——. *Food Plants of Coastal First Peoples*. Victoria: Royal BC Museum, 2006.

——. "Plants of the Nootka Sound Indians as recorded by Captain Cook." *Sound Heritage* 7, no. 1. Victoria: Provincial Archives of BC, 1978.

Turner, Nancy J., John Thomas, Barry Carlson, and Robert Turner Ogilvie. *Ethnobotany of the Nitinaht Indians of Vancouver Island.* Occasional Paper no. 24, British Columbia Provincial Museum, 1983.

Tyler, David B. *The Wilkes Expedition*, Philadelphia: American Philosophical Society, 1968.

Vancouver, George. *The Voyage of George Vancouver: 1791–1795.* Edited by W. Kaye Lamb. London: The Hakluyt Society, 1984.

Varner, Collin. *The Flora and Fauna of Coastal British Columbia and the Pacific Northwest.* Victoria, BC: Heritage House Publishing, 2018.

Vaughan, Thomas, and Bill Holm. *Soft Gold, the Fur Trade and Cultural Exchange on the Northwest Coast of America.* Portland, OR: Oregon Historical Society, 1990.

Victoria Natural History Society. *A Net of Naturalists.* Victoria: Victoria Natural History Society, 1968.

——. *Victoria and Southeastern Vancouver Island Checklist of Birds.* Victoria: Victoria Natural History Society, August 2017.

Wade, M.S. *The Overlanders of '62.* Victoria: Heritage House, 1981.

Wagner, Henry R. *The Cartography of the Northwest Coast of America to the Year 1800.* Berkeley, CA: University of California Press, 1937.

——. "Journal of Tomás de Suría of His Voyage with Malaspina to the Northwest Coast of America in 1791." *Pacific Historical Review* 5, no. 3 (September 1936).

——. *Spanish Explorations in the Strait of Juan de Fuca.* New York: AMS Press, 1971.

Wagner, Henry R., and W.A. Newcombe, eds., Captain H. Grenfell, RN (trans.). "The Journal of Jacinto Caamaño." *British Columbia Historical Quarterly*, July 1938, parts 2 and 3.

Waiser, W.A. *The Field Naturalist: John Macoun, the Geological Survey, and Natural Science.* Toronto: University of Toronto Press, 1989.

Walbran, Capt. John T. *British Columbia Coast Names 1592–1906: Their Origin and History.* Ottawa: Government Printing Bureau, 1909.

Warre, H., and M. Vavasour. "Extract from a report by Lieutenants Warre and Vavasour dated 26 October 1845." *Papers Related to the Colonization of Vancouver's Island,* no. 5.

Washington, Rear Admiral John (Hydrographer). *Hydrographic Instructions for Capt. George Richards about to Proceed to Vancouver Island,* Misc. file 2, folder 3, item 2. Taunton, UK: British Hydrographic Office, March 10, 1857.

Wenstob, Stella. "The Profusion of Potatoes in Pre-Colonial British Columbia." *PlatForum,* vol. 12, 2011, University of Victoria.

Wheeler, A.O. "The Alpine Club of Canada in Strathcona Park." *Canadian Alpine Journal* 5 (1913): 82–95.

Wheeler, E.O. "Mount Elkhorn, Strathcona Park." *Canadian Alpine Journal* 5 (1913): 44–48.

Wilkes, C. *Narrative of the United States Exploring Expedition.* 5 vols. Philadelphia: Lea and Blanchard, 1845.

Williams, Glyn. *Naturalists at Sea: Scientific Travellers from Dampier to Darwin.* New Haven, CT: Yale University Press, 2013.

Williams, Judith. *Clam Gardens: Aboriginal Mariculture on Canada's West Coast.* Vancouver: Transmontanus-New Star Books, 2006.

——. *High Slack: Waddington's Gold Road and the Bute Inlet Massacre of 1864.* Vancouver: Transmontanus-New Star Books, 1996.

Williams, Margaret. "Game Bird Imports." *Daily Colonist,* Sunday, September 12, 1965, pp. 6–7.

Wood, Surgeon Charles B. Manuscript report to Capt. G.H. Richards, RN, June 14, 1862. BCAR GR 1372, F-1215. Also *British Colonist,* December 13, 1862.

Woodward, S.P. *A Manual of the Mollusca; or a Rudimentary Treatise of Recent and Fossil Shells.* London: John Weale, 1851.

Wright, William Greenwood. *The Butterflies of the West Coast of North America.* San Francisco: Whittaker & Ray, 1905.

Yip, Mike, and James Miskelly. *Vancouver Island Butterflies.* Nanoose Bay, BC: Mike Yip, 2014.

LIST OF ILLUSTRATIONS

Note: Some of the images have been cropped and/or digitally adjusted for legibility.

ACKNOWLEDGEMENTS

Many people have been of much-appreciated assistance with the text and collection of images for this book. They include Robert Amos, Steve Ansell, Katherine Bernick, Don Bourdon, Lugene Bruno, Eva Bullard, Malcolm Chalmers, James Clowater, Jurgen de Vries, John Dewhirst, Nick Doe, Matt Fairbarns, Rhonda Ganz, Lorne Hammond, Peter Hancock, Jackie Hildering, James Holkko, Keith Holmes, Courtnay Janiak, Peter Johnson, Gary Kaiser, Grant Keddie, Leslie Kennes, Tristram Lansdowne, David Leeming, Trishya Long, Gabriel Lu, Ken Marr, Neil McDaniel, Andrew McKorney, Michael McNall, James Miskelly, Lorna Mitchell, Gary Nafis, Charles Nelson, Ann Nightingale, Carey Pallister, Eric Pekonen, Sherri Robinson, Hans Roemer, Nicole Smith, Karl Stevenson, Jeanette Taylor, Nancy Turner, Frederike Verspoor, TJ Watt, Carolyn Webber, and Mike Yip.

I am indebted to the executors of the estate of E. J. Hughes for use of his watercolour on the cover and on page 246.

I am particularly grateful for the diligence and enthusiasm provided by Sharon Keen in researching sources for me in various archives.

Taryn Boyd and her team at TouchWood Editions maintained their encouragement, energy, and professionalism to bring this book to publication.

My dear wife, Jean, has again contributed untold support, editorial skill, and judgment throughout the creation of this book.

My heartfelt thanks to them all.

INDEX

Haro, Gonzalo López de, 15, 50, 53
harpoons, hunting with, 39
Harvey, Robert, 229, 231, 232
Harvey, W.H., on Lyall's algae collection, 136
Hasell, Dr. Edward S., 206, 207, 211
Haswell, Robert, 43-44, 251 n.4-2
hats, denoting status as whaler, 41
hawk, Cooper's, 77, 156, 157
Hawkins, Lieutenant Colonel John S., 131, 139
HBC (Hudson's Bay Company). *See* Hudson's Bay Company, expedition; Hudson's Bay Company (HBC), charter for Vancouver Island
Hecate (ship), 135
Heiltsuk Peoples, oral history of human habitation, 10
Hepburn, James, 153, 155-159
Herald (ship), 126
herring, 17, 20, 25, 51, 73, 76
Herschel, Sir John, 127
Heuchera micrantha (small-flowered alumroot), 62
Higgins, Mary Ann, 199
Hooker, William Jackson
　adviser to HBC, 98, 111
　background of, 97
　on collecting botanical specimens, 127
　secures botanist for Boundary Commission, 131
　species named by, 102, 104, 107, 118
Horetzky (photographer), 166
Hoskins, John, 44
Hudson's Bay Company, expedition
　mandate, 97
　natural history recorded on, 101, 102, 104, *104*, 105, 106, *106*, 107
　relations with Indigenous Peoples on, 105, 106
　route of, 100–102, 104–7
Hudson's Bay Company (HBC), charter for Vancouver Island, 115, 128
Hughes, E.J., 246
humans, habitation by, 10, 13
hummingbirds, 25, *27*, 36, 37, 77, 156, 242, 252
humpback whale, 14
hunchback salmon, 104, *104*
hunting
　birds, techniques for, 14–15, *16*, 17, 25, 37
　seasonal practice of, 105
　skills for, 14
　whales, techniques for, 14

I

Indigenous Knowledge
　of natural world, 9
　recognition of, 3, 5, 9, 21, 248
　and sustainability, 5
　transmission of, 20
Indigenous Peoples
　arrival on Vancouver Island, 5
　intertribal conflict of, 106
　Mowachaht culture, documentation of, 76, 77–78
　as naturalists, 3, 9, 247–48

　regard for pygmy owl by, 138–39, *140*
　regard for sea otters, 103
　spirit bear, significance of, 160
　value of devil's club to, 148
Indigenous Peoples, food of
　archaeological record of, 25–26
　clams, cultivated by, 18, *19* (*see also* clam gardens)
　diet, 77–78, 159
　trade, 13
Indigenous Peoples, languages
　Chinook Jargon, dictionary, 107
　Mowachaht, dictionary, 76
　study of by Tolmie, 118
　on Vancouver Island, 13
In Nature's Realm (music), 3
insects, species recorded
　by Colnett, 47
　by Haenke, 61
　by Menzies, 88
　by Pantoja, 52
　by Spreadborough/Macoun, 178, 181
　by Taylor, 227
intertidal species, *139*, *234*
　recorded by Lord, 138
　recorded by Maldonado, 75
invertebrates, species recorded, *124*
　by Colnett, 47
　by Scouler, 106, *106*
　by Spreadborough/Macoun, 178
　by Wilkes, *124*
Island in Bird's Eye Cove, An, 246

J

jay, Steller's (blue-fronted), 35, 46, *142*, 154
Jeffrey, John, 118–19, 121, *121*
Jeffrey pine *(Pinus jeffreyi)*, *121*
Jenns, P., 207
Johnstone, James, 82

K

Kamchatka *(Medeola notkana)*, 79
Kane, Paul, 15
Kellett, Captain Henry, 126
Kellogg, Louise, 238, 240, 245
kelp, 10, 12, *12*, 13, *96*, 136, *137*
Kennedy, Arthur Edward, 150
Kermode, Francis, 185, 186, 207, 212, 219, 258 n.15–38, 259 n.17–24, n.17–26
Kimmerer, Robin Wall, 20
kingfisher, *34*, 35, 44, 72, *142*
Kwakwaka'wakw Peoples, 17, 18, 59
Kwaxistalla (Clan Chief Adam Dick), 18, n.1–124

L

Labouchere (ship), 158
Ladies' Botany (Lindley), 190
ladybug *(Coccinella)*, 226

Lady Washington (ship), 43
Lamb, W. Kaye, on Menzies, 87
Langley, E., 203
language
　Chinook Jargon, dictionary, 107
　Indigenous, groups of, 13
　Mowachaht, dictionary, 76
　study of by Tolmie, 118
　on Vancouver Island, 13
Lansdowne, J. Fenwick, 51
La Pérouse, Jean-François de Galaup, comte de, 44
Larrison, Earl, 156
Lawson, George, 164
learned societies, 99
LeConte, John L., on Lord collection, 225
Ledyard, John, 39
Leptasterias macounii (mottled sea star), 187
Lilium parvifolium (tiger lily), 199
lily, chocolate *(Medeola notkana)*, 79
lily, Easter, 146
lily, fawn, conservation of, 212
Lindley, Dr. John, 135, 190
Lindley, W., 203
ling cod, 75
linguistics. *See* language
littoral, 11, *12*, 13
Logier, E.B.S., *113*
Lopatecki, M., 207
Lord, John Keast, 131, 137–39, 225
Loxia curvirostra (red crossbill), 78
loxiwey, 8, 17–19, *18*
lupin, blue, *197*
Lyall, Dr. David, 131, 136, 137, *137*, 156
Lysaght, Averil, 37

M

Mackenzie, Alexander, 102, 104, 105
MacMillan, Conroy, 237, 238
Macoun, Ellen, 164, 166, 186
Macoun, James (son of John)
　death of, 186
　early training of, 169
　employed by Geological Survey, 178
　Macoun expeditions, 178, 185
　Strathcona Park expedition, 184
　Vancouver Island, collecting on, 183, 184–85
　at Victoria Memorial Museum, 180
Macoun, John, *168*, *180*, *182*
　background of, 163–64
　children of, 164
　collection of, 167, 168, 184, 186
　death of, 186
　as Dominion Botanist, 169
　finances of, 166
　on height of trees, 170
　Manitoba and the Great North-west, 169
　marriage of, 164